"I loved this book! It teaches wisdom and values, and that is what people need to learn today."
—Alvin Dark, former Major League Baseball player and manager

"These sixteen rules for a lifetime of success will inspire all who read this book."
—Bobby Richardson, former New York Yankees star

"Unparalleled passion and enthusiasm in page after page of insight into R. E. Littlejohn's unique approach to life."
—Bob Vander Weide, CEO, RDV Sports

"Must reading for any individual, whether you are established or up and coming in your profession."
—Mike Martin, head baseball coach, Florida State Univ.

"Many of the rules for success in sports and life were taught to Pat by his godly mentor, R. E. Littlejohn. Through this well-written book you can now learn the same valuable lessons."
—Tim LaHaye, coauthor, best-selling "Left Behind" series

"Must reading for anyone really interested in becoming a success in life."
—Ruly Carpenter, former president of the Philadelphia Phillies

"Reading and studying this material is time well spent and a most enjoyable experience."
—John Wooden, former UCLA basketball coach

"Through this wonderful book you can experience the lessons Pat Williams learned from Mister R. E."
—Clyde King, former Major League Baseball pitcher and manager

"A ton of profound wisdom. Get it and read it. You'll be glad you did."
—Steve Brown, author, professor, Reformed Theological Seminary

"Those who try to live by these rules will find they are living better and glorifying God more."
—James M. Boice, senior pastor, Tenth Presbyterian Church, Philadelphia, Penn.

"Enjoyable reading. Personal, practical, and purposeful."
—Andre Thornton, former Major League Baseball star

"At a time when mentoring is becoming an empty buzzword more talked about than done, Pat Williams shows us the real thing vividly and attractively."
—Os Guinness, author, *The Call*

"Pat Williams continues on his literary journey with another winning book on life and success."
—Mark H. McCormack, chairman and CEO, International Management Group

"This book is not just food for thought; for some of us it is an entire banquet. Truly a must read!"
—Joe Theismann, former NFL quarterback

"A marvelous book about success—not short-term success, but success that has eternal power."
—Robert H. Schuller, founding pastor, Crystal Cathedral Ministries

"Mister R. E. has impacted me through this wonderful book. You will not be the same person after you finish it."
—Ann Meyers Drysdale, basketball Hall of Famer, TV analyst

"This story of success is full of courage, commitment, and humor."
—Denny Doyle, former Major League Baseball infielder

"A work of passion and commitment. I recommend this book highly and without hesitation."

—Richard E. Lapchick, civil rights activist, scholar, author

"A vital resource for overcoming any obstacle that may present itself."

—Ron Wolf, vice president and general manager, Green Bay Packers

"Pat Williams knows how to read the road map to a successful, fulfilling life. If his life is any example, these sixteen rules work."

—Jim Bunning, United States senator

"R. E. Littlejohn's life passes through Pat to us. Read this, grow, and pass it on!"

—Joseph M. Stowell, president, Moody Bible Institute

"Bound to have a special appeal to those who love sports and seek to know the Lord."

—D. James Kennedy, senior minister, Coral Ridge Presbyterian Church, Fort Lauderdale, Fla.

"A must read for those seeking wisdom to enhance themselves spiritually and professionally."

—Steve Alford, head basketball coach, Univ. of Iowa

"A practical, entertaining, and deeply spiritual book. This is a welcomed volume."

—Adrian Rogers, senior pastor, Bellevue Baptist Church, Memphis, Tenn.

"A story of lifelong devotion, of two worthy souls who loved unconditionally. With that shining through, the principles take on new meaning."

—Bill Curry, former NFL player and college football coach

"Pat Williams attributes his remarkable achievements to a willingness to put himself in the hands of Jesus Christ—and then let go. Pat shows that nothing could be simpler—or more predictive of success in even the most intimidating tasks."

—Gary L. Bauer, Republican presidential candidate 2000

"A powerful, practical guide to success in every dimension of life."

—Kathleen Parker, nationally syndicated columnist

"Guaranteed to have an impact on anyone who reads this book."

—Carmen Policy, president and CEO, Cleveland Browns

"Inspiring and motivational. Shows that the positive impact we have on others is the true meaning of success."

—Dot Richardson, 1996 U.S. Olympic gold medallist, softball

"A wonderful book, loaded with practical ideas and wisdom."

—Brian Tracy, motivational speaker and author

"Heartwarming, uplifting, and inspirational. Hats off to Pat Williams for sharing the life, words, and wisdom of his role model with us."

—Donna Rice Hughes, author, *Kid's Online*

"An interesting book about a man I respect: Mr. R. E. Littlejohn."

—Jerry Richardson, owner, Carolina Panthers

"A story worth studying. We will all be improved by reading this book."

—Bobby Jones, former NBA star

"Gives anyone who has lost a mentor the hope that they will find another. A road map to success."

—Lou Holtz, head football coach, University of South Carolina

A Lifetime of Success

MR. R. E. LITTLEJOHN
(1913–1987)

Mr. Littlejohn's Secrets to
A Lifetime of Success

Pat Williams

with
James D. Denney

Fleming H. Revell
A Division of Baker Book House
Grand Rapids, Michigan 49516

© 2000 by Pat Williams

Published by Fleming H. Revell
a division of Baker Book House Company
P.O. Box 6287, Grand Rapids, MI 49516-6287

Printed in the United States of America

Library of Congress Cataloging-in-Publication Data is on file with the Library of Congress, Washington, D.C.

ISBN 0-8007-1772-4

For current information about all releases from Baker Book House, visit our web site:
http://www.bakerbooks.com

To our eldest son,
James Littlejohn Williams,
who is growing to become
Mr. R. E. Littlejohn's namesake
in more ways than one

Contents

Acknowledgments

I want to express my heartfelt appreciation to my wife Ruth for her loving support and her suggestions, which added so much to this book; to my friend Jim Denney for lending his skills to the shaping of these ideas; to Bob Vander Weide and my RDV Sports family for their encouragement of this project; to my old pal Ken Hussar, proof-reader and reviewer extraordinaire; to my valuable assistant Melinda Ethington; to Bill Petersen, John Phipps, Brian Phipps, and Twila Bennett at Revell; and to Mr. Littlejohn's many friends and cowork-ers who were so generous in sharing their memories and reflections with me.

Prologue

My Second Father

I was seven years old when my father, Jim Williams, took me to Shibe Park in Philadelphia to see my first big-league game—Connie Mack's Philadelphia Athletics hosting the Cleveland Indians in a double-header. That was in 1947, and it was one of the happiest days of my life. On that day, my future course was dialed in. From that moment forward, I knew that the rest of my life would revolve around professional sports.

My mom and my dad were big sports fans, especially baseball, and they supported my manic, single-minded passion for competitive sports. Dad coached at Tower Hill, a private school in Wilmington, Delaware, and he was an enthusiastic, proud papa—always taking snapshots and hollering at my games and telling people, "That's my boy!" He was so loud and exuberant at times that it got to be embarrassing. He was my biggest fan, and looking back, I wish I had gotten to know him better and appreciate him more at the time.

My time with my dad was all too short.

After high school, I moved from Delaware to Winston-Salem, North Carolina, to attend Wake Forest University. There I caught for the baseball team and kept my eyes on the prize—a career in the major leagues. It was the only goal I'd ever known since that day in '47 when my dad took me to Shibe Park and filled me up with hot dogs and soda and dreams of baseball glory.

During my senior year, Wake Forest fielded an excellent baseball team; we won the Atlantic Coast Conference championship and made it to the NCAA regional tournament. All we had to do was beat Florida, West Virginia, and Florida State in the double-elimination tourney and we would be on our way to the College World Series. My family drove down from Delaware for the games—my mother and sisters in one car, my father in another. The tournament got under way, and we easily mowed down Florida and West Virginia in the opening rounds. But in the deciding game, Florida State won on a close play at the plate in the bottom of the eleventh inning. Our season was over—and so was my college career.

I hated to see it end like that. I was filled with a deep, hollow ache and I didn't want to see anyone or talk to anyone, not even my family. When my dad came up to me after the game, I thought, *Doesn't he know I don't want to talk?* Yes, I was self-centered and self-absorbed, I see that now. But at the time, all I knew was that I was hurting.

"Tough break, son," he said.

"Yeah, tough. . . . Listen, Dad, could you check with Mr. Carpenter and see what my chances are with the Phillies organization?" Bob Carpenter was the owner of the Phillies and a friend of Dad's. His son, Ruly, was my best friend.

"Bob Carpenter knows you," my father replied. "When you get home, you can talk to him yourself."

"I guess so," I said gloomily. "Well, g'bye, Dad. See ya back home."

Looking back, I deeply regret that this was the last conversation I ever had with my father. There was so much more I should have said—and would have, had I only known.

Losing One Father, Finding Another

Dad took my sister Carol in his car and headed home by way of Washington, D.C.; there, he dropped off Carol, then continued on his way, driving all night. My mother and my sister Ruthie took a more direct route back to Wilmington. I would be coming home a day later with four friends from school.

The next morning, my friends and I slept late, took our time loading the car, then hit the interstate north at a leisurely pace. That evening, we stopped in Richmond, Virginia, watched a Triple-A baseball game, and stayed overnight. We got a late start the next morning, and arrived in Wilmington around five o'clock in the afternoon. There were a bunch of cars parked in front of our house and people in our yard. My mother hurried over to the car as we pulled into the driveway.

"Oh, Pat," she said, "something terrible's happened. Your father had an accident after he left Carol off in Washington."

Fear clutched my chest. "An accident? How bad?"

"Pat, your father was killed."

My father had fallen asleep at the wheel, and his car had struck a bridge abutment on the Washington-Baltimore Expressway. I've often wished in the years since that I had thought to say a proper good-bye. After the funeral, I followed the last piece of advice my father had given me—I called Bob Carpenter. He was very sympathetic over my loss, and he also told me there was an opening for a catcher on the Phillies' farm club in Miami. So I joined the Miami Marlins—a Class D club in the Florida State League. It wasn't the big leagues—but it was pro ball.

In 1963, after two years with the Marlins, I began to face facts: It would take more than a .295 batting average in the low minors to get me to the majors. So, reluctantly, I let go of the dream that had seized me as a seven-year-old boy. But that didn't mean I was through with baseball or with sports. No way! It just meant that a whole new realm of the game was about to unfold—the front-office world of sports promotion.

I spent the '64 season as assistant general manager of the Miami club, and the following year I took an assignment as general manager of the Spartanburg Phillies in South Carolina. I loaded all my possessions into my car and drove to Spartanburg. I didn't know a soul in town, but I had been told to look up one of the team owners—a man named R. E. Littlejohn. On a rainy Sunday in February 1965, I pulled up in front of a well-kept red-brick home. I instantly knew it was the right place because the house numbers were affixed to a metal cutout in the silhouette of a tanker-trailer rig. R. E. Littlejohn owned a prosperous petroleum tanker company and was known as the Tanker Tycoon.

Mrs. Littlejohn answered my knock. She was a warm and gracious woman in her fifties. Her name was Marion, but she insisted

I call her by her nickname, Sam. She said, "Mister R. E. was called out of town unexpectedly, but please come in." That's what she called her husband—"Mister R. E." Sam was a gracious hostess, offering refreshments and engaging me in conversation. Near the end of our talk, as I was preparing to leave, she said something I will never forget. "You'll never meet another man like Mister R. E.," she told me. "You'll never again work for anyone like him, no matter how long you're around. He's the greatest man in the world."

I later learned that this was no hyperbole on the part of an adoring wife. Mrs. Littlejohn was exactly right about her husband.

In 1974, when our first son was born in Atlanta, we named him James Littlejohn Williams—James after my birth father, Jim Williams, and Littlejohn after the man who became, in a very real way, my second father, my spiritual father, and one of the most profound influences on my life and career. (Incidentally, Mister R. E. and Sam came to the hospital the day Jimmy Williams was born and presented him with a one thousand dollar savings bond.)

From R. E. Littlejohn I learned everything I needed to know about how to be a success, how to make life count, and how to have a true, lasting sense of purpose and meaning in life. I ended up running the Spartanburg team for four years, from 1965 to 1968, and during those years, Mister R. E. became my mentor, my teacher, my spiritual guide, and my best friend. What Mrs. Littlejohn told me on my first day in Spartanburg was absolutely true: I have never met anyone like Mister R. E.—not before and not since.

Wisdom, Values, and Class

Over the years I knew him, I came to realize that the life of this great but humble man was built on a sturdy foundation of three pillars. The three pillars of R. E. Littlejohn's life were wisdom, values, and class.

Wisdom: As I look around this world, I see a lot of people who are bright and well-educated—but I see very few people who are wise. True wisdom is a deep understanding of what is true, right, and lasting. Many of the smartest people in the world are completely lacking in wisdom. Wisdom comes with age but sometimes age comes alone. Outwardly glib and successful, they're inwardly a shambles; their relationships are in ruins, and they are hollow and unhappy inside.

Mister R. E. was outwardly and inwardly successful, reaping the rewards not only of material success but of spiritual contentment and a rich, loving family life. He was a walking paragon of these Old Testament words: "Wisdom is supreme; therefore get wisdom. Though it cost all you have, get understanding" (Prov. 4:7).

I learned a lot about the difference between knowledge and wisdom simply by sitting at Mister R. E.'s knee and observing his life: Knowledge likes to speak; wisdom prefers to listen. Knowledge studies; wisdom observes. Knowledge knows how to take things apart; wisdom understands how to put things back together. Knowledge is proud of all it has learned; wisdom is humble and always thirsts to learn more. Ralph Waldo Emerson once wrote, "Raphael paints wisdom, Handel sings it, Phidias carves it, Shakespeare writes it, Wren builds it, Columbus sails it, Luther preaches it, Washington arms it, Watt mechanizes it." And R. E. Littlejohn *lived* it.

Values: In Mitch Albom's best-seller *Tuesdays with Morrie,* he quotes Morrie Schwartz, who said, "We put our values on the wrong things, and it leads to very disillusioned lives." That is a very accurate observation.

Roy Disney, Walt Disney's brother and business partner, once said, "When your values are clear to you, making decisions becomes easier." That's absolutely true. I'm convinced one reason Mister R. E. acted so confidently and decisively was that he had a firm grasp of his values. His principles dictated his decisions. I don't remember a single occasion when Mister R. E. floundered, dithered, or agonized over a decision. He knew what to do in every situation because his values and principles did not oscillate on a sliding scale.

We live in an age that has lost its moral underpinnings. The great preacher Vance Havner said, "Americans know the price of everything and the value of nothing." These days people want to do well; Mister R. E. wanted to do what was right. These days people say, "Do what feels good"; Mister R. E. said, "Do good—and you will never regret it." These days people care about *looking* good; Mister R. E. cared about *doing* good, even when no one was looking. Abraham Lincoln once told a friend, "When I do good, I feel good. When I do bad, I feel bad."

I enjoy listening to Dr. Laura Schlessinger's advice show on the radio. One day I heard her say, "Values inform our conscience, which influences our behavior. Our behavior determines the quality of our lives and the meaningfulness of our personal contributions to others, to life, and to history."

Someone once said, "You can tell the values of a man by the way he treats his wife and daughters, by the way he treats his subordinates, and by the way he treats someone who can do nothing for him." I observed R. E. Littlejohn on a daily basis for four years, and I saw how he treated his wife, his subordinates, and the many people who received his gracious help and kindness, for which he asked nothing in return. He was a man of good and godly values.

Class: You know class when you see it—but what is it? Coach John Wooden describes class this way: "Class is an intangible quality which commands rather than demands the respect of others." It's dignity, grace, polish, good taste, good manners, and just a touch of elegance. To have class is to have confidence in every social situation. It's the ability to relate easily to everyone, from kings and queens to scrubwomen and ditchdiggers. A person of class may make mistakes, but never makes excuses. A person of class never builds himself up by tearing others down. A person of class is so comfortable with himself that he puts everyone around him at ease.

Real class has nothing to do with "social class." A person of aristocratic blue blood may be a no-class boor while a so-called "hayseed" from the backwoods of nowhere could be the classiest person you'd ever want to know. To know R. E. Littlejohn was to know real class.

Mr. Littlejohn's Sixteen Rules for Success

My father died in 1962, when I was twenty-two. Mr. Littlejohn became my surrogate father when I was twenty-four, and he remained a guiding father-figure in my life until his death in 1987. Rarely can a man say of another man, "He loved me unconditionally." But that was the kind of relationship I had with Mister R. E.

He cared for me in a way I can probably never fully understand. When an older man takes you under his wing and treats you like his own son, that's rare, that's special. I once heard Gene Stallings, when he was the head football coach at the University of Alabama, say, "I have yet to see a young person go wrong who had one good adult friend." Mister R. E. was that kind of friend to me, and he had a lot to do with shaping the direction of my life.

Perhaps part of what led him to take such an interest in me was the fact that he had no sons of his own. He had two beautiful daughters, Carolyn and Dixie, and he was very close to them and to his two sons-in-law, Jimmy Ballew and Bobby Pinson. But on more than one occasion, Mrs. Littlejohn told me that I was the son her husband never had.

When I met Mister R. E., I certainly was not looking for a substitute father. But in retrospect, now that I'm sixty years old, I can see that this is what our relationship became. He saw me as a young man in his midtwenties with a lot of potential—but also with a lot of growing up to do. I was young, I was impetuous, I was impatient. My attitude was, "I want to *do* everything now, and I want to *have* everything now!" Mister R. E. loved the eagerness, enthusiasm, and drive he saw in me, but he knew that those qualities needed channeling and refining for me to reach my full potential. So he invested in me. Day by day, through the things he showed me and taught me, R. E. Littlejohn made an incalculable investment in my life.

In 1968, during my fourth year in Spartanburg, I received an offer to become the Philadelphia 76ers basketball team's business manager. When I told Mr. Littlejohn and his partner, Leo Hughes, about it, they agreed it was a big step up for me, and Mister R. E. told me I was ready to make the move—but he hated to see me go. "In fact," he said, "if you will stay here in Spartanburg, Mr. Hughes and I will give you the ball club."

I couldn't believe what I was hearing. "What do you mean—*give* me the ball club?"

"I mean we'd sign everything over to you. You'd own it. It's all yours—if you want it. All you have to do is stay."

I was stunned. I had known all along that he was the kindest, wisest man I'd ever met—but at that moment it really hit me that

Mister R. E. truly loved me as a father loves a son. In today's terms, a class A club like the Spartanburg Phillies would be worth three million five or more, easy—and he was offering it to me on a silver platter if I would just stay. Many times I've wondered if I shouldn't have taken him up on it, but I believed it was time for me to move on. So I went to Philadelphia in 1968 and moved to the big leagues, to the National Basketball Association.

Even so, for the next three decades, as I moved into management with the 76ers, the Chicago Bulls, the Atlanta Hawks, and the Orlando Magic, I never made a major personal decision or career move without first talking to Mr. Littlejohn. I called him often and visited him whenever I could. I sought his counsel, I bounced ideas off him, and stayed very close to him.

One of my most memorable visits with Mister R. E. took place after the 1973–74 basketball season, during my one year with the Atlanta Hawks. The season ended in March, and I headed down to Clearwater, Florida, to recuperate and watch some Phillies spring training games. Mr. Littlejohn would always relax in Clearwater during spring training. He was, after all, a huge baseball fan as well as an owner. I spent the better part of a week with Mister R. E., going to the ballpark, hanging out with him, sharing dinners with him, talking and listening, and having a wonderful time.

One night over dinner with Mister R. E. and Sam, I said, "You know, I went to Wake Forest for my B.S. and Indiana University for my M.S., but I got my Ph.D. from Littlejohn University." He laughed—but I was serious. I had learned more from him than from all my years of schooling combined.

"You know what I'd like to do tonight?" I continued. "I'd like to write down everything I've learned at Littlejohn University. I don't mean just those four years I was in Spartanburg, of course. I'm also thinking of all the years since, while I've been with the NBA, while I've been married and starting a family. You know, every time I've talked with you, you've been teaching me something, educating me, advising me with that great wisdom of yours."

Humble man that he was, Mister R. E. would smile and deflect my compliments—but I didn't mean them as empty flattery. What I had said was true, every word. So we continued to sit for a long time over that leisurely dinner at a seafood restaurant in Clearwater. I pulled out my pen and turned over the place mat, and as we chatted, I wrote down thoughts and ideas and life lessons I had learned during my years of doctoral studies under Professor Littlejohn. We spent hours talking, refining, bringing dozens of lessons down to a point.

And when the evening was over, I had written on the back of that place mat sixteen rules for a lifetime of success. A few days later, when I got back to my office in Atlanta, I had my scribbles and scrawls neatly typed onto a single sheet, and I've carried those sixteen rules in my wallet ever since. As I write these words, it's been two, going on three decades since that night in Clearwater, and even more years since Mister R. E. first began teaching me these principles—yet they are as practical and valuable today as when I first learned them.

I have read nearly every motivational book and business manual that's been written, gone to countless advanced education classes and success seminars, and personally visited with many of the great inspirational and motivational speakers and writers of the past few decades—from Norman Vincent Peale to Og Mandino to Stephen Covey to Zig Ziglar to Lou Holtz. I'm here to tell you: Mr. Littlejohn knew it all, taught it all, and lived it all decades ago. He was a master motivator and business educator long before these concepts were formalized by others. In this book, I'm going to share the distilled essence of his wisdom with you. I have taken those sixteen principles I copied down in a Clearwater seafood restaurant in 1974, and I have turned them into sixteen chapters:

1. Sell yourself.
2. Work hard.
3. Keep the communication lines open.
4. Seek out wisdom and advice from others.
5. Be aware of your influence on others.
6. Seek agreement but respect disagreement.
7. Control what you can control—and let go of what you can't.
8. Avoid snap decisions—be patient.
9. Keep it simple.

10. Manage your personal life well.
11. Care about the people you work with.
12. Don't run from problems.
13. Surround yourself with greatness.
14. Be a good listener.
15. Pay your dues.
16. Have faith in God.

The examples and stories in this book are drawn from all aspects of life—from sports, business, ministry, and family situations. Whether you are a CEO, a salesman, an entrepreneur, a coach, an athlete, a writer, a pastor, a stay-at-home mom, or a street-sweeper; regardless of your age, gender, race, creed, or religion; whether you work in the penthouse or the boiler room; whether you want to be a successful executive, entrepreneur, minister, or spouse and parent—*these sixteen success secrets will transform your life,* just as they have transformed mine.

In 1987, Mister R. E. left this world for a better one—but before he left, he invested some of himself in me and in thousands of other lives he touched. You may have never heard of R. E. Littlejohn before you picked up this book, but just as his wife told me one rainy afternoon in 1965: You'll never meet another man like him. So let me tell you about the greatest man I've ever met and the things he taught me.

And the first thing Mister R. E. taught me? You've got to sell yourself.

ONE

Sell Yourself

His name was Richard Erlic Littlejohn, though most people called him by the affectionate nickname of Mister R. E. I usually called him Coach, because that was the role he played in my life. He was a mentor, a cheerleader, a motivator, an energizer, a teacher, and above all, a coach. And one of the first things he taught me was, "You've got to sell yourself."

Now, that may seem contradictory, coming from a man as genuinely humble as he was. (Whenever we'd go out to eat, Mister R. E. would always order the lowest priced meal on the menu.) Fact is, I don't remember Mister R. E. ever bragging or blowing his own horn. He believed that people who toot their own horns always get the pitch too high and are seldom asked for an encore. But bragging and horn-tooting is not at all what he meant when he told me, "Pat, you've got to sell yourself."

R. E. Littlejohn was born in the little South Carolina town of Cross Anchor, in the parsonage of his grandfather, a Baptist preacher.

His father was a shopkeeper of modest means, who changed jobs and residences several times while young Richard was growing up. When Richard was eleven, his father accepted a job managing the grocery store for a mill in the little Carolina village of Tucapau.

"We had an old Model T Ford back then," Mister R. E. once told me, "and even though I was only eleven, I used to drive that car all the time. Once, I drove my dad to Tucapau so he could see about getting a job at the mill. Along the way, we must have had ten or eleven flat tires. Back then, you didn't buy a new tire when you had a flat—you just patched it and pumped it up again. I remember it was a hot, humid summer day, and when we finally got to Tucapau, one of the tires was completely ruined—there was no way it was going to take one more patch. So we had to buy a new tire and put it on.

"Well, as it happened, when that tire blew, we pulled over right in front of a house where two girls were sitting on the front porch. Those girls sat and watched while I changed that tire. They didn't talk to me, and I didn't talk to them. As it turned out, one of the girls was named Marion. After my father got the job at the mill, our family moved in across the street from Marion's house. Some years later, in 1935, I asked that little girl to be my bride—and she said yes."

At the time Richard went to Furman University, an entire year of education, including tuition, room, and board, cost only $350. As cheap as that seems today, he could afford only two years of college. Though he was a standout player on the basketball and baseball teams, he had to leave school at the end of his sophomore year because he had spent all the money he'd saved working after school and summers at the mill.

He wanted to be an accountant, so in 1933, in the depths of the Great Depression, he applied for work at the accounting office of Union County's Buffalo Mills. Unfortunately, a baseball injury from his college days made it painful for him to write for a lengthy time, so he had to give up his accounting job. Next stop: a career in sales.

"I had an uncle in Atlanta," Mister R. E. recalled. "He was doing well, despite the depression, by selling equipment and supplies for gas stations—compressors, pumps, hoses, nozzles, and so forth.

After I left Buffalo Mills, I talked to my uncle and secured the rights to sell his products in a new territory. Because of my bad arm, I couldn't lift the products to show them to the customers. So I drove around to the gas stations and showed my products to customers from the trunk of my car.

"That's when I learned what selling is all about. It's all about trust. It's about building relationships. I got to know my customers and they got to know me. And when they knew me, they trusted me. When they trusted me, they bought from me. I made my living from repeat business and from all the friendships I made along the way. I didn't sell products. I sold myself—and when my customers were sold on me, they just naturally bought from me rather than from some other fellow." Famed sports agent Mark McCormack says, "Every interaction in essence, is a selling situation."

With the beginning of World War II, Mister R. E. saw a new opportunity open up in the petroleum market. Wartime regulations prevented petroleum companies from hauling their own oil and gasoline products, requiring them to use common carriers. When a number of oil jobbers got together and asked Mr. Littlejohn to go in with them to form a new petroleum-hauling carrier (they knew him well and trusted him because of their long association with him through his equipment business), he readily agreed. He was elected president of the newly formed War Emergency Cooperative Association, which was begun with $2,500 and fifteen leased tanker trucks.

After the war, Mr. Littlejohn applied to the Interstate Commerce Commission for permanent authority to operate a petroleum carrier under the name of Associated Petroleum Carriers. "At our first hearing before the ICC," he recalled, "the big boys had assembled an army of eighteen attorneys to argue against us. The railroads and other haulers didn't want the competition, and they tried to shut us down. Our application went all the way to the United States Supreme Court, where we finally prevailed in 1950." In the meantime, he perfected and patented a new trailer design that prevented leakage, and he founded two other companies, Littlejohn Equipment Company and Rhymer-Littlejohn Incorporated, which specialized in repairing oil tanks and trailers. He was also named director of First Federal Savings and Loan of Spartanburg.

Over the years, his business interests grew. From a startup with fifteen leased trucks, APC grew to a fleet of 650 trucks transporting more than ten million dollars' worth of oil products a day. By the time I met him in the 1960s, he was operating six companies, plus a Class A baseball club, the Spartanburg Phillies. He was intensely involved in such organizations as the Fellowship of Christian Athletes and the Boy Scouts of America. He also served as a deacon in First Baptist Church of Spartanburg and was largely responsible for spearheading the church's far-reaching television ministry. He generously endowed scholarships at Furman University, where he had attended only two years, and he became one of the university's trustees.

Quite an impressive list of accomplishments, don't you think? But it all started with *sales*. Mister R. E. learned at an early age that, to get anywhere in life or accomplish anything of note, *you've got to sell yourself*. He told me, "There are thousands of one-shot salesmen. The key is selling yourself to the same people over and over again."

Five Great Rules of Selling

From Mister R. E., I learned the five great rules of selling. I'm sure you've encountered these same rules yourself many times over the years. There's nothing deep or mysterious here—it's rather like Vince Lombardi's famous locker room statement to his Green Bay Packers, a statement about the fundamentals of the game: "Gentlemen," he said, "this is a football." Your first response to these five rules of selling might well be, "Duh!" But both Lombardi and Mister R. E. knew that, every so often, you need to get back to basics and study the fundamentals of the game. And the fundamentals of the game of selling are these:

1. Get your client's attention.
2. Convert attention into interest.
3. Convert interest into conviction.

4. Convert conviction into desire.
5. Close the deal.

Mr. Littlejohn knew what he was talking about when he shared those rules with me. He was a salesman. He started out selling gas station equipment. He built a fuel-hauling company on selling. He built his baseball team on selling. In minor-league baseball, that's all you do. You're selling, selling, selling all the time. He taught me that if you can't *sell* in minor-league baseball, you can't *succeed* in minor-league baseball—let alone the major leagues. Remember the message of the movie *Field of Dreams*? "If you build it, they will come." Wrong, all wrong! Just because you build it doesn't mean they'll come. *Field of Dreams* is a fantasy. But the reality of baseball is selling.

In minor-league baseball, you can't sell winning. If you have a winning team, that helps. But you can't count on winning, because you have no control over your ballclub. The big-league team calls the shots. It sends the players down and moves the players up. As soon as you have a player who's on a hot streak and making a name for himself and becoming a crowd-pleaser, the organization moves him up to the next level.

So when you sell minor-league baseball, you have to sell a good time, win or lose, big-draw talent or no. You have to sell promotions and fun and pregame shows. People have to know that no matter how the team performs, they're going to have a great time and get their money's worth at the ballpark. That can be a tough sell—and I know *exactly* how tough it can be.

But I look back on those days of selling minor-league baseball as some of the happiest, most exciting days of my career. I wouldn't trade that experience for the world. I'll always be grateful that Mister R. E. burned those five rules of selling into me, then turned me loose to sell my brains out! The practical sales lessons I learned in those early years of my career have stood me in good stead throughout the decades since, through my years with the 76ers, the Atlanta Hawks, the Chicago Bulls, and especially the founding and development of the Orlando Magic. It's all about selling. You've got to sell yourself to people again and again. Nothing happens until a sale is made.

As David Mahoney, chairman of Norton Simon Incorporated, once said, "Ever since Moses came down from the mountain with the tablets, the world has been moved by salesmen. I'm a salesman."

Well, so am I! And you should be, too! So let's take a closer look at each of these five life-changing rules of selling.

1. Get Your Client's Attention

Getting your client's attention begins with *you*. A great salesperson makes a great first impression—and you know the old saw: You never get a second chance to make a great first impression. Being neat and well-groomed is part of the battle—but only part. A great first impression goes beyond mere appearance, all the way to personality. A great salesperson must be genuine, pleasant, easy to talk to, a good listener, someone who puts other people at ease. And you know, when you want to attract attention, it doesn't hurt to have a gimmick.

Take, for example, Orville Redenbacher, the popcorn king. He died a few years ago, but everyone still remembers him from his TV commercials—that hokey name, that natural folksy style, his trademark suspenders and bow tie, his hair parted down the middle. He looked like he had just stepped out of a barbershop quartet, circa 1901. That was his gimmick, his trademark, his shtick—and that's one of the reasons he was one of the top salespeople in the world.

Orville Redenbacher knew how to get your attention—and that folksy, honest, sincere image went a long way toward building trust and getting people to try his product. The best thing about Orville's shtick was that it wasn't just shtick, it wasn't a put-on. Those who knew him best said that he had always worn the bow tie and suspenders, long before he was the popcorn king on TV. That's just who he was.

The key to getting your client's attention is to open with something the client already is vitally interested in—himself, his needs, his finances, his family. Stir up the notion that you have something the client desperately needs or wants. It might surprise you to find the perfect example of this kind of salesmanship in the ministry of Jesus Christ. In John 4, he was sitting by a well when a Samaritan woman came to draw water, and he offered her something he called "living water."

"Whoever drinks the water I give him," he said, "will never thirst." Well, that got her attention! "Sir," she eagerly replied, "give me this water." And that was the opening he needed to share his message of eternal life with her. He started not with his own message, but by keying in on *her* needs, priorities, wants, and thirst—and that is how he got her attention. By the end of the story, he had clinched the "sale" and transformed her life.

So what is it that you want to sell? A message? An idea? A candidate? A product? It all starts with you. You must sell you. You must make a great first impression and get the other person's attention. As Ben Compaine once said in *Success* magazine, "The marketplace is not a podium in a quiet lecture hall, where everyone gets a turn to speak. It's more like a crowded bazaar in Casablanca. You must distract people from their main occupation—living—and show them that they can't live a minute longer without one of your beautiful rugs." So go out into the marketplace and make a splash!

2. Convert Attention into Interest

Once you get your client's attention, you must convert that attention into interest. People generally have a very short attention span, so unless you know how to get people to stick around and listen to you, your prospect is likely to say, "That's nice," turn on his heel, and walk away. I've found that the best way to convert attention into interest is by *focusing on the customer and his needs.* Great salespeople are fanatically dedicated to pleasing their customers. Their primary objective is not to make a sale but to make *customers.*

Demonstrate to the client that she has something to gain from listening to what you have to say. It might be as straightforward as offering a gift or incentive in exchange for "a few moments of your valuable time." Or it might be a promise that your product or idea is guaranteed to produce some benefit. Whatever you promise, make sure you deliver. This is a key transition point in your pitch. It's fairly easy to grab someone's attention for a few moments—but converting that momentary attention into genuine interest is a greater challenge. If you don't accomplish that transition, you'll never get to the close.

Mary Kay Ash, founder of Mary Kay Cosmetics, put it this way: "My advice to salespeople is this: Pretend that every single person you meet has a sign around his or her neck that says, 'Make me feel important.' Do that, and not only would you succeed in sales, you will succeed in *life*." Focus on the customer, listen to him, make him the center of your attention. People love to talk about themselves, so ask questions, draw your client out, get her to talk about herself—her needs and wants and goals. Then you will be prepared to show your client how your product, service, or idea meets those needs, wants, and goals.

3. Convert Interest into Conviction

This is another crucial bottleneck in the selling process. It's relatively easy to get someone's attention, a little more challenging to hold someone's attention—but the really tough act is *winning the client's trust*. You will never make the sale unless the client trusts you and becomes as convinced as you are of the value of your product or idea. That is why you cannot merely sell a product—you must sell yourself. You must prove to the client that not only is your product great, but *you* are worthy of the client's faith and confidence. If you have faith in your product or idea, and your client has faith in you, then you are practically home free. You convert interest into conviction by offering persuasive evidence of your own credentials (your knowledgeability, experience, and credibility) and of your product's ability to perform as promised.

If you want to win a client's trust, then—above all—treat the client with respect, never as a "mark" or a "chump." The salesperson who sets out to con people into buying a useless or fraudulent product may make a few one-time sales, but he will never be anywhere near as successful (in either the short run or the long run) as the honest, sincere salesperson who believes in her own product and who is convinced in her heart that she is doing people a favor by selling her wares.

Zig Ziglar, the legendary sales guru, put it this way: "Selling is essentially a 'transfer of feeling.' If you can make the prospect feel about the product the way you feel about the product, you've sold him. Now, if that feeling is based on factual information, you will build a solid customer base for the future. To do this you must have integrity, which gives consistency not only to your business, but to your personal and family life, too."

I received a vivid lesson in this principle early in my career. After my two quasi-distinguished seasons playing minor-league baseball in Miami, I moved up to the Miami Marlins' front office. My boss was the team's general manager, Bill Durney. One day, he called me into his office and said, "Pat, you're in charge of selling advertising in the season program."

Talk about a cold sweat! The thought of knocking on doors and selling ads absolutely terrified me. I had never sold anything in my life. I went out calling, and my approach was, "I'm selling ads in this program book—you don't want to buy one, do you?" Predictably, I flopped. Three days of knocking on doors, and not one sale. By noon of my third day, I returned to Durney's office feeling like a washout.

"I know what your problem is, Pat," said Bill. "You think you're asking merchants to do you a favor by buying an ad. That's the wrong attitude. They're not doing *you* a favor—you're doing *them* a favor! Take another look at that program. That is a great advertising medium. When merchants advertise in that program, it doesn't cost—it pays."

"I—I never thought of it that way," I admitted.

"Here's another tip: Always give your client a choice: 'Do you want your ad next to the Marlins' lineup or the visitors' lineup?' Don't ask him *if* he wants to buy an ad. Ask him *where* he wants his ad. Remember, selling is the name of the game. If you can sell, you'll always have a job in sports."

Then he patted me on the back and added, "Tell you what—go up to Mugge's Restaurant and ask for Mr. Mugge. See what you can do." To this day, I don't know if Bill Durney set it up with a call to Mr. Mugge. I only know that I left the office thinking I could sell iceboxes to Eskimos. When I got to the restaurant, Mr. Mugge bought a seventy-five-dollar ad on the spot. I celebrated by ordering a piece of Mr. Mugge's famous key lime pie.

I sold the rest of the program in just a few days—then I went back to Bill and asked, "What's my next assignment?" I was ready for anything!

Paul Karasik, author of *Sweet Persuasion,* once described the moment of his epiphany in sales: "When I was a child, I asked my father, a successful salesman, what I needed in order to become a great salesperson. Without hesitation, he said, 'You've got to believe 100 percent in yourself, 100 percent in your organization, and 100 percent in your product. When you go out the door in the morning, sell yourself, sell your organization, sell your product—and sell them in that order."

Motivational speaker Bill Gove tells a story about a fellow named Harry who runs an appliance store in Phoenix, Arizona. Harry doesn't have the lowest prices in town, and he knows that people come into his store all the time to make price comparisons. Many a time he's had couples spend an hour asking him about prices and features, knowing all along that these people are going to drive down the street to one of the discount superstores and buy the same product for a few shekels less. But Harry is philosophical about it. He patiently answers their questions, and when the customers say, "We're going to think about it," Harry gives them his pitch.

"I know you folks are looking for a good price," he tells them, "and I know you can go down to Discount Dan's and maybe save a few bucks. But I want you to think about one thing: When you buy from me, you get something you'll never get anywhere else—you get *me.* I've been at this same corner for thirty years, I'm gonna be here tomorrow, and I stand behind everything I sell. I want you to be happy with your purchase, because I want you to come back and buy from me again. I don't just want to make a sale—I want to make friends who keep coming back. So you can bet I'm gonna do everything I can to make sure you'll never regret doing business with me. But whether you buy from me or Discount Dan, I want you to have a little gift with my compliments."

That gift was Harry's pièce de résistance: a quart of creamy vanilla ice cream. "Now," Bill Gove asks in conclusion, "just how far do you think those customers are going to get with Harry's speech ringing in their ears—and a quart of ice cream in their hands on a 110-degree day in Phoenix, Arizona?"

You've got to sell yourself, you've got to build trust in yourself in order to make the sale—but there's nothing wrong with a quart of slowly melting ice cream for added insurance.

4. Convert Conviction into Desire

Help the client visualize himself already enjoying the benefit of your product. Help him see how much better his life would be if he were already using your product, or if she were living her life by the tenets of your faith or philosophy, or if he were living under the benevolent governance of your political party or candidate. Use imagery, metaphors, and word pictures to help your client glimpse a happier, more successful future using your product, whatever your product might be.

Let's say that you've captured the prospect's attention, you've even kindled her interest, she believes in you and agrees that you have a great product—but she has one objection: "I don't really need your product." Whoa! Don't let her get away. Now you must stir up a *desire* for your product:

"Wait! Did you think I was selling firewood? Oh, no! I'm selling heat and warmth and fond family memories that you can build in front of a crackling fire on a cold winter's night. I'm not just selling firewood—I'm selling a dancing fire on your hearth while you sip a cup of hot chocolate with melting marshmallows, while the snowflakes dance on the wind outside your window. I'm selling a lifetime of pleasant dreams at bedtime."

Or, "Did you think I was just selling a newspaper? Oh, no! I'm offering you the whole world on your doorstep every morning. The day's events! Weather, commentary, sports, recipes, entertainment, comics, information, insight, laughter, wisdom, all delivered to your door for just pennies a day."

You've seen the commercial: Two golfers swat golfballs around the links accompanied by these familiar taglines: "Greens fees: $116. . . . Graphite shaft clubs: $877. . . . Lunch at the turn:

$13.50. . . . Balls, tees: $36." And then the clincher as one miraculous shot bounces across the green and into the cup. "Hole in one—and a witness: Priceless. There are some things money can't buy. For everything else, there's MasterCard."

What's the product? A credit card. But the commercial arouses *desire* for that card by selling something less tangible—and much more appealing: A perfect day at the country club. A one-in-a-million shot. Smiles all around. Pride. Joy. A memory that will never fade. The commercial never shouts, "Get this card." Instead, it whispers, "Picture yourself in a perfect place on a perfect day, making a perfect memory. . . ." Remember, selling is more than pitching a product. It's spinning a dream—and helping people to visualize themselves enjoying that dream.

5. Close the Deal

Don't talk beyond the sale. Get the signature on the dotted line, congratulate your client for making such a wise decision, then find the exit and move on to your *next* sale.

Jack Kent Cooke was a Canadian-born self-made billionaire who made his fortune in the television industry. He also built a reputation as the owner of major sports franchises, including Toronto's AAA baseball team, hockey's Los Angeles Kings, basketball's Los Angeles Lakers, and football's Washington Redskins. He got his first lesson in selling at the tender age of fourteen during the depths of the Great Depression.

For obvious reasons, the life of a salesman could be pretty tough in the depression. But when young Jack learned that his mother's phone would be cut off if she didn't get two dollars and fifty cents to pay the bill, he got a job selling encyclopedias door-to-door. The encyclopedias came with an instruction book on successful selling. Jack flipped through the book, then tossed it aside, confident that he could sell encyclopedias on his boyish charm alone. He went out, knocked on door after door, and struck out every time. Returning home, he picked up the instruction book and began to read. In two hours, he had read it from cover to cover. He later said that those were the two best-invested hours he had ever spent.

Next morning, he made his first sale on his second call. The principle that enabled him to make that sale was the book's instruction on how to close. At the end of his pitch, he asked the prospect, "Where would you like us to ship the books?" After that first sale, he went back to the customers who had turned him down the previous day—and he made still more sales! At the end of the day, he plunked his commission on the kitchen table in front of his astonished mother. He had earned twenty-four dollars and fifty cents, almost ten times what she needed to pay the phone bill. "That was the proudest moment of my life," Jack later recalled. "It was better than the Redskins winning the Super Bowl."

Closing is crucial in every kind of selling. A man was away from home on a business trip, and on Sunday he visited a church near his hotel. After the service, he stopped to chat with the pastor at the door. "Good sermon, Reverend," he said, "but would you mind some advice?"

"What is that?" asked the minister.

"I'm a sales manager, and if you worked for me, I'd tell you that your voice got my attention. You made a great first impression. Your stories held my interest. Your sincerity convinced me that you mean every word. It all made sense, and I was ready to buy—but then you stopped. You didn't ask me to *do* anything. You didn't close the sale. In my business, you have to get people to sign on the dotted line or you're out of business. I bet your business is no different." From that day forward, that pastor always made sure that he "closed the sale" at the end of every sermon.

Now, you may not get to close the sale on the first call. Don't worry about it. Just keep going back. The National Sales Executive Association once conducted a survey that underscored the importance of persistence in making a sale. The survey revealed:

- Eighty percent of all new sales are made after the fifth call to the same prospect.
- Forty-eight percent of all salespeople make just one call—then cross off the prospect.
- Twenty-five percent of all salespeople quit after the second call.
- Twelve percent of all salespeople call three times—then quit.

- Only 10 percent keep calling.
- It is the persistent, determined, relentless 10 percenters who are rewarded by a sale. They collect the dividends on what their less persistent colleagues have invested.

These are lessons in selling that I learned early in my career at the side of R. E. Littlejohn—one of the wisest men I've ever met, and one of the best salesmen I've ever known. One of his enduring legacies is the message that keeps ringing in my ears: "Pat, you've got to sell yourself!"

After that lesson, the next thing Mister R. E. taught me was the importance of something that lately has gone out of favor but never goes out of style: Hard work!

TWO

Work Hard

I have never known anyone who better exemplified the work ethic than Mister R. E. I told you about a time when he was eleven years old and he drove his father in a Model T to a job interview in Tucapau, South Carolina. What I didn't tell you was that he had *bought* that Model T with his own money! Where did the money come from? Hard work. He spent hours and hours after school and during the summer working in a South Carolina mill. How many eleven-year-olds do you know who have actually worked and saved so they could plunk down cash and buy their own car?

But that's exactly what young Richard Erlic Littlejohn did.

So it's not surprising at all that one of the first lessons I learned in Littlejohn University, soon after my arrival in Spartanburg, was the importance of hard work.

I vividly remember the first time I met Mister R. E. I arrived at his office and was instantly and profoundly impressed by this gray-haired, soft-spoken southern gentleman. He immediately put me at ease and asked me question after question, taking a genuine interest in me. One of the first things he told me that day was, "I hope you like to work hard, because there's a lot of work to be done here." He was right. The season would open in just two months, and I had to hit the ground running.

My first order of business was to go out to the ballfield, Duncan Park, and survey the situation. The ballpark was located in a beautiful, green city park, fringed with huge trees. The stadium, however, was neglected, dirty, and unpainted. The office was tiny and cold, and the public rest rooms were filthy beyond belief. No wonder attendance at the games had been so sparse in recent years. I decided to take on renovation of the ballpark as a personal challenge. If we were going to sell baseball to Spartanburg, we'd have to transform that baseball-diamond-in-the-rough into a crown jewel—and we didn't have much time.

For the next two months, I worked eighteen-hour days, seven days a week. In addition to the hired help I brought in, I personally bent my back to the gruntwork. I worked from dawn till dusk, cutting grass on the field, hammering nails in the new press box, slapping paint on the outfield walls, and hosing down the rest rooms. Our masterpiece was the completely refurbished ladies room. We transformed that grim, concrete-walled outhouse into a pink palace. We air-conditioned it, painted it, wallpapered it, hung curtains and laid carpeting, put up full-length mirrors, piped in music, hired an attendant, and arranged for fresh flowers for every game.

Even though sprucing up our ballpark was job one, I still had plenty of other chores that had to be juggled: meeting with the town fathers to plead for moral and financial support from City Hall, getting programs and tickets printed, getting uniforms altered, mended, and restored, and running around town, selling advertising. Whenever I wasn't working, I was thinking and brainstorming and dreaming up eye-popping, pulse-pounding promotional ideas to bring in the crowds.

And all our hard work paid off—big-time.

Attendance at the park skyrocketed that year, from around 30,000 to 114,000 for the season. Word spread across the state about the wild, exciting promotions at our ballpark, from nighttime skydivers to big-league stars' personal appearances to beauty pageants to watermelon-eating contests to a wild and wooly barnyard scramble in which our players chased farm animals all over the field. Our fans swelled in number and in pride, and everyone had a great time. At the end of my first year on the job, I was named Executive of the Year in the Western Carolinas League; two years later, I was named Minor League Executive of the Year by *The Sporting News*.

That was one of the most important lessons any twenty-five-year-old could learn, and it has stood me in good stead throughout my career as a sports executive. It's a lesson I've tried to pass on to my kids and to anyone else who will listen—and it's a lesson that often falls on deaf ears in this gimme-something-for-nothing world we live in. But what was true for an eleven-year-old boy who bought his own Model T during the Great Depression and what was true for a twenty-five-year-old wet-behind-the-ears baseball exec in Spartanburg in 1965 is still true: If you want to get anywhere in life, nothing beats hard work. The adage "The only place success comes before work is in the dictionary" still rings true.

The Fate of the American Work Ethic

In his book *Beyond the Classroom: Why School Reform Has Failed and What Parents Need to Do*, Dr. Laurence Steinberg draws on a ten-year study of twenty thousand American high school students to uncover the factors that lead to success or failure. He concludes that one of the leading indicators of success in school is (are you ready for this?) *ethnicity*. The researchers found that the most successful students were of Asian descent, followed by non-Hispanic whites, who were in turn trailed by black and Latino students. Asian students starkly outperformed non-Asian classmates of identical socioeconomic backgrounds, and even posted top scores when attending schools that were perceived to be of substandard quality.

What does this mean? Did God pass out intelligence according to racial and ethnic lines? Of course not.

There is a very simple reason Asian students outperformed their non-Asian peers: their cultural attitude toward hard work. "They work harder, try harder and are more interested in achievement," observes British educator Tony Mooney, "the very same factors that contribute to school success among all ethnic groups. It has nothing to do with superior intelligence."[1] And Steinberg adds, "If Asian students were truly genetically superior to other students, they would not be spending twice as much time on homework each week as their peers, in order to outperform them."

The issue is not genetic superiority but cultural attitudes. The Asian culture promotes a work ethic that directly leads to academic and occupational success. Asians tend to see success as a product of hard work, while regarding failure as a direct result of poor effort. By contrast, non-Asian students tend to downplay the importance of hard work; they see success or failure as the result of the innate ability ("you're either born smart or you're not"), an easy or difficult assignment ("that homework's too hard!"), a biased teacher ("the teacher hates me—that's why I failed"), or simple luck, either good or bad. Such attitudes lead to failure in school, failure in careers, and the waste of a good life.

Tragically, the work ethic in America is under vicious assault. In many nonwhite subcultures, there is an unfortunate attitude, enforced by peer pressure, that hard work and achievement equals "acting white." These attitudes have even begun to affect the attitudes of Asian-American students. Steinberg's research shows that the longer an Asian student's family has lived in America, the worse that student tends to perform in school. In other words, Americanization, the encroachment of increasingly anti-work-ethic American attitudes, is causing the Asian work ethic in America to erode, generation by generation.

In 1998, *Time* magazine published a special report called "How to Make a Better Student: Their Eight Secrets of Success." That report underscored a number of factors that contribute to the academic and long-range occupational success of young people, including parental encouragement and involvement, a structured environment for doing homework, parents and teachers who know how to feed a child's hunger for learning, involvement in church, a strong moral and ethical framework, and more. But the number one factor cited as a key to success was something *Time* called "The Sweat Factor"—a willingness and eagerness to work hard.

One student profiled was seventeen-year-old Bismarck Paliz, nicknamed Bizzy by his friends, not only because of his given name but because of his passion for hard work. His Ecuadorian father had immigrated to Newark, New Jersey, where he started with nothing and built up a successful real estate business. His Puerto Rican mother had worked her way up from being an office clerk to being an administrative professional by taking courses to improve her skills. Bizzy Paliz credits his parents with instilling a strong work ethic in him. "They are my mentors," he says. "They've led by example. They've kept me on track."

Bizzy is an honors student and a valedictorian at Science High, a magnet school in Newark. A math, science, and computer wiz, he earns extra money trouble-shooting computer problems for the firm where his mother works. Not that he needs the money—he was awarded a forty-thousand-dollar scholarship to Rensselaer Polytechnic Institute in Troy, New York, without even applying.

Where does his ability come from? It's not an issue of genetics, says his math teacher. Bizzy, she says, is in "the top 1 percent, not just in terms of ability but in terms of positive attitude, initiative and motivation." In other words, he's in the top 1 percent in *hard work*. His chemistry teacher agrees, noting, "Students like Bismarck are not expecting things just to happen for them. . . . They know they have to do it on their own." The sweat factor pays off.[2]

The fate of the American work ethic may look cloudy right now. All too many people—many young people, of course, but also many who are old enough to know better—seem to think the world owes them a living. They expect success, security, and rewards to be handed them as their due. So it's a real encouragement to know that there are still young people like Bizzy Paliz around—and we need to do all we can to encourage more young people to put in the time and sweat, so that both they and society will reap the rewards.

As a father, I'm having an interesting time with my children on this whole issue of work. As I write these words, we have sixteen teenagers in our family. Overall, we have nineteen children in our family—four birth children, one daughter by remarriage, and fourteen adopted kids (four each from South Korea, the Philippines, and Brazil, and two from Romania). Does that make me one of the world's leading authorities on teens or what? As you can imagine, with so many teens in the house, we spend a lot of time talking about work.

One of the key characteristics of my teenagers is that they all think they're working hard—but they don't have a clue. I hear it all the time: "Dad, I'm working so hard in school this year! I'm working so hard in sports! I'm working so hard, doing all my chores and keeping my room neat!" The truth of the matter: they aren't doing diddly! That's why I love high school graduation night—because on the day after graduation, one of three things happens: they go off to college (where they encounter a level of academic stress and strain they never imagined before), or they go into the military (we have two sons in the United States Marine Corps), or they go into the workforce and start paying their own way. In the words of humorist Bob Orben, they get a case of remedial reality real quick.

I think about the kind of hard work Mister R. E. was doing at age eleven, and I think of so many other people who have worked ten, twelve-, or sixteen-hour days throughout their teenage and adult lives because they were hungry for success—and I think of what real, hard, sweat-on-your-brow and dirt-under-your-fingernails work is all about—and I tell my kids, "You think you're working hard? Listen: whether you are a fuddy-duddy like your dad or a cool teenager growing up in the 'burbs of Orlando, there are nine words that will never change: *There ain't no such thing as a free lunch!*" I call it the Tanstaafl theory: T-A-N-S-T-A-A-F-L

The great jockey Eddie Arcaro said it best in one of my favorite quotes of all time: "When a guy starts sleeping in silk pajamas, it's tough to get up in the morning." If you want a lifetime of success, nothing beats hard work.

Mr. Work Ethic

It should come as no surprise that the number one example of success in America today is also the number one role model for the work ethic: Michael Jordan. He's Superman, Air Jordan, an icon of quasi-religious fan adoration. At the height of his basketball career with the Chicago Bulls, he was the most highly paid athlete and corporate pitchman in history, pulling down more than $75 million per year, or about $8,700 per hour, twenty-four hours a day, seven days a week—a tad more than minimum wage. He is an international symbol of achievement in maximum overdrive. Everybody wants to be like Mike.

But how did Michael Jordan get to be Michael Jordan?

A lot of youthful NBA wannabes dream of reaching M. J.'s rarified altitude and extending his legendary hangtime. Many of them doubtless have as much raw ability in their arms, legs, and the motor centers of their brains to achieve Jordanesque greatness—but they are doomed to mediocrity despite their raw talent. Why? Because only a very few human beings have M. J.'s superhuman work ethic.

Millions have seen Jordan, the finished product, working miracles on court. But few have seen how that product was built and honed and polished to perfection by hours and hours of sweat and pain and struggle and grueling exertion on the practice floor. No one becomes Michael Jordan without leaving a trail of sweat—not even Michael Jordan. He didn't get to the top of his game by being a natural-born basketball genius. He got there by being Mr. Work Ethic.

As a boy growing up in Wilmington, North Carolina, young Mike was raised by two loving and incredibly hard-working parents, James and Deloris Jordan. In addition to working two and three jobs, both of the Jordans invested hours and hours of time and involvement with their five kids through Boy Scouts, PTA, school music and sports programs, and continual contact with the kids' teachers. Whenever one of the kids had an after-school game or other event, Deloris would work through her lunch hour so she could leave work an hour early and get to the event.

James Jordan's military background probably had a lot to do with the way he applied firm but loving rules and discipline with his children. Education was the number one priority in the Jordan household, and Mike and his four siblings knew it. But James Jordan also made sure his kids had plenty of exercise and fun. He leveled a space behind the family's split-level brick house and created a basketball court with hoops at both ends so the kids could play real end-to-end games.

While growing up, Michael was not considered as talented as his brother Larry, who was a year older. Larry consistently beat him in games of one-on-one. In his sophomore year, Michael was cut from the varsity team—a devastating emotional blow to the future Air Jordan. But being cut from the team only fired his intensity to work harder and make the cut the following year. One practice a day wasn't enough for Mike: he worked out with both the varsity and junior varsity teams. He'd also go to school early before class and on weekends to shoot baskets and hone his skills.

When he arrived at the University of North Carolina to begin his college career, he told assistant coach Roy Williams about his ambition to be the best in the game. A few days later, during a practice, Williams yelled at Jordan, "You're dogging it, Mike! Come on, show some hustle!"

Jordan bristled. "Hey, Coach, I'm working as hard as everyone else!"

"Sure you are," Williams shot back, "but you told me you wanna be *better* than everybody else. So you're gonna have to work *harder* than everybody else!"

Jordan was shaken. From that day forward, he determined to practice longer and harder than anyone else for as long as he played the game.

A few years later, Jordan was drafted by the Bulls. At the end of his first year in the NBA, he was voted Rookie of the Year. A lot of players would have gotten cocky at that point and started coasting. Not Mike. After the season, he went back to North Carolina and visited with Coach Williams. "You've been watching my games, Coach," he said. "What do you think I need to improve?"

Williams had a ready answer. "Your jump shot needs work. If you could get that shot down perfectly, you'd be unbeatable."

So Jordan spent the summer working intensely on his jump shot. Jordan's jumper became legendary. But it didn't come naturally. It came with a price tag—and the price was hours and hours of hard, lonely work.

Later in his career, as Jordan saw that some of his skills and abilities were slipping due to the natural advance of time, he worked on developing new skills, new shots to compensate. So fanatical was Jordan about working on these skills that he had a basketball court constructed on the set while he was filming the movie *Space Jam*. Whenever there was a break in the filming, Jordan could be found on his private court, working on his new fadeaway jump shot. By the time he was through filming and ready to return to work with the Bulls, he had his fadeaway jumper perfected.

Mike's work ethic was not just reserved for himself. He demanded hard work from his teammates. "I push players now, in some respect, more-so than most coaches," he once told an interviewer for *USA Today*. "I strive for excellence and some players don't. They strive for acceptance. I even see that with some players on [the Bulls]. If you push too hard, they don't take it very well."[3]

Everybody wants to be like Mike, but only a few will ever come close. Why? Because only a few know what it really means to work hard to achieve a goal.

Words of Working Wisdom

In the closing years of the nineteenth century, Charles Michael Schwab, the right-hand man of Andrew Carnegie of the Carnegie Steel Company, formulated what he called The Ten Commandments of Success. Those commandments are as valid today as when Schwab penned them:

1. *Work hard:* Hard work is the best investment a person can make.
2. *Study hard:* Knowledge enables us to work more intelligently and effectively.
3. *Have initiative:* Ruts often deepen into graves.
4. *Love your work:* Then you will find pleasure in mastering it.
5. *Be exact:* Slipshod methods bring slipshod results.
6. *Have the spirit of conquest:* Thus you can successfully battle and overcome difficulties.

7. *Cultivate personality:* Personality is to a person what perfume is to the flower.
8. *Help and share with others:* The real test of business greatness lies in giving opportunity to others.
9. *Be democratic:* Unless you feel right towards others, you can never be a successful leader.
10. *In all things, do your best:* The person who has done less than their best has done nothing.

Great words! Dr. Martin Luther King Jr. also knew the value of hard work done well: "If a man is called to be a street-sweeper," he once said, "he should sweep streets even as Michelangelo painted, or Beethoven played music, or Shakespeare wrote poetry. He should sweep streets so well that all the hosts of heaven and earth will pause to say, 'Here lived a great street-sweeper who did his job well.'" And Charles Kingsley made this observation about the character-building value of hard work: "Thank God every morning when you get up that you have something to do that day which must be done, whether you like it or not. Being forced to work, and forced to do your best, will breed in you temperance and self-control, diligence and strength of will, cheerfulness and contentment, and a hundred virtues which the idle never know."

And of course, I also want to leave you with the wise words of R. E. Littlejohn. He taught me that to be successful one has to be willing to sacrifice some ease and pleasure to win what really counts. On more than one occasion he said to me, "The man who rows the boat generally doesn't have time to rock it."

This is not to say that we should work in a driven or obsessive way. Mister R. E. worked hard, but he was not a workaholic. Workaholism is an unhealthy addiction that causes people to neglect their marriages, their kids, their relationship with God, and their own mental, emotional, and physical health. Mister R. E. knew how and when to relax, and he often quoted the words of Vance Havner: "If you don't come apart, you'll come apart." So come apart from your work now and then, so you won't come apart at the seams. Work hard—but pace yourself. Life isn't a hundred-meter sprint. Life is a marathon—and as someone who has run a few marathons, I can tell you that the only way to go the distance is to pace yourself.

Finally, let me pass on the most important thing Mister R. E. ever taught me about work: Our work should have a high purpose, a noble goal. He taught and lived the New Testament wisdom of Colossians 3:23–24: "Whatever you do, work at it with all your heart, as working for the Lord, not for men, since you know that you will receive an inheritance from the Lord as a reward. It is the Lord Christ you are serving."

That is the goal of my own work, and I trust you will make it yours.

The third thing Mister R. E. taught me was the importance of keeping the lines of communication open.

THREE

Keep the Communication Lines Open

On January 13, 1982, a Boeing 737 idled on the runway at National Airport in Washington, D.C. Because of heavy snowfall, that flight—Air Florida Flight 90 to Fort Lauderdale—was preparing to depart almost two hours behind schedule. Though the copilot was experienced in icy-weather flying, the pilot was not. As the plane waited to take off, the copilot repeatedly tried to warn the pilot about the bad weather and point out the ice buildup on other planes.

"Look how the ice is just hanging on the tail of that plane—see that?" asked the co-pilot. "See all those icicles on the back there?"

"Yeah," said the pilot, unconcerned.

Time passed. "It's been a long wait since the last de-icing," the copilot worried aloud. "A lot of time for new ice buildup in this storm.

You know, this is a losing battle, trying to de-ice these things. It just gives you a false feeling of security."

The pilot apparently did not share the copilot's concerns. He went about his preflight checklist and prepared for takeoff. After a few minutes, Flight 90 was cleared for takeoff. The pilot throttled up the engines and the plane rumbled forward.

The copilot nervously watched the instruments as the plane lifted heavily off the runway. "Look at that indicator! That doesn't seem right, does it?" he asked, pointing to the console. "Uh, that's not right."

"Yes it is," the pilot answered confidently. "There's eighty."

"No, I don't think that's right," the copilot fretted as the aircraft wallowed into the air, reached an altitude of about two hundred feet and banked left. He paused uncertainly. "Well, maybe it is." Another long pause. "I don't know—"

Just then, the "stickshaker" stall warning system began to sound. At that moment, the pilot realized he was in trouble. The plane was descending.

"Come on, forward! Forward! Climb!" he pleaded. Ten seconds of fear crept by. "We're falling," moaned the pilot.

The stickshaker continued to yammer in their ears.

"Larry, we're going down!" yelled the copilot. "Larry—!"

"I know it—" said the pilot. Those were his last words.

The very next instant, the belly of the plane plowed through six automobiles and a truck on the 14th Street Bridge over the Potomac River, ripped out the bridge railing, and plunged nose-first into the ice-crusted river. The plane almost vanished beneath the surface of the river—all that showed was the blue Air Florida tail. Four of the five crew members died, including the pilot and copilot. All but four of the seventy-four passengers died. Four more people were killed in their cars on the bridge.

In all, seventy-eight people died because of poor communication.

A Failure to Communicate

The dialogue above came from the black box recordings of the cockpit conversation. Crash investigators who first listened to those recordings instantly understood what had gone wrong: The copilot on Flight 90 knew that the icing conditions were dangerous and that the de-icing procedures prior to the flight were not adequate, and he tried to warn the pilot. But his warnings were indirectly stated—almost hints rather than warnings—and the pilot failed to heed them. In fact, the pilot didn't even seem to grasp what the co-pilot was telling him. Investigators have since learned that similar communication problems have contributed to other air disasters.

Communication problems are widespread throughout our society—in corporations, on sports teams, in churches, in schools, in clubs and service organizations, and in families. The results: a business failure, a losing season, a church split, a failing grade, an organizational collapse, a marital breakup. Poor communication underlies much of the failure in our lives; effective communication is a key to achieving success.

There are many barriers to effective communication that must be recognized in order to be overcome. We need to understand why bosses and subordinates sometimes have a hard time talking to and understanding one another. We have to understand the differences in thinking and communication style between generations, between cultural and racial groups, and between men and women.

"No matter what you're doing," Mister R. E. often told me, "whether it's business or sports or talking to your wife and kids, you have to keep the lines of communication open. You have to make sure there is understanding all around. Never take it for granted that, just because you said it, the other person heard what you meant."

The problem of indirect communication that brought down Flight 90 is a two-sided problem. You could say, "It's the copilot's fault. He should have said what he meant. He should have said, 'I know this weather, and it's dangerous to take off with that much ice on the wings. Captain, we have to get this plane de-iced again.'" Certainly, the copilot was worried about the ice—but he also was worried about dealing with the man who was the boss on that plane. He was concerned about not hurting his career, and he was concerned that Flight 90 was already two hours behind schedule.

You could also say, "It's the pilot's fault. The copilot made himself clear enough. He specifically said, 'This is a losing battle, trying to de-ice these things. It just gives you a false feeling of security.' The pilot should have listened to his copilot and drawn upon his greater experience in cold-weather flying."

There are two sides in every dialogue—a speaker and a listener. Both are responsible for the communication process. The speaker is responsible for expressing his message clearly enough to be understood, and the listener is responsible for detecting nuance, concerns, emotions, and meaning. The failure in the cockpit of Flight 90 involved both sides. And in all probability, so does that failure in your business, on your team, in your church, with your child's schoolwork, in your organization, or in your family. And the result of a communication failure can be disastrous.

Styles of Thinking and Communicating

We tend to assume that communication is merely the process of conveying information from one person to another. But it's really much more than that. Communication is the process by which we build relationships and trust, share meaning and values and feelings, and transcend the aloneness and isolation of being distinct, individual human souls. Communication is not just a data dump. Communication is *connection*.

So it is crucial that we understand how communication works, what causes it to break down, and how to restore it. It is important that we understand the differences between the way we communicate and the way others communicate. If we fail to bridge that gap of understanding, we will continually tangle the lines of communication, and we will continually create disaster after disaster in our personal and business lives.

Jack was an elder in a large church. His longtime friend Renee also served as an elder in the same church. A conflict arose between two groups over a major change in the direction of the church's ministry. Though good friends, Jack and Renee found themselves on opposite sides of the issue. Jack and Renee strongly believed that their respective positions were right.

But during a congregational meeting, Renee made a public statement about Jack and his views that deeply offended Jack. He felt she had attacked his reputation for integrity. With the pastor acting as an intermediary, Jack and Renee agreed to meet to resolve their differences in a Christian manner. They met in the relaxed, neutral atmosphere of the pastor's backyard. The pastor opened with prayer, then asked, "Who would like to speak first?"

"There's something I'd like to say," said Renee.

"Okay with me," said Jack.

"First, I want to say, Jack, that I really admire everything you do as a leader in this church." And she went on to pile on compliments and commendation and flattery for the next couple of minutes. The longer she went on, the more Jack fidgeted. He was sure he knew where Renee was headed. At the end of the compliments would be a "but"—and then the criticism would begin. Listening to her compliments was like waiting for the other boot to drop. Finally, he interrupted her.

"Renee," he said, "can we just cut to the chase?"

Renee looked stricken. "What?"

"Look, I don't need all this flattery. You and I have a problem, so let's just get down to business and solve it, okay?"

She stared at him for several seconds, wounded and furious. Then she stood up. "Forget it."

Jack spread his hands. "What did I say?"

"Just forget it." Renee turned and left.

Jack looks back on that day with regret. "We had been friends for years. She never spoke to me again after that."

What went wrong? Jack failed to understand that men and women tend to have different styles of communicating. Renee, using the communication style typical of her gender, tried to build rapport with supportive statements. Jack, typical of a man, was eager to get down to brass tacks. Today, he wonders if he wasn't mistaken in anticipating what Renee was going to say next. What if she was actually leading up to an apology, instead of more criticism, as he assumed? He'll never know. He aborted the conversation before he could find out. In the end, nobody won, everybody lost. And a friendship, a holy Christian relationship, was destroyed.

Similar disasters often take place in business environments. Judith is the editor of a corporate public relations magazine. Brad is a new staff writer who reports to Judith. He has just turned in a manuscript that is, in Judith's view, unusable, because he didn't follow the instructions she gave him when she assigned it. So she calls Brad into her office.

"Brad," she says, "I think you are a terrific writer."

Brad smiles. "Thank you."

"I mean it. Some of these lines really sing. You held my interest throughout. The lead is a grabber, and you have a powerful finish. And you're a good interviewer—you got some great quotes from the sales manager."

"Thanks."

"Now, Brad, do you remember the angle we talked about when I assigned you this piece? You sort of got away from that. You focused in on the sales manager. I wanted you to focus on the new product. After all, that's what we're trying to sell."

"Oh, yeah, I see what you mean."

"So, could you do a rewrite, focusing on the product?"

"No problem! I'll have it for you by tomorrow morning, first thing."

"Well, Brad, I would think it would take you at least a couple of days—"

"Not at all! Tomorrow morning—promise."

So Brad leaves Judith's office. The next day, she finds the revised manuscript in her in-box. She flips through it, page by page, and everything is the same as the original draft. Not one word changed— oh, here it is! He's added a new paragraph just before the close. He spends all of three sentences at the end of the piece talking about the product.

Enraged, Judith calls Brad into her office. He enters, smiling. "How did you like it?"

"How did I—?" Judith sputters. "Brad, you didn't rewrite it! You only added one paragraph near the end!"

"Well, that's all you asked for," Brad replies, a look of defensiveness erasing his smile. "You told me the whole thing was great—it just needed a little added emphasis on the product and it would be perfect."

"I said no such thing!" Judith shoots back. "The whole point of calling you in and talking to you about this piece is that you completely missed the angle I told you to go for. I wanted you to interview the sales manager about the new product—but what you turned in is just a puff piece on the sales manager himself! You were supposed to rewrite the whole piece, top to bottom, and promote the product."

"You never said that," Brad asserts. "All you said was you liked my writing, but you wanted me to fix one little thing. So I fixed it. I did exactly what you told me to do."

What went wrong? Judith and Brad were approaching the situation with different communicating styles (or, as John Gray, author of *Men Are from Mars, Women Are from Venus,* would say, from different planets). Judith thought she was building rapport and softening the criticism by opening with a few compliments. She didn't want Brad to feel put down or discouraged, so she gave him some face-saving flattery at the beginning. Brad, however, assumed that Judith was opening with her main feedback on the piece and took her flattery to mean that she overwhelmingly approved of the piece. Brad took her final criticism—which Judith considered the main thrust of their meeting—to be nothing more than a minor postscript to a main theme of "Well done!"

Clearly, a lot of people would have responded well to Judith's tactful feedback and would have considered a "let's-get-down-to-business" blunt approach to be unfeeling and cold. But some, like Brad, would consider the blunt approach to be honest and sincere, while the tactful approach appears to them muddled and vague. He left Judith's office muttering to himself that his editor was irrational and devious, never realizing that she had actually attempted to be kind and caring in their previous discussion.

In the end, each side blamed the other—and the result was a pattern of frustration, personality clash, and wasted effort.

Who Gets the Credit?

Communication experts such as Deborah Tannen, John Gray, and Tom Kochman tell us that most of the world's cultures prize indirect communication. The indirect approach used by Renee and Judith is typical of many Asian cultures—but it's also typical of the way most women, including Western women, communicate. The indirect approach avoids confrontation and unpleasantness, mixes small talk and business talk, softens criticism with praise and affirmation, and prefers to ease into business matters rather than jumping in with both feet. The indirect approach places a priority on establishing a relationship and warm feelings before moving on to matters of hard information and negotiation.

American men, by contrast, see communication as a matter of direct data transfer, achieving goals and quotas, solving problems, and closing the deal. Sure, a little small talk (comparing golf scores or "How about that Magic game!") is acceptable to lubricate the conversation—but the overriding attitude is, "Keep it brief, snap it up, c'mon, c'mon, time is money."

Communication, to a man, is often focused on competition, status, power, and position in the pecking order. To a woman, communication is about cooperation, relationships, feelings, and offering support to others. Men tend to be more concrete and fact-oriented; women tend to be more abstract and feelings-oriented. Women tend to soft-pedal their certainties; men tend to downplay their doubts. Men communicate to fix problems and reach goals; women communicate to make connections. Men tend to ask, "What do you *think* about this?" Women tend to ask, "How do you *feel* about that?" Men tend to place a premium on getting credit for accomplishments, while women place a premium on maintaining an image that is not too boastful, bossy, or pushy.

A research team led by psychologist Laurie Heatherington designed an experiment, reported in the journal *Sex Roles* in 1993, in which the researchers asked hundreds of incoming college freshmen in two groups to predict their grades in the coming year. The first group was asked to make sealed, written predictions. The other students made their predictions in a group setting.

The results: "More women than men predicted lower grades for themselves if they made their predictions publicly. If they made their predictions privately, the predictions were the same as those of the men—and the same as their actual grades. This study provides evidence that what comes across as lack of confidence—predicting lower grades for oneself—may reflect not one's actual level of confidence but the desire not to seem boastful."[4]

If a woman talks to a man about a problem, it is likely that all she wants is emotional support and caring. But when a man hears a woman express a problem, he tends to perceive it as a plea for help—so instead of offering her support and caring, he gives her advice on how to fix the problem, which is not at all what she wants. If, on the other hand, a woman offers advice to a man, she probably sees it as a sign of caring and support to him. From his competitive, status-oriented perspective, however, he views her unsolicited advice as criticism, implying that she doesn't think he's competent to solve the problem himself—and the result is often conflict, misunderstanding, and miscommunication.

These, of course, are generalizations. Individuals vary, and so do situations. But in my own experience—in my family and career—I have often seen that these generalizations provide a fairly accurate approximation of real encounters between men and women. The origin of these gender-based differences can be traced to childhood.

"Although both girls and boys find ways of creating rapport and negotiating status," observes Deborah Tannen, "girls tend to learn conversational rituals that focus on the rapport dimension of relationships whereas boys tend to learn rituals that focus on the status dimension. . . . The result is that women and men tend to have different habitual ways of saying what they mean, and conversations between them can be like cross-cultural communication: You can't assume that the other person means what you would mean if you said the same thing in the same way."

Tannen cites as an example a focus group meeting she attended at a major multinational company. The participants sat in a circle, evaluating a new company policy. The consensus was that it was a good policy with some room for improvement—and it was a very productive meeting. Tannen reports that at the conclusion of the

meeting, she left with the impression that one of the male participants, Phil, had generated most of the suggestions adopted by the
focus group. Later, however, she typed up her notes and made a
surprising discovery: most of the key ideas had actually been put
forward by a female participant, Cheryl. Phil had merely picked up
Cheryl's ideas and supported them, speaking at greater length than
Cheryl had.

It was not a case of Phil stealing Cheryl's ideas or hogging credit—
fact is, he never claimed her ideas as his own. For her part, Cheryl
later reported feeling she had made an important contribution, and
she was grateful for Phil's support of her ideas. There was a genuine
attitude of teamwork and cooperation between Cheryl and Phil.
The focus group accomplished its mission; case closed—right?

Well, not so fast. Deborah Tannen went back to the group and
polled the participants on their impression of Phil's and Cheryl's
contributions. Asked who was more responsible for the ideas put
forth in the group, the two other women accurately named Cheryl
as the originator of the ideas, while all the men (except Phil) in-
correctly credited Phil.

Why this disparity in perceptions? Gender differences in communication. Cheryl was more deferential, less vocal, less direct,
while Phil was more assertive, more vocal, more direct—and he inadvertently ended up getting credit where no credit was due. "Men
tend to be sensitive to the power dynamics of interaction," Tannen
concludes, "speaking in ways that position themselves as one-up
and resisting being put in a one-down position by others. Women
tend to react more strongly to the rapport dynamic, speaking in
ways that save face for others and buffering statements that could
be seen as putting others in a one-down position. These linguistic
patterns are pervasive. . . . They affect who gets heard and who gets
credit."[5]

The point is that faulty communication patterns take place hundreds of times every day in offices across the country—and as a result, the contributions of talented, capable workers (generally
women) tend to be under-recognized and unrewarded. This places
women at a distinct disadvantage in the workplace—but is it anyone's fault? The fact is, both the speaker and the hearer, both the

manager and the subordinate, both the male employee and the female employee have a responsibility to improve communication in situations such as these. Workers like Cheryl, if they want to be recognized and advanced, need to make sure that they make themselves heard, clearly and forcefully. And managers need to develop the skills of listening and observing, so that talented, capable, creative people like Cheryl will be rewarded and retained for the good of the company.

Keeping Lines of Communication Open

Whether you are a man or a woman, a boss or a subordinate, a coach or a player, a leader or a follower, here are some practical suggestions for keeping open lines of communication with the people around you.

1. *Set the tone.* If you are an owner, a boss, a leader, or a manager, set a tone that is conducive to good, open communication. The best way to have open lines of communication is to have *short* lines of communication. The boss should be accessible to the subordinates—walking the factory floor, eating in the lunchroom with employees, walking the corridors and hallways, greeting workers by name.

In February 1997, the management of the Orlando Magic had the tough job of releasing head coach Brian Hill. I personally hated to see him go. He is a fine human being, a great family man, and a very capable coach. When he was given the news that he was being let go, he understandably wanted to know why. Answer: "Lack of communication." Hill was surprised. "But," he said, "my door was always open and the players knew that." I've often thought about that statement, and I know he was sincere—but it occurs to me that having an open door is not enough. Even if the players know they are welcome, they won't come in. A great coach, a great leader, a great manager doesn't wait for people to come to him; he must go out to them. Employees don't enjoy going up to the boss's office, but they feel appreciated and more at ease when the boss comes out on the shop floor. Gen. George S. Patton captured this idea when he said, "The more senior the officer, the more time he has. Therefore, the senior should go forward to visit the junior rather than call the junior back to him."

It's the same when you're a parent. You can tell your kids, "You can always come to Dad; I'm always here for you." But that's not enough. I've noticed, especially as my kids have gotten older, that they don't come to me very much anymore (except for money or to borrow the car keys). If I want to have a relationship with them, if I want to keep the lines of communication open, I have to go to them.

2. *Make people feel important.* As a boss or manager, make sure everyone knows he or she has a right to express an idea or opinion. If certain people seem shy or self-effacing, draw them out. Invite candor. Make sure employees feel that their opinions and ideas matter and that their contributions are valued. Make the people around you feel important.

An Englishwoman once dined separately with two great statesmen—Gladstone and his chief political rival, Disraeli—on two successive nights. Asked to compare the men, she replied, "After spending the evening sitting next to Mr. Gladstone, I came away thinking he was the cleverest man in all England. But after spending an evening sitting next to Mr. Disraeli, I came away thinking *I* was the cleverest *woman* in all England. To tell you the truth, I'd rather be with Mr. Disraeli!" That's how a good leader makes subordinates feel—not that *he* is so astoundingly clever and brilliant, but that *they* have something brilliant and valuable to offer.

3. *Show support.* As the boss, sit in on meetings, even if you don't have to be there. Be there not to intimidate but to show support, ask questions, affirm good contributions, and encourage good communication. Be a cheerleader. Show that you are interested, involved, and accessible. Keep the group's creative juices flowing with encouragement: "Great idea! Why don't you flesh that out a bit?" Or, "Okay, those two ideas won't fly, but you're thinking in the right direction—let's see what else you can come up with!" Use your position in the organization to keep ideas and information flowing freely.

Carly Fiorina is now the CEO of Hewlett Packard. But when she was at Lucent Technologies, she gathered a small group of executives in her office to celebrate a third straight year of record profits. Amid the good-natured banter, she asked, "So, where do we go from here? I know you won't want to rest on your laurels." One of the executives thought it was a telling demonstration of her leadership. Carly, the boss, didn't say, "Great job, but I'm not satisfied." Instead, it was, "You're wonderful. And I know you want to do even better."

4. *Express yourself clearly.* As a leader, always express yourself clearly, directly, confidently.

5. *Always put people at ease.* Nothing stifles good communication like feelings of anxiety and intimidation. When people tense up, they clam up. Communication usually is distorted whenever people feel ill-at-ease or apprehensive.

6. *Build relationships.* Build horizontal relationships rather than vertical power structures. Good communication flows from feelings of camaraderie, shared goals, shared commitments, shared relationships, and a sense of teamwork. Information flows freely when everyone feels committed to a common good. Information pipelines get clogged when people feel as though they are merely occupying a space in the corporate pecking order.

While writing this book, I attended an Orlando Magic staff retreat in Holland, Michigan. Owner Rich DeVos stood up and addressed all of the executives. He told us the story of Amway Corporation, a $7 billion company which had just celebrated its fortieth anniversary and of which he is cofounder. "As I think back over the successes we've had," he said, "I realize that the key to everything is *encouragement.* All I ever did as a leader was go around and encourage people. I went to our manufacturing plants and our distribution sites, here in the States and around the world, and I shook hands with people and told them I appreciated what they were doing. Those people are the reason for our success, and I wanted to encourage them and let them know they are appreciated. When people ask me what my role at Amway is, I tell them, 'I'm the head cheerleader.'"

7. *Listen.* Listen carefully to the nuances of those who express themselves indirectly. Does their communication style betray a lack of confidence—or merely a desire not to appear too pushy? Try to

draw such people out. Encourage them to speak freely and directly. Applaud them when they express themselves in clear, assertive, unambiguous terms. Let them know they have nothing to fear in stating themselves in a direct way.

8. *Welcome ideas.* Make sure everyone knows that new ideas and unconventional solutions are welcome. Great ideas often come from the unlikeliest places. No one should be left out of brainstorming sessions. When there is open communication in an organization, everyone feels that his or her ideas are valued, from executives and managers to mailroom clerks and secretaries. Often, it is the people in the lower echelons of an organization who are closest to the customers and know what the customers want.

Ron Wolf, general manager of the Green Bay Packers, put it this way: "Never, ever stand up in front of your employees and say, 'This is my operation, and this is how we're going to do it, period.' If you do, you'll shut down the lines of communication. You'll send a message that what they think and say really doesn't matter, because you'll do it your way no matter what. Your business is only as strong as its ability to tap into the strength of its employees."

9. *Welcome respectful dissent.* This is not easy in most organizational structures. Corporate structures generally discourage dissent. In fact, employees in many companies live in fear of doing or saying anything that might be a "career ender." What does that do to communication? It shuts it down! Open, honest communication requires that people feel free to express themselves, reasonably and respectfully but also candidly, without fear of punishment.

10. *Create networks.* As a leader or owner, create a network of human connection in your organization. Make effective use of such tools as teleconferencing and E-mail to keep all the levels of your organization in touch and in sync.

11. *Keep people informed.* Make sure all in the organization are well-informed, and they will keep you informed—and they will do a better job. It's a mistake to hide information from employees. Never say, "You don't need to know that." Solutions to problems often come when diverse and seemingly unrelated pieces of information (from unexpected sources!) fall into place. So share information and keep it flowing.

12. Give feedback. Provide a steady stream of feedback in addition to formal performance reviews. Let people know how they are doing and how much you appreciate them. A continuous "feedback loop" builds worker confidence, reinforces good habits, and stimulates enthusiasm and creativity.

Bill de Genaro, an expert in espionage, once noted, "The lack of recognition is a common thread among both political defectors and disenchanted employees. People can turn on you or leave you if they feel their contributions don't matter." So, to keep your best people, give them positive feedback and make sure they feel valued and recognized.

13. Contribute. If you are a subordinate looking to move up the ladder, make your contributions felt in meetings and team situations. Put yourself forward, talk to the boss or manager, ask questions, and share ideas. In social situations, practice your small-talk skills. If you tend to be shy, work on assertiveness and communication skills so you can display more confidence and competence.

14. Build trust. Build trust by practicing integrity. Always tell the truth. Practice openness. Avoid hidden agendas. Communication is always enhanced when each side trusts the other. When in doubt, always tell the truth.

I once interviewed the great major-league baseball manager Sparky Anderson on my radio show. He told me about his first interview in the big leagues, sitting across the desk from Bob Howsam, president of the Cincinnati Reds. Howsam asked him, "If you tell your ace pitcher he needs to go out and get his wind sprints in, and he says, 'I'm your best pitcher, I don't do wind sprints, and you can't make me,' what would you do?" Sparky said, "I don't know—but I'd figure something out." Rather than try to con Howsam, he just answered candidly—and he got the job. "When 'I don't know' is the honest answer," Sparky concluded, "it's the *only* answer. I think that's probably why Bob Howsam gave me the job—he appreciated my frankness."

15. Build rapport by practicing humility. Mister R. E. often said to me, "Pat, never give the other fella the impression that you know more than he does. If you do, you'll break his spirit and destroy your influence with him. If you want to keep the lines of communication open with others, keep a humble spirit." Great advice. Lord Chesterfield put it another way: "Be wiser than other people if you can—but do not tell them so."

16. Finally, make communication fun! How do you do that? Well, let me tell you a story. . . .

Fun Times in Toyland

When John Amerman took over as CEO of California-based Mattel Toys in 1987, the company and its stockholders were still reeling from a $113 million one-year loss. Several new Mattel toy lines had bombed badly. Morale was in the tank. Amerman knew that desperate times call for drastic changes. On his first day on the job, he wandered around the Mattel headquarters and one fact stood out to him: Here was a company whose mission was to manufacture and sell fun—yet nobody at Mattel was having any fun! It was as though Santa's workshop had become a slave-labor camp full of miserable, depressed elves! Well, something had to be done about that!

So on John Amerman's second day on the job, he called his employees together and announced a new policy: Henceforth, Mattel was going to be a fun place to work. From then on, all employees were under orders to relax and enjoy themselves on the job. To make sure the lines of communication were wide open, Amerman would take time out every day to walk through the facility, eat lunch in the cafeteria with the rank-and-file, and generally schmooze with the workers.

Not only was Amerman a hit, but morale quickly zoomed—and so did profits. In just three years, Mattel rebounded from a $113 million loss to a record $91 million profit in 1990—and paid every employee a bonus equivalent to two weeks' pay. To announce the company's rosy earnings picture to employees in 1989, Amerman delivered his message in a down-and-funky rap routine, backed up by a group of secretaries dubbed the Rappettes. Mattel workers howled when they saw their white-haired CEO doing his homeboy thing:

> Yo! Supersonic motivatin' toys we're creatin'!
> Everybody knows that Mattel is devastatin'!

Immediately afterward, Amerman was swarmed by employees wanting to hug him. He later recalled, "It was like I hit the home run in the ninth inning of the seventh game of the World Series!"[6]

Now, I never saw Mister R. E. do a rap act. But in his own way he was a great communicator, and his ability to state himself clearly and directly, to gently level with people, to put people at ease, to make people feel valued, and to inject *fun* into the workday—these qualities all contributed mightily to his success in business, and his success as a great and wise human being. He taught me the importance of good communication—but more important, he lived it.

For example, during my years in Spartanburg, Mister R. E. and I had a January ritual. New Year's Day is a big event among southerners. The Littlejohns would invite me over for a traditional supper that had great symbolic meaning. There was roast pork to symbolize health, black-eyed peas to represent coins, turnip greens to represent dollar bills—and Mrs. Littlejohn would throw in some rice and gravy, ripe cantaloupe, and sweet iced tea for good measure. Then Mister R. E. and I would sit in front of the TV and watch the bowl games—after which I generally would fall asleep on their couch.

New Year's Day also was the day Mister R. E. and I would negotiate my salary for the coming year. Those discussions were unlike any negotiating sessions I had before or have had since. Mister R. E. would have me write on a piece of paper what I would like in the way of salary. At the same time, he'd write down his idea. Then we'd exchange papers. Amazingly, his number was always higher than mine. We would always go with his number.

Now, that's what I call communication!

But that wasn't all Mister R. E. taught me—not by a long shot. The next thing I learned from him was the importance of seeking the wisdom and advice of other people.

FOUR

Seek Out
Wisdom and Advice
from Others

I was twenty-two years old when I first met Bill Veeck.

In case you're wondering, "Who's Bill Veeck?" let me just say that he was one of the greatest owners, executives, and promoters in the history of major league baseball. From birth, baseball was in his blood. The son of a Chicago sportswriter who later became president of the Chicago Cubs, Veeck got started in the game by selling peanuts, popcorn, and scorecards in the stands at Wrigley Field. He worked alongside Cubs' manager Charlie Grimm in the late '30s and early '40s and later became famous for buying struggling teams and turning them into winners—the AAA Milwaukee Brewers, the Cleveland Indians, the St. Louis Browns, and the Chicago White Sox.

But Bill Veeck was more than a hall-of-fame sports promoter. He was a hall-of-fame humanitarian. In a time when racism was institutionalized in our society, Bill just flat-out didn't care if you were white, black, or plaid. He looked at people as *people,* and he looked at players as *players.* That's why in 1947 he hired Larry Doby to play for the Cleveland Indians—the first black player in the American League. And that's why he brought Satchel Paige up from the Negro League to play for Cleveland—a gutsy move in those times.

One of the many lessons I absorbed from Bill Veeck was the importance of giving people a great time at the ballpark. He prized entertainment and fun right up there with winning and making money. He was the Walt Disney of baseball, and his passion for creating excitement and making people happy showed in everything he did. As he reflected in his 1962 autobiography, *Veeck as in Wreck,* "My philosophy as a baseball operator could not be more simple. It is . . . to draw people to the park and make baseball fans out of them."

I saw in Bill Veeck a man who always mingled with the fans, who never closed the door of his office, who answered his own mail, and who never screened his phone calls. He was a marvelous human being, and he made a powerful impression on me. To this day, I try to run my office the way Bill Veeck ran his.

After I completed my first year with Mr. Littlejohn as general manager of the Spartanburg Phillies, I gave Bill Veeck a call and told him that I was feeling like a failure because of the team's losing season. I was so focused on the team's lackluster performance that I failed to see that we'd had a very good season at the gate. As I poured out my frustrations over the phone, Bill listened quietly. When I was finished, he said, "Pat, just how many people did you draw to the ballpark this season?"

I told him: 114,000.

"How many of those people were entertained and had a good time?"

"Well," I said, "I think they all had a good time."

"Can you think of one other thing you could have done this summer to provide that much fun and entertainment to that many people?"

I couldn't think of anything.

"Pat," he said, "you never have to apologize for giving people a great time."

That bit of advice—like so many others I received over the years from Bill Veeck—transformed my outlook. He was a friend and a mentor to me, and I am incredibly richer for having known him.

A Few of My Mentors

One of the most profoundly important mentors in my life was R. E. Littlejohn. I drew so much inspiration and strength from him that to this day, years after his death, he is one of the guiding influences of my life. Again and again when I'm faced with making a decision, I ask myself, "What would Mister R. E. do in this situation?"

But there were other influential mentors and advisers in my life. One was a man named Chuck Hall. Chuck first came into my life when I went to Philadelphia in 1968 as the 76ers' business manager. Shortly after I arrived, I got a call from a man I had never met, never even heard of. "My name is Chuck Hall," he said, "and I'm a former coach, now in the financial planning business, and I'd like to take you to lunch sometime."

So we met and had a nice chat. I found out that he was a strong Christian, and we talked about spiritual matters and sports matters, and we had a pleasant lunch, and that was that. Nothing much came of it at the time. I moved on to become general manager of the Bulls, then the Hawks, and then returned to Philly in 1974 for a second run with the 76ers, this time as general manager. Again, Chuck called on me, and he became my financial planner from that time until his death in November 1998.

But Chuck was far more than a financial adviser. Over the years, he became a close and trusted friend. He was a very strong-minded and opinionated man, and if he saw something that was not right, he'd speak right up and say so. He never hesitated to tell me what he thought, and I was glad to have such a candid and forthright friend in my corner. We all need friends like that who will not schmooze us but will confront us and hold us accountable for our own good. Even after I moved to Orlando, Chuck continued to oversee our family's financial affairs while continuing to be a good friend far beyond the boundaries of a business relationship.

In the fall of 1994, I got a full read on what a great friend Chuck really was. My first marriage was falling apart, and even though I wasn't saying anything about it to anyone, Chuck sensed that something was wrong just from the tone of our phone conversations. He was incredibly perceptive—and incredibly caring. He dropped everything, flew to Orlando at his own expense, and took my then-wife Jill and me out to dinner to see if there was anything that could be done to resolve the situation and prevent a divorce. Even though Jill eventually filed against me, and Chuck's efforts to keep us together came to nought, it meant a lot to me that he cared enough to try to help us. Chuck was a wise counselor and a great friend, and his death was a great loss to me.

And then there is Jay Strack—twelve years my junior, but in wisdom and insight, my mentor. Based in Orlando, he's a former pastor, a motivational speaker, and an author. Jay and his wife, Diane, have become extremely close friends to my wife, Ruth, and me. He performed our marriage ceremony and has been a constant spiritual guide, reminding me of the words of Euripides: "Some wisdom must thou learn from one who is wise." Well, Jay is wise, and I have learned much wisdom from him.

Jay has the ability to see through superficialities and focus on the core issues. He's not at all hesitant to confront me, to hold me accountable, and to tell me in a way that makes me feel incredibly valued and cared for, "Pat, what you are doing is really not the best way. Here's what you should be doing. . . ." We share an interest in sports (he's a huge Orlando Magic fan), and he never hesitates to tell me what we're doing wrong with the team. He loves to laugh—and he even laughs at my jokes (which is hard to do).

These are just a few of the people who have invested in my life by mentoring me. I can't imagine where I would be right now if not for the wise advice and counsel of people like Bill Veeck, R. E. Littlejohn, Chuck Hall, and Jay Strack. But I know one thing for sure: Without them, I wouldn't be anywhere near where I am today. Any success I have, any accomplishment I've ever achieved, any contribution I've ever made to this world, I owe in large part to the special people who went before me, taught me, encouraged me, and shared their lives with me.

Part Genius, Part Madman

Wisdom doesn't come naturally. It must be learned—either from experience (which is learning the hard way) or from wise people. Here's the story of a man who listened to his mentor—and learned.

They call him the Walt Disney of Beaverton, Oregon. In the late 1950s, he was a middle-distance runner at the University of Oregon (he ran the mile in 4:09). Back then, they called him Buck Knight, but today the sixtyish, sandy-haired founder and chairman of Nike is just plain Philip Knight. He presides over an athletic attire empire that has virtually conquered the world of sports.

If you visit the seventy-four-acre Nike corporate campus in Oregon, you'll find a beautiful lush park with green stands of trees, shimmering man-made lakes, manicured running trails, and sparkling fountains. The heartbeat of the Nike campus is the complex of multistory buildings with names like the John McEnroe Building, the Dan Fouts Building, the Alberto Salazar Building, the Mike Schmidt Building, the Bo Jackson Fitness Center, and the Joe Paterno Day Care Center. Along the Nike Walk of Fame are bronze bas-relief images of legendary athletes and coaches, ranging from wheelchair athletes to pro sports legends. The roll call of legendary sports figures who have endorsed Nike products includes Michael Jordan, tennis stars Lynn Jennings and John McEnroe, baseball great Nolan Ryan, football legend Troy Aikman, and track stars Carl Lewis, Joan Benoit, and Jackie Joyner-Kersee.

The Nike empire has made Philip Knight a very wealthy man. His net worth is somewhere in the billions—an overkill prosperity that enables him to indulge a passion for fast cars (his collection includes a Lamborghini Diablo, a Porsche 911 Turbo, and a Ferrari Testarossa).

Knight is quick to share credit for the success of his sports attire kingdom with his mentor, Bill Bowerman, who was Knight's running coach at Oregon. Their meeting in 1957 would lead to a change in athletic competition throughout the world. Knight calls

Bowerman "part genius, part madman, and the best coach I ever had" and credits Bowerman with the innovation that led to the Nike shoe design.

Coach Bowerman was never satisfied with the off-the-rack shoes his Oregon runners wore, so he personally customized their shoes with tape, glue, and hand-cut pieces of rubber. One day, Bowerman poured liquid latex into his wife's waffle iron—creating the rubber waffle soles that were to become the key to Nike's success. He cut out the rubber waffles and glued them to the bottom of some flat-soled track shoes, creating a new kind of shoe with vastly improved traction plus extra cushioning and comfort.

After leaving Bowerman and the University of Oregon, Philip Knight went on to Stanford Business School—but he never forgot Bowerman's innovative shoe designs. At Stanford, Knight wrote a term paper outlining a plan for starting a running shoe company using affordable imports from Japan. After obtaining his degree from Stanford, he went to Kobe, Japan, and met with the Onitsuka Tiger shoe company to cut an import deal. The Japanese businessmen asked the name of the company Knight represented, but Knight didn't represent a company, only himself. Thinking quickly, he answered, "Blue Ribbon Sports." Then he went back to the States, started a company by that name, and began importing Tiger shoes.

Knight's Blue Ribbon Sports store was a hole-in-the-wall shop next to the Pink Bucket Tavern in Portland. He operated the store as a sideline while teaching accounting at Portland State University. The start-up capital was a mere one thousand dollars—half from Knight and half from Bowerman. The coach designed the shoes, Onitsuka Tiger manufactured them in Japan, and Knight sold them in the store or from a card table at track meets. Representatives from Adidas, the running shoe giant at the time, would stop by Knight's card table just to have a good laugh. Within a few years, however, nobody was laughing at Philip Knight—least of all Adidas.

Soon, Knight hired his first full-time salesman, a Stanford runner named Jeff Johnson. It was Johnson who, in 1971, came up with the idea of renaming the company after the Greek goddess of victory (Johnson later retired a millionaire, thanks to being in on the ground floor of the business). Also in 1971, Knight hired art student Carolyn Davidson to design the now-famous Nike "swoosh" logo, one of the most recognized logos in marketing history (the swoosh represents the wing of the goddess). For that design, which now identifies billions of dollars' worth of Nike products, Davidson was paid the mutually agreeable sum of $35.

In 1972, after a dispute between Knight and Onitsuka Tiger, Blue Ribbon Shoes launched the Nike brand at the U.S. Olympic Trials. By 1979, Nike had surpassed Adidas as the number one athletic shoemaker in the world.

Was it brilliance or blind luck that led Knight to sign future NBA superstar Michael Jordan to an endorsement contract when Jordan was fresh out of the University of North Carolina? Nike's star soared on a parallel track with Jordan's. Nike even designed a special shoe for Jordan, the Air Jordan, which was ruled illegal by the league (only white shoes were NBA-approved; Air Jordans were black and red). Though he was fined one thousand dollars every game in which he wore them, Michael laced up his shoes, paid his fines, and set the sports world on fire. The controversy sent sales of Air Jordans skyward.

Coach Bowerman remained Nike's chief shoe designer until his semiretirement in 1987. Even after Bowerman retired a wealthy man with a thick portfolio of Nike stock, Philip Knight continued to seek out Bowerman's advice and to quote from the coach's treasure trove of wisdom—quotations such as "Nobody ever remembers number two," and, "Play by the rules, but be ferocious," and the coach's admonition to combine humility and toughness: "It's all right to be Goliath—but always act like David."

Philip Knight can rightly claim a lot of credit for his success, but he wisely reserves a lion's share of the credit for his old coach and longtime mentor, Bill Bowerman. Knight has offered many tributes to the man who taught him so much about running, about making a great shoe, and about building a great company. One of the most visible of those tributes is the location of Nike's international headquarters at One Bowerman Drive in Beaverton.

If you were to ask Philip Knight how to be successful, I'm sure he'd tell you: Have a wise mentor—and listen to the mentor's advice.

Mentors and Learners

I am convinced that every successful person I've ever met is a person who has consciously allowed other people to impact his or her life. So if you want to be successful, be teachable and coachable. Instead of trying to impress others with what you already know, show that you are always eager to learn more. Seek out advice. Ask for help. Accept coaching and mentoring with patience and humility.

Humility really is the key, isn't it? You have to be humble to seek advice and take it. These days, a lot of people look upon humility as a sign of weakness. It's not. Only those who are strong, confident, and secure in themselves have the capacity to learn and be humble. Arrogance is a sign of weakness and insecurity. If you would be strong, be humble. If you would be wise, confess your ignorance. If you would succeed, admit that you need help and advice from those who have gone before you.

Most of our children are grown or away at school, but a few of them still live at home with Ruth and me. I do my best to be not only a dad but a mentor, helping to meet their individual needs, investing in their growth and their future. Let me tell you about two of them.

Bobby has just turned twenty-two. He's decided to pursue a career in baseball as a coach, manager, or instructor. Being an old baseball guy myself, that's right up my alley. Hardly a day goes by that Bobby doesn't get a newspaper or magazine clipping from me on some aspect of success or playing the game. Ever since he was a Little Leaguer, I've been there to coach him and instruct him to the limits of my ability and to put him in touch with coaches and instructors who can do a better job of teaching him than I can. After playing ball at Rollins College, he sees clearly that he (like his dad) doesn't have the gifts to be a major-league player. But he also knows there are plenty of options for someone with his drive and passion for the game. So I've tried to mentor him, guide him, and open some doors for him—and it has been a thrill to watch him respond and take advantage of the advice and opportunities I've sent his way. I wouldn't be at all surprised to see Bobby Williams as the manager of the Cincinnati Reds or a similar organization someday.

And then there's Karyn. She loves broadcasting. She wants to be the Katie Couric of the twenty-first century. Well, I just love it! Broadcasting is in my blood, and I still do a radio sports talk show every week in Orlando. So I give Karyn advice, send her articles, open a door or two, and introduce her to successful people who can give her advice and help her get some experience. I tell her, "Karyn, I'm looking forward to the day I turn on the *Today* show and see you there."

If it wasn't for mentors and teachers willing to pass on their store of knowledge and wisdom to the next generation, civilization would never progress. Humanity would remain stuck in place while each succeeding generation attempted to reinvent the wheel. Everything we now enjoy, everything that enriches life, from art to literature to music to drama to science to technology to sports—all of these and more—are the result of the accumulated wisdom that has been passed down from mentors and teachers to young, eager, hungry minds.

One person who knows this well is the Tony Award-winning singer and actress Betty Buckley. Though TV audiences may best remember her as the wholesome stepmom in TV's *Eight Is Enough* (1977–81), she has enjoyed a shining second career on Broadway as a major acting talent. With a voice that has been described as "supple steel," she is also a singer who can fill a theater with the power and energy of her voice. She won the 1983 Tony for her performance in *Cats*, singing Andrew Lloyd Webber's "Memory" as Grizabella the Glamour Cat. She wowed audiences as the haunting Norma Desmond in *Sunset Boulevard,* and she has starred in stage productions of *1776, The Mystery of Edwin Drood,* and *Pippin.*

Betty Buckley gives credit for her success to her many teachers and mentors, but especially her voice and acting teacher, the legendary Stella Adler (who also taught such luminaries of stage and screen as Robert DeNiro, Marlon Brando, Richard Dreyfuss, Cybill Sheperd, and Melanie Griffith). "Everything I do onstage," Betty Buckley says today, "I learned from great teachers or directors, and I want to pass that on." Today, Betty Buckley has become a mentor and teacher in her own right, giving workshops and classes, handing down the skills, insight, and knowledge she has acquired from those who went before her. She also passes on her human compassion as an advocate for numerous humanitarian causes, including AIDS research.

Seeking a Mentor

"Those who seek mentoring," said the sixth century B.C. Chinese historian Su Ching, "will rule the great expanse under heaven." But how do you find a mentor? How do you seek out and build a relationship with someone who can teach you and advise you and instill in you the wisdom you need? Here are some suggestions.

1. Adopt the mindset of a learner. Once you are willing and ready to learn, you will find yourself encountering people who are willing and ready to teach. It's like the transformation that occurs when you decide it's time to buy a new car. Normally, people don't pay that much attention to other cars. But once you decide you're in the market for a car, you stop at a red light and look around at the cars in the next lane. You pull into a parking space, and you give the car next to you a good going over. Instead of flipping past the car ads in a magazine, you linger over the clean, appealing lines of that Lexus or that Town Car. You have adopted the mindset of a car buyer.

It's the same when you adopt the mindset of a learner. You begin looking differently at the people you encounter at work, at seminars, at church, or people you read about in the newspaper or magazines. You begin to think, *I bet this person or that person would have a lot to teach me. I wonder.* . . . Adopting the mindset of a learner is the first step to finding a mentor.

2. Do your homework. Research the top individuals in businesses, organizations, and trade associations in your chosen field. Identify the accomplished leaders through newspaper, magazine, and Internet articles that have been written about them. Ask around and find out as much as you can through word of mouth. Identify the leaders who demonstrate the qualities and accomplishments you most admire and want to emulate.

3. Don't be shy. Many people hesitate to approach a potential mentor, thinking that they would be imposing on that person's time.

But I've found again and again that most people who have reached a point of accomplishment and success in their career or their ministry are eager to share their wisdom, knowledge, and skills with others. When you ask someone to be your mentor, you offer the highest praise and affirmation possible. You are saying, "You are important. You are accomplished. You are a role model to be admired. I want to be like you." When you convey that message to a person, you are not merely asking for a favor, you are doing one.

There was a time when mentors selected a protege to follow in their footsteps. You could only have a mentor if you were fortunate enough for someone to come along, notice you, and choose to be your mentor. Today, however, the concept of mentorship has become widespread, particularly in the business world. You no longer have to wait and hope that a mentor will find you. It is perfectly acceptable for you to take the initiative and seek out a mentor who will meet your needs for learning and growth.

For years, Apple Computer Incorporated offered a formal mentoring program as part of its staff development effort. In the mid-1990s, however, the company scaled back its mentoring program. But as Cheryl Dahle reported in the magazine *Fast Company,* a number of Apple employees, "including Subhana Ansari, 47, decided that if Apple would not bring mentoring to them, they would bring mentoring to Apple. Ansari, an area administrator, approached other women at Apple with a proposal: With no funding, no support, and no materials, Ansari and other volunteers would build a formal mentoring program."

Ansari began a series of Tuesday afternoon classes for people who wanted to find a mentor. Twenty people signed up, fifteen women and five men, and Ansari instructed them in how to seek out and build a relationship with a mentor. By the fourth week of the six-week course, two people had dropped out, but the remaining eighteen all had mentors. Within four months after completion of the program, fully one-third of the group's members had been promoted—an amazing result.

Perhaps the most important benefit of the program was realized by Ansari herself, because it started her on an entirely new career. She left Apple and became a training project manager for Adecco

Employment Services in Redwood City, California. "Creating the mentoring program redirected my career," she reflected. "It was the most fun I ever had at work."[7]

4. *Introduce yourself.* If possible, arrange for an introduction through a mutual acquaintance. If that is not possible, introduce yourself in a brief letter that reflects the homework you have done. For example, you might write, "I have been following your achievements in the field of _____, and I eagerly read your book on _____. Like you, I am very concerned about the issue of _____, and hope to make a contribution in these areas myself someday. I am looking for a mentoring relationship, and I would be grateful if you could spare thirty minutes of your time to discuss such a possibility with me."

If the person you contact meets with you, follow up the meeting with a brief, gracious, handwritten note of thanks. Underscore your learner's attitude by stating that you found the person's advice helpful and that you intend to follow it. By showing appreciation, you offer back something of value to the mentor: the satisfaction of knowing that the insights gained from his or her years of experience are being passed along to someone who can put them to good use.

5. *Select a mentor who is a good role model.* Look for someone who not only is famous or wealthy or successful but who also has a reputation for character and integrity and honesty. Look for someone you can admire and respect as well as emulate.

6. *Select a mentor who is a good listener.* It is not enough to find a mentor who is a good talker. The best mentor is one who gets to know you, your skills and strengths and weaknesses, your personality, and your aspirations. A mentor who asks no questions and never listens is not truly interested in you; he is only interested in hearing himself talk. A good mentor should serve not as a mere lecturer but as a sounding board and a person who will want to know about your struggles, issues, and challenges—someone who will help you clarify your concerns and problems.

7. *Select a mentor who levels with you.* A good mentor doesn't just flatter or affirm you. He or she also will let you know when you are going in the wrong direction. He or she will tell you when you are

doing right, but also when you are doing wrong—and will show you how to do something better. It is also a good sign if your mentor is candid and open about his or her own life. Anyone who has accomplished anything has made mistakes along the way. A good mentor will talk freely about those mistakes to alert you to the pot-holes and pitfalls in your path.

8. *Look for someone who is unlike you in some important way.* Our tendency is to gravitate toward those with whom we have a lot in common. But in searching for a mentor, it is wise to seek out people who have strengths that we lack. For example, if you are shy and introverted, look for someone who is bold and gregarious. Try to soak up some of his or her confidence and outgoing nature. The more your mentor resembles you, the less you can learn from him or her. So pair up with someone who, instead of reinforcing your weaknesses, will challenge you to acquire new strengths.

9. *Be open to finding a mentor in unlikely places.* Our natural in-clination is to think of a mentor or teacher as someone with some gray hair and a lot of mileage on the chassis. Not necessarily so. A mentor can be anyone who has something to teach, and could be your age or even younger. If you come across someone in your or-ganization, company, or church who has gained valuable insights and experience you lack, be open to the possibility that this is some-one who could advise you and encourage your growth—and be humble and receptive enough to benefit from the association.

Many people at a lower place on the corporate ladder or at a lesser educational level often have much to teach us. During my years in sports promotion, some of our most creative and successful pro-motional ideas have been suggested by fans, vendors, ticket takers, and even kids. Comedian Bill Cosby put his finger on it when he said, "No matter where you work, seek out the janitor. The janitor knows everything and everybody. Don't ever think you know more than someone who is mopping the floor."

Cal Ripken Jr.—the iron-man third baseman of the Baltimore Orioles—only recently was introduced to the Internet, but he's started taking a laptop computer with him when he's on the road. "I'm a little intimidated by the technology," he says, "but my daugh-ter Rachel is at the age where she can teach me. She's seven years old." Here's a man who's not ashamed to learn and take advice from his elementary school-age daughter.

Mr. Littlejohn knew the importance of listening to advice from his employees. He told me that he had acquired quite a number of money-saving ideas—even those which improved the safety of his fuel-hauling tankers—by listening to his mechanics. So seek advice and wisdom wherever it may be found.

10. Recognize that you are never too old to have a mentor. I have come to recognize that, while I have a lot to offer others, I still have plenty left to learn. I am a mentor to a number of people, but I still consider myself very much a student—despite my graying hair.

One of my mentors is Rich DeVos, of Amway fame, who, you'll recall, is the principle owner of the Orlando Magic. Rich has a true love for people, and that's what makes him such an empowering, encouraging individual to others. He has an amazing touch when it comes to inspiring and motivating people.

Whenever Rich comes to Orlando, he always seeks me out and talks to me. I don't mean the usual surface chatter that most of us use in our social contacts. He gets right down to reality and wants to know about me, my family, my work. He asks questions and offers sincere encouragement: "Is there anything you need? Is there anything I can do to support you? Is there anything I can be praying about for you?" Whenever I walk away from an encounter with Rich DeVos, I feel I can accomplish anything.

Do you have someone like that in your life? If not, seek one out. Better yet, seek out two or three or a dozen. You might find a special mentor in your church, at the office, in your neighborhood, at your university, or on your sports team. We all need that kind of person in our lives—and we need to become that kind of person to others.

That's my goal—to somehow pass along a measure of the encouragement, insight, knowledge, skill, confidence, values, inspiration, and strength that has been given to me by my mentors. So much has been invested in me by others over the years—how can I do any less than pass it on to the next generation? That is why I continually try to bequeath the things I have received to my own children, to the athletes and staff members of the Magic organization, to the young people in our church, to the various groups I speak to, and to the readers of my books. I *have* to live that way. We *all* have to live that way, so that the wisdom and knowledge we have received from the past will be transmitted into the future.

Our goal is not to simply build a mentoring relationship but to maintain a *mentoring mindset,* which produces an ongoing, ever-growing network of many mentorships. Our aim is to be continually learning, continually growing, and continually reaching out to help others learn and grow.

This is what I learned from the most influential of all my mentors, R. E. Littlejohn. And the next thing he taught me was something I saw him live out on a daily basis: Be aware of your influence on others.

FIVE

Be Aware of Your Influence on Others

I hardly ever saw Mister R. E. even mildly annoyed, much less angry. But on one occasion I made a suggestion to him that—well, let me tell you what happened.

Our ballpark in Spartanburg was something of a rarity in the baseball world: It was a "dry" park. We didn't serve beer in the stands—and what's more, we didn't even have any signs advertising alcoholic beverages at beautiful Duncan Park. When I arrived in Spartanburg, I didn't realize that the exclusion of beer from the ballpark was a policy of Mister R. E.'s. Though I was a nondrinker, I had nothing against other people enjoying a beer, and I was always looking for ways to enhance revenue for the organization. So one day early in my tenure, I approached Mr. Littlejohn and said, "We could bring in a lot more money if we sold beer in the park and put up some wall ads for beer."

He looked up sharply, frowning at me as if I had just spit on the carpet. "If we do that, Pat," he said sternly, "I'll have to sell the team."

Whoa! I instantly knew I had hit a very raw nerve. I later learned that Mister R. E. was highly sensitive to his influence on others, especially young people. He believed that beer and ads for alcoholic beverages had a corrupting effect on young people, so he simply refused to allow any hint of alcohol on the premises. I never brought up the matter again.

I did, however, manage to make one somewhat related mistake. Eddie Grasso ran a little nightclub in town. He was a big baseball fan, and I sold him a program ad. When the program came off the press with the ad for Grasso's club printed in it, Mister R. E. called me into his office. He was very unhappy.

"Pat," he said, "you accepted an ad in our program for a tavern. A tavern!"

"Well," I stammered, "it's a little nightclub. They have music and—"

"And they serve drinks," Mister R. E. said. "Pat, I have nothing personally against Eddie Grasso. But advertising a tavern! That's *not* the image we're trying to convey with our ballclub. That's not the impression we want to make on the families, and especially the children, who come to our games."

I never did it again.

And I learned an important lesson: Always be aware of the influence your actions have on others.

No "Little People"

After moving to Orlando in the summer of 1986, our family started attending First Baptist Church. In Orlando we have Disney World and Sea World, so it is only natural that a huge church like First Baptist in Orlando should be known as Baptist World. One of my first reactions to that church was a feeling of being awed by the massive 118-rank Schantz pipe organ. The power of that massive instrument permeates your senses, penetrates your soul, and resonates in the marrow of your bones. One Sunday morning after the service, I went up to the organist, Ken Varner, and introduced myself.

"Oh, yes," he said, "I know who you are. I'm from Spartanburg, South Carolina, and we have a mutual friend."

"Who's that?" I asked.

"Mr. R. E. Littlejohn," he said.

"Wow!" I said. "You know Mister R. E.? He's like a second father to me."

"Well, my family has known him for years," said Ken. "In fact, Mister R. E. knew there was no way I could afford to go to college, but he saw that I had talent to play the organ, so he paid my way through school."

I thought, *Isn't that just like Mister R. E.?* And to this day, Ken Varner still pulls out all the stops and rattles the rafters of Baptist World, glorifying God with a talent that was nurtured by Mr. Littlejohn's generosity and love for others.

"He was always encouraging other people and helping other people," Mister R. E.'s secretary, Marilyn Scruggs, once told me. "He made everyone feel appreciated and special. He gave his full attention to whomever he was talking to at the moment. The last dozen years or so of his life he had health problems, and he experienced a lot of headaches—yet his mind was never on his own pain, but on the needs of others. *Your* problem, *your* difficulty, *your* welfare were always uppermost in his mind. He was infinitely patient and extremely generous with people. Mister R. E. gave away enormous amounts of time and money, and he helped hundreds, maybe thousands of people— but he was also careful to give people exactly what they needed to become self-sufficient. He gave people a hand *up,* not just a handout."

His longtime friend, Robert Odom, told me, "Mister R. E. had two hobbies: baseball and people—people of all walks of life. No matter how busy he was, he always had time to respond to the hundreds of requests he received from people asking for advice on whether to buy this business or sell that business, whether to change jobs or take a promotion. He always had time for others. He was always moved by the needs of others. He was always influencing others for the better."

Dr. Julian Williams, Mister R. E.'s physician, told me, "Mr. Littlejohn was more than a patient. He was a friend. I benefited immensely from knowing him. He was quiet and reserved, yet the light of Christ shone through him onto all the others with whom he had contact. He faced health crises—first, a coronary artery bypass surgery, then some years later, treatment for cancer—with courage and a calm peace. Through it all, his primary concern was for others in all walks of life, regardless of status or station."

That was the way Mister R. E. was—no person was beneath him. He wouldn't treat a janitor or a waiter any differently than he would treat the president of the United States. Every person he met received his full attention and his full respect. He drew no distinctions of rank, class, power, or privilege. Columnist Dave Barry once observed, "A person who is nice to you but rude to the waiter is not a nice person." I am reminded of a story related by supermodel Kim Alexis in her book, *A Model for a Better Future:*

> I was once out to dinner with some wealthy friends in Florida. During the meal, the waiter came around and refilled our water glasses. As he filled mine, I said, "Thank you." No big deal, I always thank people when they do something nice for me.
>
> But the man sitting across from me said, "You don't have to thank those people! You're better than they are."
>
> I was shocked! I had never in my life thought of myself as better than anyone else. "God made all of us," I said. "That waiter is just as important as I am. It's just common courtesy to say thank you when someone does something nice for you."
>
> The man looked at me as if I was speaking in another language, like he could not even comprehend what I had just said. "Really, Kim!" he said, shaking his head at (so he thought) my utter naiveté. "Don't you understand? That guy gets paid minimum wage to fill people's water glasses! You're on the cover of *Vogue* and *Sports Illustrated*. You've done so much more than people like that! Of course, you're better than they are! You should realize who you are!"
>
> That conversation was a real eye-opener to me. Since then, I've encountered many people who consider themselves better than others—and I find that completely baffling. Aren't we all God's children? Aren't we all equal in His sight?[8]

We live in a culture that worships the self. But when I met R. E. Littlejohn, I discovered a man who was always about others, never about self. Again and again, the message of his life was others, others, others. That truly was the centerpiece of his life. Mister R. E. treated *everyone* with courtesy and respect, even people who could do nothing for him in return. That approach was not a matter of good business to him. It was simply the essence of who he was. It was not in his nature to treat people any other way.

As I worked alongside Mister R. E. and broke bread at his table and watched his life, I learned some valuable lessons in relating to others.

1. Always Show Respect to Others

Many years ago, a ten-year-old boy walked up to the counter of a soda shop and climbed onto a stool. He caught the eye of the waitress and asked, "How much is an ice cream sundae?"

"Fifty cents," the waitress replied.

The boy reached into his pockets, pulled out a handful of change, and began counting. The waitress frowned impatiently. After all, she had other customers to wait on.

The boy squinted up at the waitress. "How much is a dish of *plain* ice cream?" he asked.

The waitress sighed and rolled her eyes. "Thirty-five cents," she said with a note of irritation.

Again, the boy counted his coins. At last, he said, "I'll have the plain ice cream, please." He put a quarter and two nickels on the counter. The waitress took the coins, brought the ice cream, and walked away. About ten minutes later, she returned and found the ice cream dish empty. The boy was gone. She picked up the empty dish—then swallowed hard.

There on the counter, next to the wet ring where the dish had been, were two nickels and five pennies. The boy had had enough for a sundae, but he had ordered plain ice cream so he could leave a tip.

The moral of the story: There are no unimportant people in the world. We should *always* treat others with courtesy, dignity, and respect. This point came home to me in a story I found some years ago in *Guideposts*. Written by a nurse, Joanne C. Jones, the story related that during her second year of nursing school, one of her professors surprised the class with a pop quiz. Joanne breezed through all the questions—then was stumped by the last one: "What is the first name of the woman who cleans at this school?"

At first Joanne thought it was a joke. She had seen the woman many times, scrubbing floors, cleaning the restrooms, and doing other chores. But her name? Who knew? She was just a cleaning woman. The nursing student left the last question unanswered.

A student later asked, "Will the last question count toward our grade?"

"Absolutely," the professor replied. "In your nursing career you will meet many people. Each one is significant. Each deserves your personal attention, even if all you do is smile, call the person by name, and say hello."

Nurse Jones recalls, "I've never forgotten that lesson. I also learned that the woman's name was Dorothy."

2. Recognize and Reward the Contributions of Others

The desire to be recognized and feel significant as a result is one of the most basic of human drives. When that desire is fulfilled, people are motivated to accomplish great things. When that desire is thwarted, the effects can range from a debilitating loss of morale to a seething hostility that can destroy an organization. Our success depends on our ability to recognize and reward the attainments of those who contribute to that success. It is a vain, small, and immature person who steals credit for the work and ideas of others, or refuses to share credit for a group achievement. Those who cannot be generous in giving recognition and rewards for the accomplishments of others merely demonstrate their own insecurity and self-centeredness.

Cordell Hull served as secretary of state under President Franklin D. Roosevelt. One of his great skills as a diplomat and leader developed out of his ability to give credit to others—even when credit was not due. On one occasion, he won the support of the anti-American foreign minister of Argentina with the skillful use of public recognition. Before the Pan-American Conference in Peru in 1938, Hull wanted to enlist Argentina's support of an agreement between twenty-one American nations to keep fascism out of the Western Hemisphere. When the Argentine foreign minister balked, Hull responded, "Now, Mr. Minister, we want the best leader in Latin America to propose this program in the conference. I believe you are that leader. If you would offer the proposal, the United States would give you all the support, recognition, and praise you are due. Will you take this bold step on behalf of the people of North and South America?"

What could the man say? He accepted. The Pan-American Conference was a success—and the bridges of friendship Cordell Hull forged in the process later played a key role in the founding of the United Nations in 1945. For his work in bringing about the dream of a world body of nations, Cordell Hull was awarded the Nobel Peace Prize. By giving recognition to the Argentine foreign minister—even when it was undeserved—recognition eventually came back to him. Lester Pearson, former Canadian prime minister, used to say, "Diplomacy is letting someone else have your way." Similarly, Ronald Reagan kept a sign on his desk in the Oval Office throughout the eight years of his presidency. It read: "There is no limit to what a man can do or where he can go if he doesn't mind who gets the credit."

3. Get Along with Others

A sports executive once made this observation about a famous team owner who happened to be one of the most controversial men in professional sports: "He never compliments you or offers praise. He never asks you for your input or ideas. He never lets you complete a thought or a sentence. He never deals with you on a personal level or shows interest in you as a person." What a tragic statement! May it never be said of you or me. And what a contrast between a man like that and a man like Mr. Littlejohn, who always valued and praised others, who listened carefully to their ideas and input, and who always dealt with everyone as a feeling human being and as an equal.

Theodore Roosevelt showed enormous wisdom when he observed, "The most important single ingredient in the formula of success is knowing how to get along with people." Financier John D. Rockefeller agreed: "The ability to deal with people is as purchasable a commodity as sugar or coffee, and I will gladly pay more for that ability than for any other under the sun."

One of the greatest assets in getting along with people is a cheerful disposition. B. C. Forbes, founder of *Forbes* magazine, once wrote an editorial suggesting the cultivation of cheerfulness as a fitting New Year's resolution. "Cheerfulness," he wrote, "is among the most laudable virtues. It is good for your mind; it is good for your health. It helps you to win success. It gains you the goodwill and friendship of others. I have never been able to understand why cheerfulness is not a more conspicuous attribute of daily business. We are all smiles in our social activities, but we are often all frowns in our business activities. Why need there be less cheerfulness in our daily rounds than in, say, a round of golf? The following resolution is hereby submitted: I shall consistently seek to be cheerful."

For a concise course in getting along with people, I offer this advice from the CEO of Marriott Hotels International, Bill Marriott Jr.:

The six most important words: "I admit that I was wrong."
The five most important words: "You did a great job."
The four most important words: "What do you think?"
The three most important words: "Could you, please?"
The two most important words: "Thank you."
The most important word: "We."
The least important word: "I."

4. Be a Positive Role Model to Others

Mister R. E. always stressed to me that every one of my words and actions was leaving either a positive or negative impression on people. If we are aware of our influence on others, we will strive to be a positive role model. That means we must be people of character and integrity. Your inner reality must match or exceed your outer reputation. If not, you are a walking lie. This world desperately needs people who are committed to telling the truth, even when there is a price to pay. This world desperately needs people willing to place personal honor above momentary gain. Some people will tell you that character and integrity don't matter anymore. Don't you believe it. Even though some people seem to get away with every crime under the sun, character still matters—and always will.

Integrity means agreement between your walk and your talk. Sure, you're human and you'll fail and fall short of the mark from time to time. But a person of integrity constantly picks himself up from lapses and failures and keeps striving toward the high goal of a fully honest and integrated life. He attempts to demonstrate character in all matters, no matter how great, no matter how small.

Others are watching us all the time. Our children see us if we pocket the money when the clerk gives us too much change, if we disobey the speed limit, if we fudge on our taxes. Our employees learn about our integrity from the way we keep the ledger and treat our customers. Our coworkers watch how we use the company's office supplies, the copy machine, and the company car. Business expert Tom Peters once wrote, "There are no minor lapses of integrity." There is no such thing as a small lapse of character. We either have integrity or we don't. As Ron Willingham writes in *Integrity Selling*, "The kind of person you are sends loud and clear signals to people. It communicates on the instinctive or intuitive level, but it communicates. . . . That is why integrity, honesty, and genuine concern for your customers and their needs powerfully influence your ability to develop trust with people!

"When I get right down to it, who I am communicates! Sooner or later most people will get the message about the level of integrity I have. And they often get the message pretty quickly."[9]

In their book *The Power of Ethical Management*, Ken Blanchard and Norman Vincent Peale offer a template for testing decisions in the business world to ensure wise and principled actions. It is a three-question quiz they call the Ethics Check:

1. *Is it legal?* Will this decision be legal—not only according to laws of society but according to the practices and policies of my organization or company?
2. *Is it balanced?* Is this decision fair toward all parties—or does it create a winner and a loser? Would there be a better decision that would create a "win/win" solution?
3. *How will it make me feel about myself?* If my decision were known to the world, would I be proud of it—or ashamed? What if my spouse knew? What if my kids knew?

A father once received a letter from his college-age son which began, "Hey, Pop! This letter is free! The post office didn't cancel the stamp on your last letter to me, so I reused it."

A few days later, the son received a letter from his dad. Unfolding the letter, he found an uncanceled stamp pasted at the top—but his father had drawn a big, bold X through it in black ink. Beneath the stamp were these words: "Dear son, your debt to the United States government has been paid. Love, Dad."

This father was teaching his son an important lesson in the meaning of character and integrity. The matter of a postage stamp may seem like a small thing to make such a fuss over, but I submit to you that if you practice complete integrity in the smallest details, you will never lose your integrity in the big issues.

Living for Others

During World War II, in Auschwitz, a Nazi death camp in southern Poland, guards discovered that a prisoner was missing. In retaliation the guards assembled the prisoners and randomly selected ten to die a horrible, lingering death in the starvation bunker.

"My poor family!" sobbed one of the condemned, Sergeant Gajowniczek, as the guards stripped him and herded him to the bunker.

"Stop!" someone shouted. Out of the mass of prisoners, one man stepped forward and faced the camp kommandant. "I volunteer to die in the place of one of these men," the prisoner said.

"In whose place do you wish to die?" asked the commander.

"That one," the prisoner replied, pointing to Gajowniczek. "The one with the wife and children."

The commander examined the identification number on the prisoner's clothing. "Who are you, Number 16670?"

"Just a Catholic priest, sir," replied the prisoner.

The commander considered for a moment, then replied, "Accepted."

So Father Maximilian Kolbe took his place with the other nine. Gajowniczek was allowed to live.

Who was this man who exchanged his life for that of a stranger? Before his arrest in 1941, Father Kolbe was a Polish Franciscan priest who denounced Nazism from the pulpit and over the radio. He was sentenced to Auschwitz for the "crime" of aiding Jews. In prison, he daily encouraged his fellow prisoners and cheerfully shared his meager rations with them. Finally, when he had nothing else to share, he shared his life.

During the next couple of weeks, a worker regularly went into the starvation bunker to check on the doomed men and hauled out any who had died, so that the bodies could be fed to the crematorium. The worker later reported that going into that bunker was like "descending into the crypt of a church." Instead of the usual moans and curses that came from the starvation bunker, this worker reported hearing prayers and hymns led by Father Kolbe.

One by one the prisoners in the bunker died. Whenever a man seemed on the verge of unconsciousness or death, Father Kolbe prayed with that man, administered last rites, and bade him farewell. As time passed, the hymns and prayers grew fainter. After two weeks of starvation, four men remained alive. Of the four, only Father Kolbe was conscious. Finally, the door of the bunker was flung open and a group of SS guards and the camp doctor entered. The doctor administered a syringe of carbolic acid to the four, putting them out of their misery—not as an act of kindness but because the starvation bunker was needed for a new group of victims.

Father Kolbe prayed aloud as he held out his arm to receive the injection. A few moments later, he was dead. His life was poured out, but not wasted. Even the hardened SS guards were amazed as they watched this great man die. Sergeant Gajowniczek survived Auschwitz, was reunited with his family, and was one of a number of death camp survivors who told the world about a man named Father Kolbe—and his love for others.[10]

Father Maximilian Kolbe lived his life for others. Then he gave his life for others. His story is a challenge to us all: Live for others. And if need be, die for others.

The next important lesson I learned from Mr. Littlejohn was the key to handling disagreements and conflicts.

SIX

Seek Agreement but Respect Disagreement

A few years ago, I was out for my morning run, getting in shape for the Disney Marathon in Orlando, when I spotted a group of junior high kids waiting for the school bus. Something was wrong. Two of the boys were going at each other with bare knuckles, really duking it out.

I dashed over to them and placed myself between them, separating them with my hands. They continued flailing away, trying to reach around me to get at each other. With scarcely a moment to think, I shouted the first thing that came into my head: "Penny Hardaway wants you boys to know four things!"

That stopped both boys in their tracks. "What do you mean?" asked one of the boys. "Do you know Penny?"

"Sure I do," I said. "I work with the Magic. Penny's a friend of mine."

At that point, I had their undivided attention. The other boy asked, "What do you mean Penny wants us to know four things?"

I thought furiously. In the next few seconds, I had to come up with four things Penny Hardaway, one of the NBA's most recognizable stars, wanted them to know. I quickly thought back to some of the breakfast table discussions we've had in the Williams household during times of conflict—and then it came to me.

"First," I began, "Penny wants you to know that you've got to keep your mouth shut. Problems always start when you've got your mouth running. Second, he wants you to know you have to keep your eyes off each other. Stop staring each other down like a couple of pit bulls. Third, keep your hands to yourself. Fights always start when one kid pushes or hits another kid. Fourth, walk away from trouble. When you see trouble coming, go in the other direction."

One of the kids eyed me skeptically. "Penny Hardaway said all that?"

"You bet," I said, crossing my fingers behind my back. "What's your name, son?"

He was African-American. "Dwayne," he answered.

I turned to the other—a blond, blue-eyed Norwegian-American, from all appearances. "And what's your name?"

"Wayne," he replied.

"Well, Dwayne and Wayne," I said, "I think you guys are ready to shake hands and become friends. What do you say?"

Dwayne put his hand out. But Wayne just jammed his hands into his pockets.

"Oh, did I forget to mention? There's just one more thing that Penny Hardaway wants you both to know."

Wayne squinted up at me. "What's that?"

"He wants you both to come to an Orlando Magic game as his guests—but there's a catch. You two have to sit together. You have to share the armrest. You have to share a box of popcorn. And you have to get along. And right now, you have to shake hands."

Both boys extended their hands and shook.

"Fine," I said. "Let me know when you can come to a game, and I'll have Penny set it up." We had just finished exchanging phone numbers when the bus pulled up to take the boys and their classmates off to the Maitland Middle School. And me? Well, I jogged off down the street and mentally awarded myself the Nobel Peace Prize.

Healthy Conflict: Both Sides Win

Conflict is a part of life—in business, government, church, and family life. You can't get away from it—especially if you are in a leadership role. In fact, disagreement can be a positive force in your organization. Well-managed, honestly resolved conflict often can be a catalyst for change, growth, and creativity. Andrew Young, former mayor of Atlanta and a protege of Martin Luther King Jr., recalls that King used to invite diverse points of view to stir up creative thinking and synergistic solutions to problems. "He would ask somebody to express as radical a view as possible," said Young, "and he would ask somebody to express as conservative a view as possible. He figured that the wider variety of opinions you got, the better chance you had of extracting the truth."

In my large and diverse family, which includes fourteen kids adopted from countries around the world, bringing together different ages, cultures, and backgrounds, there's plenty of potential for conflict every day. My job as a father is to do all I can to make relationships function smoothly. I don't believe in papering over or repressing conflict; when fights and arguments rear their ugly heads, we have to resolve issues and forgive wrongs. But we also have learned that many needless conflicts can be avoided.

I might say, "You two never agree on this, so just don't talk to each other about it. Stay off this subject and you'll be okay." Or, "You know the rules, you know the chores you've been assigned. Everyone keeps his or her assigned roles—no switching, no negotiating, no arguing." By creating an atmosphere in which conflicts are resolved in a healthy way at the lowest possible level of intensity, we manage to avoid a lot of brawling.

Conflict is inevitable in every dynamic relationship and in every organization or company. Relationships and organizations are made up of individuals, and every individual is a unique bundle of backgrounds, cultural mindsets, ideas, personalities, beliefs, and tastes. Mix all those ingredients together, add a little stress and pressure, and you are bound to end up with tension, friction, and an occasional open clash. A certain amount of dynamic tension is normal and healthy. Differences of opinion and diverse points of view challenge us to learn, change, and grow. So our goal should not be to eliminate conflict but to manage it.

Stephen Covey, in *The Seven Habits of Highly Effective People,* identifies six common patterns people use to deal with conflict. The first four are unhealthy patterns, usually producing destructive results; the fifth and sixth are healthy ways to manage conflict.

1. Win-lose (destructive). The person with a win-lose mindset approaches conflict saying, in effect, "I'm going to win; you're going to lose. I'm going to get my way; you're going to get nothing." This is the approach of naked aggression. It demonstrates a complete disrespect and contempt for the other person, and is destructive to relationships.

2. Win (selfish). This approach is similar to win-lose—but with a subtle difference. The winner doesn't necessarily want the other person to lose—he frankly doesn't care about the other person at all. He's not competitive, just selfish. This person says, "All I care about is getting what's coming to me. Whether you get what's coming to you is up to you—I couldn't care less."

3. Lose-win (self-destructive). This is the way of appeasement. The loser says, "I'm a doormat. Go ahead, wipe your feet on me. I'm a loser and you win." Issues are not resolved—only postponed until the next round. People may bury their feelings and deny their needs for a while, thinking that by doing so, they are keeping the peace. But the reality is that there is no genuine peace. The longer they remain in the lose-win stance, the more resentment and bitterness they accumulate.

4. Lose-lose (vindictive). When two win-lose aggressors butt heads and one loses, the loser often shifts into the lose-lose position: "Okay, I've lost—but I'm gonna make sure you lose, too. I'll get even with you, if it costs me everything I have!" An example is the newly divorced man who, after his ex-wife won a judgment against him for half of everything he owned, took a chain saw and cut his house in half. He didn't care about winning—just revenge.

5. *Win-win or no deal (healthy compromise)*. This approach isn't always satisfying, but it's often the best compromise in a conflict. It says, "Let's come up with a mutually agreeable solution. If we can't, then let's at least agree to disagree agreeably and part on good terms." Both parties recognize that if they insist on getting their own way, it will damage the relationship. If both can't come out winners, at least no one winds up a loser.

6. *Win-win (healthy resolution)*. This is the optimal goal of all healthy conflict. No aggressors, no doormats, no losers. We seek a creative solution in which everyone comes out a winner, everyone maintains his or her dignity, and the relationship is strengthened and affirmed, not destroyed.

Rules for Healthy Management of Conflict

Disagreements are inevitable in any relationship—family, team, or organization—so we had best prepare for it. If people can agree ahead of time to some simple ground rules, they will find their disagreements easier to manage and resolve. Here, then, are some suggested rules for bringing stronger relationships and creative solutions out of times of conflict.

1. *Focus on assertively stating your views—not on aggressively blowing off your anger*. Conflict is inseparable from anger, and most people have difficulty accepting anger, either their own or someone else's. It's important to realize that anger is a feeling, not a behavior. During conflict, feelings of anger are normal. No one can completely control feelings, but we can all learn to control our behavior. Some people think that venting anger—exploding in someone else's face—is a healthy way to "get the anger out." Wrong. Venting and giving way to feelings of anger trigger strong, unhealthy physiological responses, such as increased levels of adrenaline. Stress goes up. The ability to think rationally becomes clouded. Communication becomes tangled—and solutions to problems move out of reach. Anger tends to spiral upward once it's unleashed.

If you feel angry, don't vent—verbalize instead. It's fair and honest to admit, "This problem makes me feel angry," then go on to say, "but I don't want to stay angry. I want to be a partner with you in solving this problem." When angry, don't direct your anger at the other person but at the problem. State your feelings in a way that respects the other person's feelings and human dignity.

Remember to put behavior ahead of feelings. Contrary to what many people think, behavior doesn't have to be dictated by feelings. God gave us a rational brain, a cerebral cortex, which enables us to *think* our way to mastery over our feelings. Make a commitment to act rationally when you feel angry. Feelings follow behavior. Even though you momentarily feel like putting your fist through a wall, if you talk out your anger, respect the other person's point of view, avoid inflammatory statements or abusive language, and outwardly maintain your composure, you will soon find that you have begun to cool off inwardly as well. And you'll be that much closer to a solution to the disagreement.

2. Avoid lecturing, accusation, personal insults, and generalities. When discussing issues, focus on concrete examples. A common flashpoint in disagreements is the generalized accusation: "You're *always* so stubborn," or, "You *never* do anything right." What is a person supposed to do with a comment like that? He or she feels personally attacked but has no specific behavior or issue to work with. When attacked, people naturally become defensive. Communication shuts down and conflicts become much more difficult to solve.

During disagreements, be specific. "I needed that report by three o'clock yesterday. I lost the deal because I didn't have the figures from your department." Or, "It created a serious problem for me when you showed up a half hour late for our appointment." When you focus on specific issues or behaviors instead of making a broadside assault on someone's overall character, the other person is much more likely to respond by dealing with that issue or changing that behavior.

3. Stay in the present. Don't dredge up old disagreements or past conflicts. Equally important, don't borrow trouble from the future.

Focus on the present conflict, the issue that is on your plate right now—and resolve it.

4. *Take responsibility.* You can often head off conflict by apologizing—and remember, you don't have to be in the wrong to apologize. Saying "I'm sorry" doesn't necessarily mean you are confessing to an evil act. Sometimes you may inadvertently and quite innocently do things that annoy or inconvenience someone else. It doesn't make you a bad person. It's just one of those "oops!" situations. And it's perfectly in order to say, "I didn't mean any harm; I didn't realize I did something that irritated you—so I'm sorry. I'll try to be more aware of how you feel about such things, and I won't let it happen again."

5. *Avoid assigning blame.* Avoid condemning or judging the other person. A person who has to assign blame is thinking win-lose, not win-win. What practical good does it do to make the other person a loser? Why not find a way to resolve the conflict so you both can win?

One way to avoid blaming and condemning is to consciously frame all your statements as an "I" message, not a "you" message. Instead of saying "You make me mad," say, "I feel angry when this issue comes up." Instead of saying, "You always do such-and-such," say, "I find it annoying when such-and-such occurs." This technique enables you to communicate your concerns and feelings without raising the other person's defenses by making him or her feel attacked.

6. *Focus on one issue at a time.* State a single problem in a clear, specific, factual manner. Don't bounce from issue to issue. This only causes frustration, confusion, and increased levels of anger as participants in the disagreement see the discussion getting out of hand. By staying focused on one issue at a time, you are more likely to see real progress in resolving the conflict.

7. *Maintain rigorous honesty and candor.* In conflicts as in every other aspect of life, honesty is the best policy. Put your cards on the table. Avoid hidden agendas, snide innuendoes, and sarcasm. Say only what you mean, and mean what you say. Treat times of conflict as opportunities for honest, open exchanges of truth and information.

8. Listen to the other person's concerns. Don't just wait out the other person while mentally formulating your counterattack. Really listen. You might learn something. A good technique in times of conflict is *active listening.* After the person has spoken, you repeat what the person said, putting it in your own words. Begin with, "What I'm hearing you say is _____." If you got it right, the person will be gratified to know that you understood, and that his or her concerns were actually heard. If you got it wrong, the person will have a chance to correct the misimpression. Speaking is only half of the communication process; the other half is listening.

9. Think win-win. Make sure all sides can benefit and feel a part of the resolution of the conflict. Be flexible. Be creative. Be willing to look at the problem from new angles and perspectives. Don't just try to win an argument; try to win a friend.

10. Replace the "I versus you" mindset with an "us versus the problem" mindset. Remember, your goal is not to defeat the other person. It is to clarify issues and resolve problems so mutual goals can be achieved. Don't focus on the petty details and annoyances of the argument. Instead, keep your mind on the bigger picture. Make a point of stating, "I don't want to defeat you; I want to support you. I'm committed to you and to your success. Let's not allow this problem to divide us."

In his autobiography, *My American Journey,* retired Gen. Colin Powell relates a story that illustrates the mindset we should all have in times of conflict. Powell writes about the troops carrying out Operation Desert Storm in the Persian Gulf region in 1991—especially a young black private who was interviewed by ABC correspondent Sam Donaldson on the eve of the ground war. "How do you think the battle will go, soldier?" asked Donaldson. "Are you afraid?"

"We'll do okay," the GI answered without hesitation. "We're well-trained." He gestured with one thumb toward his buddies. "I'm not afraid of anything because I'm with my family."

The other soldiers shouted, "Tell him again! He didn't hear you!"

"This is my family," the soldier repeated. "We take care of each other."

Our goal, whenever conflict or misunderstanding arises, should be to treat it as any other external problem or threat: We will meet it and beat it together, because we are a family, we are a team, we are partners, and we take care of each other. No conflict, no argument ever should be bigger than our commitment to one another.

The next important lesson I learned from Mr. Littlejohn was that there are things we can control and things we can't control—and we all need to learn the difference.

SEVEN

Control What You Can Control—and Let Go of What You Can't

I was the ulcer king of Spartanburg.

To me, every baseball game at Duncan Park was opening night on Broadway. I was in a frenzy over every detail: "What did the weatherman say? Fifteen percent chance of rain! Ohmigosh, I hope it doesn't rain. A couple of rainouts of key dates and we're ruined! And how about the team? We've lost four in a row—we're gonna lose our fans. Nobody's gonna come!"

After a few weeks of watching me chew my fingernails down to the second knuckle, Mister R. E. took me aside and said, "Take it easy, Pat. You need to learn to control those things you *can* control—and let go of the rest."

"What do you mean?" I asked.

"Ask yourself a simple question," he said. "'What can I control?' Now, what's the answer?"

"Well," I said, "I can control how the ballpark looks."

"That's good. And after the refurbishing job you did, the ballpark looks great, doesn't it?"

"That's true. And I can control how the staff treats the fans. And I can control the promotional activities and the quality of the concessions—"

"Exactly, Pat," said Mr. Littlejohn. "But can you control the weather? No. Even with all your worrying, you can't turn off the rain or turn on the sunshine. And can you control how the team plays, and whether it wins or loses? No. This is the minor leagues, Pat. Everything is controlled at the big-league level. The big brass moves the players around from team to team, and we have no say in the matter. You can call the Phillies' front office and whine and fuss, but you can't control a thing."

Mr. Littlejohn was right. There were some things I could control, and some I couldn't—and I needed to learn the difference.

Another lesson he tried to drum into my thick head was *delegate, delegate, delegate!* That was one of his biggest themes, and he hammered it relentlessly—but for some reason, I just couldn't get it.

When I started in minor-league baseball, operating the Spartanburg Phillies, I did everything myself. I was so driven, so obsessive about details, and so cotton-picking green as a sports executive that I simply didn't understand you can't succeed as a one-man band. On my belt, I wore the biggest key ring I could find, because I had to carry the keys to the ballpark, the office, the storeroom, the rest rooms, the bank box, as well as my personal keys. I did the selling, I did the game-night promoting, I did the publicity, I took the gate receipts to the night deposit slot at the bank. I even got the brooms out after the game so the cleanup crew would be ready to go the next morning. I didn't trust anyone else to do the job. I figured if I didn't do it myself, it wouldn't get done right. Trouble was, I was running myself right into the ground—and paying a high price in stomach lining.

Learning to Let Go

After I left Spartanburg, I took those same bad habits into my duties with the Philadelphia 76ers and the Chicago Bulls. Though I had graduated to the big leagues, my thinking was still bush league. For years, I continued banging out press releases and writing promotional materials that easily could have been farmed out to someone with better writing skills.

Over my years in the NBA, it gradually dawned on me that, as the basketball business got bigger, I had to parcel out more of my job description to others. I had to push a lot of tasks and decisions down the chain of command. If not, these things wouldn't get done and I wouldn't survive, because there were only a finite number of hours in the day. I had to learn to trust people. Maybe they wouldn't get it done the way I would do it myself (although I discovered that some people did things better than I could), but one way or another it would get done. I began to discover that I had hired some pretty competent people. And they were happier and better motivated because they finally felt that I had confidence in them and that they were making a contribution.

I didn't become a delegator by choice. I was forced to trust other people to get the job done. I was forced to give up my obsessive control over the details. Why? Because with each new promotion, I acquired more responsibilities and a bigger job description. The bigger my job got, the more urgently I needed to learn the art of delegating so I could concentrate my efforts where they were needed most. I have to admit that delegating responsibility is still not my strongest suit, but I've been working at it ever since leaving Spartanburg—and I'm a lot better at it than I used to be.

I believe the biggest barrier to delegating for most people is fear. Some business people think that if they let someone else do things, they'll become expendable. That's nonsense. Delegating enables you to get more done—and that makes you look like a genius.

In retrospect, I realize that the more secure and confident I felt in my job, the more comfortable I became in delegating responsibility—and the more accomplished I felt. I looked around and saw that the brightest, most accomplished people are all master delegators. Gen. George S. Patton of the Third Army Corps once said, "Never tell people how to do things. Only tell them *what* to do— and they will surprise you with their ingenuity." Writer and publisher Elbert Hubbard put it this way: "It's a fine thing to have ability, but the ability to discover ability in others is the true test." A good leader should make it a habit to continually ask, "Can the work I'm doing right now be handled by someone else?"

I don't care how talented and hard-working you are, how charming and persuasive your personality, or how well-motivated and confident you may be. If you want to advance far and accomplish much in any field, you must learn to work through others. You must learn to control what you can control—and let go of everything you can't control.

Hire the Best

In the more than half century since the late David Ogilvy founded the Ogilvy and Mather Advertising Agency, he became a worldwide legend, having shaped the images and guided the fortunes of the most recognizable brand names in the world: American Express, Sears, Ford, Shell, IBM, Kodak, Dove Soap, and Mattel's Barbie, to name a few. Ogilvy always believed the key to success was to hire the best people, then trust them to do the job better than he could do it. He sought out people who were more talented and more capable than he was and helped them to succeed. He knew that his success hinged on their success.

Ogilvy instilled this concept into all of his top-level managers. Whenever he promoted someone to a management position, he sent that person a Russian *matroyshka* doll. The wooden doll opened to reveal a smaller doll inside. That doll opened to show an even smaller doll—and on and on, the dolls getting smaller and smaller. Inside the smallest doll, the manager would find a handwritten note from David Ogilvy: "If each of us hires people who are smaller than we are, we shall become a company of dwarfs. But if each of us hires people who are bigger than we are, we shall become a company of giants."

David Ogilvy's lesson was not lost on his managers. Today, Ogilvy and Mather remains a company of giants.

Many managers and executives are tempted to hire only second-rate talent, thinking that by doing so they will avoid being outshone. But those who have truly succeeded can testify that the path to success is to hire the best and the brightest. Former President Ronald Reagan put it this way: "Surround yourself with the best people you can find, delegate authority, and don't interfere as long as the overall policy that you've decided upon is being carried out." Carol Taber, publisher of *Working Woman,* agrees: "Hire the best people—then delegate." Leo Rosten, author of dozens of books, from *Captain Newman, M.D.* to *The Joys of Yiddish,* observes, "First-rate people hire first-rate people. Second-rate people hire third-rate people."

John C. Maxwell, author of *The Success Journey* and *Developing the Leader within You,* offers this insightful assessment of a great steel magnate from a bygone era: "I am drawn to Andrew Carnegie's humility, as well as his talent. He didn't try to do it all or to own it all. He once said: 'I owe whatever success I have achieved, by and large, to my ability to surround myself with people who are smarter than I am.' He knew his own limitations, but that only spurred him on to find associates who didn't have the same ones." Carnegie once joked that his tombstone should be inscribed: "Here lies a man who knew how to enlist the service of better men than himself."

Nationally syndicated talk-show host Bruce Williams once received a call on his show from an entrepreneur with a problem: The caller was a control freak—he *had* to be at the shop all the time, looking over his employees' shoulders, leaving his imprint on every item that left his establishment. He couldn't delegate. Though wealthy and successful, this man couldn't even take a vacation for fear that his business would go into the tank without his daily micro-management. Bruce responded, "From what you've told me, I can tell that you are a failure."

"A failure!" the caller remonstrated. "You don't understand! I run a very successful business."

"Maybe the business is successful," Bruce replied, "but *you* are a failure. If you can't leave your business in the hands of your employees long enough to take a vacation, then no matter how much money you're making, you've failed as a businessman."

Bruce went on to tell his own story. Not only is he a radio talk-show host, he also operates several businesses in various states. "Now, do you think while I'm here doing this radio show that I'm worrying about those businesses? No, sir! I've hired good people; I keep in touch with them; I visit my businesses on a regular basis—but I trust the people I've hired to do their job. You see, I don't have people working *for* me. They work *with* me. They respect me; I trust them; and business is good."

He went on to recall an incident that happened some years earlier. "I was landing an airplane, going about 160 miles an hour, when I hit a tree. Spoiled my day, nearly ended my life. I was in a coma for weeks. I was marginally aware but unable to speak or respond. Now, do you think for one moment that I cared how my various businesses were being run? No way. I was only focused on staying alive and getting well.

"But you know what? When I began to mend, I found out that while I was in a coma, my company had its best quarter ever. Why? Because I had hired good people and I could trust them with my business."

If you can't do that, then you have failed. The ability to delegate is a crucial test of leadership. A successful leader is one whose office or business or organization continues to function and thrive—even when he or she is not there. If you aren't delegating, you aren't leading. Craig O. McCaw, founder of Cellular One and Nextel, put it this way: "My belief is that if you pass autonomy as far down in any grouping of people as you can, you will get extraordinary results if you ask for a lot. The greatest burden you can put on someone is trust." So if you want to be a success, hire the best and brightest—and trust them to do their job. When they perform brilliantly, they will make *you* shine.

What You Can Control and What You Can't

In sports, you quickly learn you can control some things but there are others over which you have no control. Before taking his team to the Super Bowl in January 1999, coach Dan Reeves of the Atlanta Falcons offered this advice: "Don't worry about what you can't control. Just make sure you are on top of the things you *can* control. Control the draft. Control your players. Control mistakes. Control the clock. If you can do all that, chances are you'll do okay."

UCLA's great basketball coach John Wooden had a lot to say about what you can control, what you can't control, and how to tell the difference between the two. Here are some typical Woodenisms on the subject of control:

> It goes back to focusing on what you can control. We had no control over the many possible variations an opponent might use in a game. We did have control, total control, over preparing to execute our game. To me, it made more sense to concentrate on that.

> My dad used to say, "If you get caught up in things over which you have no control, it will adversely affect those things over which you have control." You have little control over what criticism or praise outsiders send your way. Take it all with a grain of salt.

> Focus all your efforts on what is within your power to control. Physical conditioning is one of those things. How your mind functions is another.

Another great basketball coach, Pat Riley of the Miami Heat, put it this way: "Am I a control freak? No. Do I believe in organization? You bet. In discipline? In being on time and making sure everything at the hotel is ready and right? Definitely. I don't control players. I try to control the environment around the players so they can flourish."

Race car drivers work in an environment full of factors that clearly are beyond their control. One of the legends of racing, Mario Andretti, understands it's impossible to control every factor. "If everything seems under control," he says with a laugh, "you're just not going fast enough." Another legendary driver, Richard Petty, observes that adaptability in the face of unforeseen, uncontrolled factors is the key to winning: "You can never control circumstances, so you have to be prepared, in your own mind and with your equipment, to take advantage of circumstances as they unfold."

One of my best friends is Orlando businessman Jimmy Hewitt—a man who reminds me a lot of Mr. Littlejohn. Jimmy was one of the first to envision an NBA franchise in Orlando, and he worked tirelessly with me and others to make the Orlando Magic a reality. One day we were talking about one of Jimmy's passions, Florida

State University football, and after we had thoroughly analyzed the performance of his cherished Seminoles, I said, "Jimmy, what are the keys to running a successful business?"

"Well, Bubba," he said (he calls everybody Bubba), "let me tell you what I think." And he proceeded to lay out a formula for success that will work in any business.

1. *You can't control the marketplace, but you can respond to it.* Before starting a new business, the marketplace must be ripe for your product or service. Your business must be the right fit for the marketplace.

2. *You control the timing and the location of your business.* If you start a new business in a good market setting but at the wrong time of the year or in the wrong location, you will fail. When and where you open your business are factors you control.

3. *You control the startup capital.* Because you can't control market conditions and downturns, you must have sufficient capital to carry you through the lean times that are inevitable in any business startup.

4. *You can't control the cash flow—but you can grow it.* An aggressive, energetic approach to marketing, promoting, and sales can take you far, even during adverse market conditions. If you can show a strongly positive cash flow for at least five years, odds are that you're going to make it for the long haul.

5. *You can control the staffing of your company.* Don't say good help is hard to find. If you do your homework, if you screen enough applicants, if you provide a positive work environment, and if you offer generous incentives, you will attract quality people who can work together for your success. Don't think money is the only issue in attracting good people. Most workers would rather make decent money in a great workplace than make big money in a tense workplace surrounded by nasty people.

6. *There will always be unexpected situations you cannot control.* Such developments as a catastrophic illness, an accident, a global recession, a fire at your factory or office, and other unforeseen circumstances are among aspects of our lives completely beyond our control. "So," Jimmy Hewitt concludes, "the most important ingredient for success is this: Trust in the Lord and seek his will in

every aspect of your business. Put him first and make him chairman of the board. No matter what happens, even when things are out of your control, you can have peace in knowing that he is always in control."

Freaking Out over Control

It is normal for a person to want as much control over life as possible. But it is dangerous and unhealthy to be so obsessive over control as to damage key relationships and lose the ability to tolerate a little chaos. The term *control freak* definitely is not a compliment.

A boss who is a control freak is a danger to himself, his employees, and his business. He usually ends up driving his best people crazy—or worse, he drives them to his competitors. A spouse or parent who is a control freak can do lasting damage to relationships and to family members' emotional well-being.

A control freak tends to be extremely self-centered. He isn't interested in a mutual relationship with shared benefits, shared responsibilities, and shared power. Because the control freak must have total control, he cares only about a relationship that serves *his* needs, *his* wants. He doesn't care about the feelings of people around him; in fact, he resents the fact that the feelings, ideas, and behavior of others interfere with his total control. What's so damaging about this is that the people who have to live and work around a control freak feel devalued and resentful, and sometimes even fearful. The control freak cannot have mutual, intimate relationships. He sees relationships only in terms of maintaining his own control and power. When disagreements arise, the control freak feels his power and control are threatened, so he often reacts in an explosive and angry way. Living and working around a control freak can be a miserable experience. Being a control freak can be just as miserable.

Judith Viorst, the distinguished author of children's books (including the classic *Alexander and the Terrible, Horrible, No Good, Very Bad Day*) and adult poetry, fiction, and nonfiction, has written an important book for those who live with or work around control freaks. In *Imperfect Control: Our Lifelong Struggles with Power and Surrender* (Simon and Schuster, 1998), she says it is normal and reasonable to want to feel in control of our lives and careers. A lot of us, she says, have at least a little bit of the control freak in us.

"But a full-fledged control freak," she writes, "is someone who can't stop controlling, controls inappropriately, and controls all the time. They're really scared, and if they don't control every piece of a situation, the world will turn to dust, the project will fail, their life will be ruined. And some of them are very anxious about being controlled, so it's a pre-emptive strike. If I don't control you, you'll control me. You see this a lot in marriages. . . . Some control out of a staggering arrogance that they know much better than you. After all, how can they deprive you and everyone of their wisdom, competence and advice?

"There have been a huge number of studies showing that people who feel they can control a situation are healthier, happier, better able to pick themselves up after disaster strikes. But a whole lot less is said about the damaging effects of believing you have a huge amount of control over a situation. So people stay in an awful marriage or they stay in a dead-end job, thinking, 'I know I can make my boss a better person.' You're banging, banging, banging your head against a stone wall because you don't know there's such a concept as 'Enough already!'"[11]

One Thing You Must Control: Yourself

John Wooden was once asked, "As a coach, did you ever lose your temper?" His reply: "I always told my players to control their tempers, and I couldn't very well expect them to if I wasn't setting a good example myself. I lost my temper once in a while. But I never lost control. I never threw anything. I never threw a chair." Wooden was talking about a form of control that all of us should have at all times: *self-control*.

In a September 20, 1998, segment of ABC's newsmagazine show *20/20*, reporter John Stossel interviewed Dr. Roy Baumeister of Case Western Reserve University. Baumeister said, "If you look at the social and personal problems facing people in the United States—we're talking drug and alcohol abuse, teen pregnancy, unsafe sex, school failure, shopping problems, gambling—over and over, the majority of them have *self-control failure* as central to them. Studies show that *self-control does predict success in life* over a very long time" (emphasis added).

The report also included video of an experiment Stossel conducted at a nursery school. "By testing how well four-year-olds can resist temptation," Stossel explained, "researchers say they can predict what kind of adults they're likely to be. In the experiment, the kids are given a choice: They'll get five pieces of candy if they can wait ten minutes until the teacher comes back into the room—or just two pieces if they can't wait and give in to the temptation before the ten minutes are up. So the kids tried. It wasn't easy. Most fidgeted and looked as if they were being tortured. Some touched the candy. One boy counted the candy—maybe to remind himself that five is more than two. One girl looked heavenward as she waited, seeming to ask for God's help. Seven of the nine kids we tested lasted the full ten minutes. Most spent some of the time with their hand hovering over the bell." Ringing the bell meant the temptation to take the candy was too strong.

Stossel interviewed one girl, a four-year-old named Heather. "Did you put your hand over the bell and think about ringing it?" he asked.

"Yeah," said Heather, "but I didn't ring the bell."

"Why not?" asked Stossel.

"Because the teacher said I could have five candies if I waited."

"And you got five?"

"Uh-huh."

"Was it worth waiting for?"

"It was hard."

Stossel was recreating an experiment conducted thirty years earlier at Columbia University. Using a much larger group of children, the Columbia study found out which kids had the self-control to resist temptation and hold out for the full reward later—and which did not. The children were checked on over the next few decades to see which group tended to do better in life. The result of the study, Stossel said, was astonishingly clear-cut: "Kids who did well on this test years ago tended to do better in life. Better in lots of ways. Their SAT scores were higher. As teenagers, the boys had fewer run-ins with the law. The girls were less likely to get pregnant."

Self-control, then, is a key indicator of whether or not we will be successful. We can't control everything in life, but if there is one thing we can control and must control, it is the self. As Dr. Baumeister concluded on *20/20*, "If we're concerned about raising children to be successful and healthy and happy, forget about self-esteem. Concentrate on self-control."

Some people think of self-control as self-denial. To be a person of self-control, they imagine, one must become a monk, living in a cave somewhere. Wrong. Self-control is simply a matter of self-management. It comes down to knowing what is important in life and what goals you want to achieve, then disciplining yourself and regulating your daily behavior so you can attain those goals. It means setting aside some momentary pleasure to obtain a more lasting sense of satisfaction.

A person of self-control says, "I can forego that piece of cheesecake and exercise instead. Having a trim, fit body for life is more important to me than a few bites of calorie-laden pleasure." A person of self-control says, "I can forego this purchase right now, because I'm saving for that dream vacation that my family and I will remember for a lifetime." A person of self-control says, "I won't go for an easy, dishonest buck in this business deal, because my self-respect and my integrity are more important to me than the money I would make from compromising my principles and values."

We live in a world which continually urges us give in to our impulses and cravings. We are barraged by commercials that say things like, "Thirst is everything—obey your thirst." So as parents, we need to drill self-control and self-discipline into our children every day. The greatest definition of self-discipline I've ever heard comes from Bobby Knight, basketball coach at Indiana University. "Self-discipline," he said, "is doing what needs to be done; doing it when it needs to be done; doing it the best it can be done; doing it that way every time you do it." My kids can recite that statement backward and forward, because they've heard it a hundred times.

Former pro football coach George Allen once said, "The secret to success, whether in athletics, business, or school, is self-discipline. Those that have it will make it, and the reason why is the competition will say, 'Oh, it's not worth it,' and they'll let you beat them out. If you want it badly enough, you'll work for it." It's true. The tougher we are on ourselves, the easier life becomes.

Those who want to succeed must first learn to control the self. John Maxwell once said, "The things that make a difference, you have control over." And the first order of business in controlling the self is to control our *attitude*. "I have a pin that I wear on my lapel every day," artist Robert Bateman once observed. "It has one word printed on it: ATTITUDE. That word is the key to success in any field, because *you* control it. You can't control the weather, or your kids, or the economy, but you can control your attitude. Life doesn't owe you anything. It's what you make it. . . . You're the only one who's got the power to improve your attitude."

Control Your Fears

Another key to success is the ability to control fears and act boldly and courageously. Many people think courage is the absence of fear. No, even heroes are afraid; their response to fear is just different from the coward's response. Courage is the healthy management of our fears. It is not cowardly to be afraid. It's only cowardly to be *controlled* by fear. As John Wayne once said, "Courage is being scared to death but saddling up anyway."

The great football coach Bill Walsh, originator of the famous West Coast offense for the Super Bowl champion San Francisco 49ers, had this to say about controlling fear in his book, *Building a Champion: On Football and the Making of the 49ers*:

> When a wildebeest or zebra is finally entrapped by the lion, it submits to the inevitable. Its head drops, its eyes glaze over, and it stands motionless and accepts its fate. The posture of defeat is also demonstrated by man—chin down, head dropped, shoulders slumped, arms hung limply. This posture is often visible as players leave the field in the later stages of the game when things are going against them. I often brought this to our players' attention using the example from nature, and we became very sensitive to it. I would remind them

never to allow this to occur. I would assert, "Even in the most impossible situations, stand tall, keep our heads up, shoulders back, keep moving, running, looking up, demonstrating our pride, dignity, and defiance."

So a crucial aspect of controlling our fears has to do with our physical bearing and the way we carry ourselves as we face the battles of our lives. If we adopt a posture of defeat, we allow our fears to control even the way we stand and walk and face the people around us. But if we carry ourselves like heroes, with shoulders squared and a gleam of defiance in our eyes, then we control our fears.

When I was general manager of the Atlanta Hawks, I got tickets to the Atlanta Braves' baseball home opener against the Dodgers. It was a night game, a complete sellout, and I'll never forget that evening—April 8, 1974. Seated immediately behind us was singer Pearl Bailey. Up at the plate: the immortal Henry Aaron. On the line: Babe Ruth's record of 714 career home runs. Aaron had tied the record and he was aiming to break it.

The story of Aaron's feat is a profile in courage. Here was an African-American player who was about to topple the great Babe Ruth—and a lot of people in the country didn't like the idea. Aaron got a lot of mail that year—more than 930,000 letters in all, far more than any other person in the country. Most were fan letters—but about 100,000 of them were crank letters. How secure would you feel if you received that many hate letters, some containing death threats? How safe would you feel walking onto a playing field surrounded by tens of thousands of people, any one of whom might be out to get you? But Aaron wouldn't let anyone or anything stop him from doing his job—and his job was to play baseball.

What happened next is etched in my memory. I was on the edge of my seat as Dodgers pitcher Al Downing hurled the ball. Aaron swung and connected. The crack of his bat echoed through the stands. That ball was gone. Babe Ruth's record was shattered. The ballpark went nuts.

As Aaron rounded second base, a couple of teenagers—both white—jumped over the retaining wall and ran onto the field, chasing Aaron. For a moment, no one knew what they had in mind—

but then it became clear: they were celebrating and cheering Aaron on. As Aaron crossed the plate, the dugout emptied as the Braves streamed onto the field to surround him, cheering and whooping it up. But amid all those ballplayers around Aaron was a short, sixty-eight-year-old black woman. She latched onto Aaron and wouldn't let go of him.

Henry Aaron turned and said to her, "Mom! What are you doing here?"

"Baby," said the mother of the new home-run king, "if they're gonna get you, they've gotta get me first!"

That's a story of courage—the courage of a devoted mother and the courage of a successful son.

We can't control all the circumstances life throws at us. We can't control all the factors in a game or a family or a business. We can't control the past. We can't control the future. We can't even control every aspect of the present. But we *must* control what we *can* control: Our fears. Our attitude. Our behavior. If we control these things, we're going to do just fine.

This is one of the most important lessons I learned from Mister R. E. The next thing he taught me is a matter that is equally vital to your success: the importance of patience.

EIGHT

Avoid Snap Decisions —Be Patient

In June 1997, I flew from Orlando to Detroit for a speaking engagement at the Ford Motor Company in Dearborn, Michigan. A limousine driver was supposed to meet me at the baggage area in the airport. He never arrived. After waiting about an hour, I got another ride to the hotel—where I was in for another wait. At the front desk, a trainee desk clerk was helping another customer. The whole process was painfully slow. It was late, I was tired, and I was—

Well, I was impatient.

It seemed to take forever to check in the other guest, and throughout the procedure, I paced, sighed, fidgeted, muttered to myself, and blew off steam. I wasn't loud about it, but I was not subtle, either. The clerk and the customer clearly could see that I was not happy. Okay, I was being a jerk.

Finally, the man in front of me was registered and it was my turn. I stepped to the desk, and the clerk said, "Just a moment, sir—I'll be right with you." He turned away to file the other guest's registration card.

The guest paused and said, in a soft tone so the clerk wouldn't hear, "You know, mister, it's not the clerk's fault that he's new on the job. He's a little nervous, he's doing the best that he can, and I'm sure all your huffing and puffing won't make him go any faster. I suggest that next time you show a little more patience."

Well, I knew the man was right—and I instantly felt about six inches tall. Before I could think of a reply, the man turned and headed for the elevator. As I watched him walk away, a thought occurred to me that gave me a horrible sinking feeling: *Oh, no! What if that guy is in the audience tomorrow when I give my speech?*

Just then, the clerk returned. Chastened, I checked in, taking extra pains to be gracious to the clerk.

The next morning I came out of my room, walked down the hall, stepped into the elevator—and wouldn't you know it? There was my friend from the night before, the fellow who had lectured me on patience.

"We meet again," he said with a smile.

"I'm glad we did," I replied. "I wanted to apologize for my behavior last night. You were right—it was inexcusable." And we proceeded to have a very nice chat.

As it turned out, he wasn't with Ford—so, fortunately, he would not be in the audience. He worked for a company that researched efficiency in hotels. He was helping to design an automated system that would enable guests to pick up a key and go right to their rooms without waiting at the front desk. It sounded like an excellent idea to me.

I had come to give a lecture, but I was the one who was lectured. I had come as a teacher, but I was the one who was taught a lesson—a lesson in the importance of patience.

Patience: The Key to Reaching Goals

Harvey Mackay, author of *Swim with the Sharks without Being Eaten Alive,* related this story in *Sales and Marketing Management* magazine:

The Japanese are masters of managing goals over time. When I visited Japan in 1983, we had a series of seminars in which we heard speeches from the leaders of Japan's largest industrial concerns, including Sony, Mitsubishi, and Matsushita Electric. When the 88-year-old president of Matsushita addressed us, he spoke eloquently and profoundly. But I was most impressed by this exchange:

Question: "Mr. President, does your company have any long-range goals?"

Answer: "Yes."

Question: "How long are your long-range goals?"

Answer: "Two hundred and fifty years."

Question: "What do you need to carry them out?"

Answer: "Patience."

Patience is a virtue—so says the wisdom of the ages. "Patience is better than pride," said wise old King Solomon (Eccles. 7:8). And the apostle Paul listed patience among the results of a life that is filled with the Spirit of God (Gal. 5:22). Helen Hunt Jackson, author of *Ramona* and the closest friend of poet Emily Dickinson, said, "Who longest waits, most surely wins." And poet Ralph Waldo Emerson agreed: "Adopt the pace of nature. Her secret is patience."

Most of us know what we want, and we want it *now!* But if we pursue only instant gratification, we may miss out on the lasting satisfaction that comes by patiently, steadily working toward goals that matter. Detroit industrialist William E. Holler, an inductee into the Automotive Hall of Fame, put it this way: "You can do what you want to do, accomplish what you want to accomplish, attain any reasonable objective you may have in mind. . . . Not all of a sudden, perhaps, not in one swift and sweeping act of achievement. . . . But you can do it gradually—day by day and play by play—if you *want* to do it, if you *will* to do it, if you *work* to do it, over a sufficiently long period of time."

Sometimes the success we want, the objective we desire, would be ours if we would only stick with our game plan a little longer. Many, unfortunately, are too impatient to succeed. Just when their plan is about to bear fruit, they impetuously leap to a new plan. "The marketing battlefields," observes Jay Conrad Levinson, author of *Guerrilla Marketing,* "are littered with winning marketing plans left behind by impatient marketing directors."

Don't sabotage your goals and your success with impatience. Work hard, work fast, work efficiently and effectively, but as the twelfth century Sufi poet, Jalaludin Rumi, Saadi of Shiraz, observed in *The Gulistan,* "Patience accomplishes its object, while hurry speeds to its ruin."

Patience: The Key to Building Greatness

Quick—name the greatest baseball team ever.

Who did you pick? The New York Yankees? Which one? The 1998 Yankees who went 114-68 and won the World Series? Or the '27 Yankees—the 110-44 Yankees of Babe Ruth (60 homers) and Lou Gehrig (173 RBIs)? Or the '39 Yankees—the 106-45 Yanks featuring a young Joe DiMaggio, who led the American League in batting (.381)? Or the 109-53 Yankees of 1961, with its pantheon of Hall of Famers: Mickey Mantle, Roger Maris, Yogi Berra, and Whitey Ford?

Or would you pick the Chicago Cubs of 1906? With a record of 116-36, the Cubbies of that summer still hold the record for most wins in a regular season.

And what about the '55 Brooklyn Dodgers? Don Newcombe on the mound, and Jackie Robinson, Duke Snider, and Roy Campanella slugging pitches out of the park with amazing regularity. Now, that was a team! Or the '54 Cleveland Indians—with pitching by Bob Lemon, Bob Feller, Early Wynn, and Mike Garcia, powerhouse hitting by Larry Doby, and a 111-43 record?

There were some great teams in the '70s. Cincinnati's Big Red Machine won four pennants in that decade, posting a 108-54 record in '75 with a lineup that included Joe Morgan, Tony Perez, Pete Rose, and the great Johnny Bench. And who could forget the 1970 Baltimore Orioles, propelled to a 108-54 record by a roster that included Brooks Robinson, Frank Robinson, Jim Palmer, and Boog Powell? And then there was the Oakland A's team that won three consecutive World Series, 1972 through 1974, led by such names as Reggie Jackson, Catfish Hunter, and Rollie Fingers.

Another great team from the days before the integration of baseball is often overlooked: the 1943 Homestead Grays, featuring Hall of Famers Cool Papa Bell, Josh Gibson, and Buck Leonard.

All of these are great teams—but my pick for best of the best: Connie Mack's Philadelphia Athletics. The first major league game I ever saw was at the Athletics' home field, Shibe Park, in 1947. Admittedly, the A's were no longer a dominant team by then, but I was seven years old and I absolutely fell in love with the game—so you can see why the Athletics hold a special, sentimental place in my heart.

Mack's organization fielded some imposing teams from 1929 to 1931. But even more formidable were the Athletics of 1905 through 1914. That was during the Dead Ball Era of baseball—so called because the game was played with a softer, squishier ball that was harder to hit out of the park. The ball was also a little battered, lopsided, and stained with tobacco juice by the end of the game, because in those days you used one ball for all nine innings. Mack's Athletics won back-to-back World Series in 1910 and '11 and led the American League in hitting and fielding averages. Pitcher Jack Coombs topped the league both years (thirty-one wins in 1910 and twenty-eight wins in '11), while Frank Baker was the league leader in homers. Hall of Fame talent was plentiful on that team, including Baker, Eddie Plank, and second baseman Eddie Collins.

Connie Mack built his organization with patience. The story of how he signed Eddie Collins to the Athletics is a textbook example of patience. While still at Columbia University, Eddie Collins was one of the hottest second basemen of his day. Connie Mack was determined to sign him—but Collins didn't want to sign. He wanted to finish college before playing pro ball.

"I didn't press him to sign a contract against his better judgment," Mack recalled, "but I didn't want to lose touch with him, either. So I made sure that not a month went by during the next year without Eddie Collins receiving a very cordial letter on Athletics stationery." Mack's steady, patient persuasion paid off. As soon as Collins graduated, he signed with the A's (Collins soon became one of the highest paid players of his era, topping out at what, in those days, was the incredible sum of fifteen thousand dollars per year).

Connie Mack used what he called his "correspondence bureau" to keep in touch with hundreds of potential players, building goodwill and connections that eventually landed many of the top talents in his dugout. "In addition to all the letters we sent out," Mack later recalled, "I made it a rule never to turn down a ballplayer if he needed a favor. If a player wanted something and I could possibly accommodate him, I went out of my way to help him out. I made and kept a lot of friends that way—and a lot of guys I kept in touch with ended up playing for me." In this way, Mack patiently built the Athletics into one of the legendary teams in major league history.

Patience is the key to building greatness in any organization, team, company, or church. And patience is also the key to building individual greatness. It takes patience and practice to acquire the skills that lead to greatness. Ignacy Paderewski, the great pianist and composer, was asked by an admirer how he had reached such a state of perfection in his field. "It must have involved a lot of patience," the admirer remarked.

"Everyone has patience," said Paderewski. "I learned to use mine."

"Patience is a bitter plant," says the ancient German proverb, "but it bears sweet fruit." True words. If we patiently, diligently apply ourselves to a daily discipline of acquiring talents and abilities and developing skills and insights, the result will be sweet indeed.

Patience: The Key to Wise Decision-Making

"Patience," said Saint Augustine, "is the companion of wisdom." Problems and crises test our wisdom, leadership, decision-making abilities, and capacity for functioning under pressure. Great leaders are people of patience, people who keep cool. By their example, they inspire others to remain calm in a crisis so they can make intelligent decisions.

In October 1987, the stock market took a sudden, frightening nosedive. The chairman of the New York Stock Exchange, fifty-seven-year-old John J. Phelan Jr., had a tough choice. Many of his top advisers urged him to shut down the exchange to "halt the bloodletting." Phelan knew that there were risks either way. Allowing the exchange to remain open could result in a selling stampede and a free fall of prices—yet closing the exchange could result in panic and loss of confidence in the market.

Phelan wisely avoided a snap decision. He listened to arguments on both sides, then withdrew and quietly considered the matter alone. When he emerged from his office, his mind was firmly made up. He called a series of press conferences and announced that he was taking a bold, decisive step: The exchange would remain open. His calm, dispassionate demeanor helped to allay fears and slow the rate of panic selling. Within days, the market had stabilized and was moving upward.

Patience is the key to wise decision-making, even in a crisis. Life is full of pressures, deadlines, and emergencies. The temptation in such situations is to make a panicky decision. We think, "There's no time for thinking or planning—I have to act *now!*" But patience, planning, and keeping cool are indispensable, especially in a crisis. A noted surgeon once said, "If I knew I had only five minutes to perform a delicate operation, I would spend the first two minutes planning the procedure." Before you act (and do something you will regret), take time to pray, prioritize, and plan. Even in a crisis, when seconds count, demonstrate the presence of mind to think through your response.

One moment of careful thought may prevent a disaster; a single moment of impatience could ruin your life. "Though I am always in haste," said the great preacher John Wesley, "I am never in a hurry." And Branch Rickey, the famed baseball executive, put it well when he said, "You can't solve everything in a minute. Make time your ally. Delay sharp action."

A few months after the successful conclusion of the American Revolution, a young Frenchman, Albert Gallatin, went to Virginia intending to buy land, settle down, and become an American citizen (he later became secretary of the treasury under President Thomas Jefferson). Gallatin attended a meeting of surveyors and settlers who were deciding the route of a road through the Allegheny Mountains. The meeting was presided over by George Washington.

Gallatin was impressed with the care with which the former commander of the Revolutionary Army approached the matter. Washington studied the maps and questioned woodsmen and hunters who were familiar with the mountain passes in the region. But Gallatin soon became impatient with what he considered a delay on Washingon's part in coming to a decision. Finally, unable to contain himself, Gallatin pointed to one particular pass on the map. "Oh, it is plain enough!" he shouted. "This is the pass! Make the decision and be done with it!"

Instantly, the room was silenced. No one had ever challenged General Washington so openly. Washington himself stared Gallatin down, obviously irked at the Frenchman's brash outburst. But he said nothing to the man. Instead, he turned his back on Gallatin and asked a few more questions of one of the settlers in the room.

A few minutes passed, then Washington turned to Gallatin, tossed the pen down on the table, and said to the Frenchman, "You are right, sir!"

Recalling the incident a few years later, Gallatin reflected, "That is the way it was with General Washington. He was slow in forming an opinion, and he never decided a matter until he knew he was right."

When you have a crucial decision to make, patience is the key to knowing when to act—and when not to act. Mark McCormack, sports agent and author of *What They Don't Teach You at Harvard Business School* and *The Terrible Truth about Lawyers,* tells of watching game warden Ian Player perform his fascinating job. Ian, the brother of one of McCormack's clients, golfer Gary Player, was the head warden of the largest game preserve in the Natal province of the Union of South Africa. The problem Ian faced was that poachers were depleting the population of endangered white rhinoceroses in the preserve. His goal: To save the remaining rhinos by rounding them up and relocating them to zoos around the world so the species could be maintained.

Each morning, Ian Player loaded up a truck with rifles and tranquilizer darts and led a crew into the bush. When a rare white rhino was spotted, he would shoot the animal with a dart, then follow it at a respectful distance. The process was tricky and demanded pinpoint timing. From years of experience, Player had developed an ability to "read" a rhino's behavior so that he knew when the animal was woozy enough to allow Player and his crew to back the truck up to it and push it into the vehicle. If Player moved too quickly, the rhino wouldn't be tranquilized, and it would charge. If Player waited too long, the rhino would fall to the ground—and rhinos are too heavy to lift into a truck.

Fortunately, says McCormack, Player "knew everything about the white rhino's movements and quickly developed the perfect combination of patience and decisive action that let him save the species. That's the image I have of Ian Player: forever watching, forever patient, forever waiting for the decisive clue, until it was time to strike."

That is the way it is with you and me, in all the crucial decisions we have to make. Patience doesn't mean complacency—a willingness to wait forever, never reaching the goal. It means a willingness to wait until just the right moment. Don't act too quickly. Don't wait too long. Wait until the opportunity ripens—then *act*. Here are five rules for patient, wise decision-making, even in times of crisis.

1. *Get advice.* Get as much information, insight, and counsel as you have time to gather. It is much easier and wiser to make an informed decision than to make a decision in a vacuum.
2. *Get alone.* After gathering advice and opinions, sit down by yourself and sort through the options in an unhurried atmosphere.
3. *Get away.* It's hard to make a wise decision when you are too close to the situation. If possible, take a breather, get away from the situation, take your mind off the matter. You may find that, while driving, running, working out, swimming, or showering, a solution will pop into your mind seemingly out of nowhere.
4. *When uncertainty persists, say no.* If, after following steps 1–3, you are still not sure which way to go, the best answer is no. It's easier to change no to yes than to change yes to no.
5. *Once you have come to a decision, act firmly and decisively.* Lee Iacocca said, "If I could sum up in one word what makes a

good leader, I'd say decisiveness." Don't look back. Don't dither or fret. Don't show indecision to subordinates. Demonstrate confidence and conviction, and do everything you can to make your decision work. Odds are that you've made the right decision—and success will be yours.

Patience in Recovering from Mistakes

One of the hardest things to do is demonstrate patience when we've made a big mistake and suffered a loss as a result. Yet patience is the key to recovering from mistakes and putting our game plan, our career, our ministry, or our lives back on track.

I've been in the sports world during four decades, and I've made plenty of mistakes. Case in point: In 1970, when I was general manager of the Chicago Bulls, we were preparing for the first college draft I had ever participated in. Our college scout was Jerry Krause, who's now the Bulls' general manager. He had zeroed in on a promising guard named Jimmy Collins from New Mexico State University. But as draft day approached, our head coach, Dick Motta, came back from an NCAA regional game raving about a guard from the University of Texas in El Paso, Nate Archibald.

So we got in touch with Nate Archibald and told him to wait in his dorm room for a call. Then Dick, Jerry, and I put our heads together and planned our strategy: We would take Collins on the first round, and if Nate Archibald was still available in the second round, we'd take him, too. Dick Motta was a little sore about that—he really wanted Archibald more than he wanted Collins. But Jerry and I were sold on Collins. I asked Dick, "What happens if Archibald isn't there by the second round?"

"Then we'll play against him." Those words would haunt me for years to come.

The draft got underway. As planned, we took Jimmy Collins in the first round. Came the second round, we anxiously awaited our turn. Then, just a few picks before ours, Cincinnati took Archibald. Dick Motta looked at me and scowled. I sank down into my chair.

In the end, our man Collins washed out after two years—but Nate Archibald went on to a brilliant fifteen-year career in the NBA and a place in the Hall of Fame. Years later, at the 1997 All-Star Game in Cleveland, the NBA honored the fifty greatest players of all time. The league published a magnificent coffee table book which was unveiled at a reception prior to the game. All the great players in that book were honored during the halftime show, so I carried my book with me, along with a felt-tipped pen, and I got my book autographed by the stars. And who was the first player I saw? Nate Archibald. I had blown the chance to draft him—and there I was, asking for his autograph.

And here's another story: As I was working on this book, I got a call from Phil Jasner of the *Philadelphia Daily News*. The paper was conducting a vote among sports fans to select all the greats of the century in Philadelphia sports—including such categories as the greatest player, the greatest team, the funniest moment. But Jasner wasn't calling me about any of those. No, he wanted my comments on what fans dubbed the worst trade in Philadelphia sports history. That trade took place in June 1986, while I was general manager of the 76ers.

It was the night before the draft, trades were flying every which way, and we ended up dealing superstar Moses Malone and Terry Catledge to Washington in exchange for Jeff Ruland and Cliff Robinson. We also traded the number one pick in the entire draft to Cleveland in exchange for Roy Hinson and $800,000 in cash. With that pick, Cleveland grabbed Brad Daugherty from North Carolina. Daugherty went on to have a great career, including appearances in five All Star games. Moses Malone went on to have more good years in Washington.

At the time, we thought we had pulled off a trade bonanza that was going to take the 76ers to another NBA championship—but it soon became known as the Edsel of all sports trades. All three players we received—Hinson, Ruland, and Robinson—turned out to be disasters. Hinson simply never panned out, while Ruland and Robinson both ended up with career-ending knee injuries. Of all the trades of the last hundred years, that one was voted the absolute worst in Philadelphia sports—and I was right in the middle of it! Some distinction, eh?

I love to read the cartoon *Peanuts* in the morning paper. One day Charlie Brown and Linus were conversing about their troubles. Linus said, "I guess it's wrong to be always worrying about tomorrow. Maybe we should only think about today." Charlie Brown answered, "No, that's giving up. I'm still hoping that yesterday will get better!"

We have to make decisions every day of our career, and some of those decisions inevitably will be clunkers. Someone once said, "The most tiring exercise in the world is carrying yesterday on your back." It's true. It's important to be patient with circumstances. It's important to be patient with other people. But most of all, it's important to be patient with yourself. When you make a mistake, learn from it, but don't beat yourself up over it. Instead, give yourself a fresh start with each new day, each new project, each new task. Keep moving forward toward your goals. Shakespeare knew. "How poor are they that have not patience!" he wrote in *Othello*. "What wound did ever heal but by degrees?" Mister R. E. would agree with philosopher Baltasar Gracian: "It is better to sleep on things beforehand than lie awake about them afterward."

If you saw the 1998 Rose Bowl game between Washington State University and the University of Michigan, you saw Michigan quarterback Brian Griese (now a quarterback with the Denver Broncos) cap an undefeated season with a Rose Bowl victory and the bowl's Most Valuable Player award. (You also saw Brian's very proud and choked-up father, ABC Sports football analyst Bob Griese, interview the victorious quarterback after the game.)

But there was one game during Griese's undefeated season with the Michigan Wolverines when it looked like defeat was inevitable: a home game against Iowa, October 18, 1997. Michigan's offense went into the first half full of confidence—and promptly began making mistake after mistake. During the entire 1997 season, Griese threw five interceptions—but he tossed three of them in the first half against Iowa. The Hawkeyes converted two of those three interceptions into touchdowns. Adding to the self-inflicted wounds of the Wolverines' offense were a fumble, a blocked punt, and a whole slew of penalties.

In the final seconds of the first half, Iowa scored a touchdown on a punt return—and the dispirited Wolverines went into the tunnel at halftime staring at a 21-7 deficit. Griese later told the media what was in his mind. "'Well,' I thought, 'I got us into this situation with those interceptions, and I'm the one who'll have to get us out.' I decided I'd have to toss out everything that happened in the first half, then come out and play the second half the way I knew I could play it. That decision was the turning point."

When Griese led the offense onto the field in the second half, people in the stands were yelling at Michigan coach Lloyd Carr to send in Brian's backup. But Carr believed in Griese. Carr took him aside and told him, "This is your time, Brian. This team is looking to you for leadership. So have fun out there—but bring us back."

"Okay, Coach," said Griese. And he proceeded to direct a sixty-seven yard, eight-play drive ending in a touchdown. Suddenly, Michigan trailed by only 7. "After that," Brian later recalled, "I was fine."

On Michigan's next possession, Griese patiently worked the ball up the field, arriving at the goal line with fourth down and inches to go. The choice: kick a field goal or risk a touchdown attempt on fourth down. Carr told Brian, "Go for it." Griese took the snap and dove over the top of the pile into the end zone. Touchdown—and the game was tied at 21.

Iowa instantly replied on its next possession with a field goal. Iowa led once more, 24-21, at the end of the third quarter. Brian and the Wolverines answered in the fourth quarter with a clock-gobbling seventy-seven yard drive, concluding with a two-yard touchdown pass from Brian to Jerame Tuman. And that's how the game ended—Michigan 28, Iowa 24.

"People always say that when you make a mistake, don't look back, just move on," Brian later reflected, "but that's easier said than done. Some guys make a mistake and it blows their confidence so bad you can never throw to them again. When you make a mistake, you just have to put it behind you and start fresh. You just have to go on from there and try to come back. Anytime somebody's in that situation, you learn something about their character. After a bad first half against Iowa, I said to myself that I was not going to get down. I know I can play this game."

Those who watched Griese play his game that day were in awe. Stan Parrish, the team's quarterbacks coach, said, "Brian is the toughest guy I've ever coached. Only one in a million can regroup emotionally to do what he did. He's as tough as they get." Wolverine tailback Clarence Williams agreed. "Brian Griese is one of the greatest leaders I've been around. He shows so much composure and confidence as a leader. It definitely rubbed off on the team. He keeps us so relaxed, and one of the prime examples was the Iowa game. He had one of the worst first halves of his career, and you would never have known by the second half. He was a totally different quarterback in the game, and not too many people could have done that."

After the game, *The Michigan Daily* made a prophetic statement: "Griese looked like a leader, shaking off a terrible first half and playing a phenomenal second. Not many quarterbacks could have pulled that off, and they are the ones who are able to usually end their seasons on New Year's Day." In football, in a career, in life, mistakes are inevitable, but the key to recovering from your mistakes is *patience*—with yourself, in sticking with your game plan, in regaining lost ground, and in rebuilding shaken confidence. Whatever mistakes you've made in the first half of your game, you *can* recover—if you start the second half with patience.

The Patience of Maturity

Is there anything as impatient as a career-minded guy in his twenties?

Mister R. E. understood my impatience and my impetuousness—certainly better than I understood it myself. He constantly preached to me, "Patience, Pat. You've got to be willing to learn and gain experience—you can't come into a new situation and jump right to the top." Well, that was a hard lesson for me to learn. Patience was never my strong suit.

I well remember the end of my first season with the Spartanburg Phillies in 1965. We'd had a wonderful year—not a great team, not a great won-lost record, but an outstanding season in terms of attendance and excitement among the fans. When I was named Executive of the Year in the Western Carolinas League—it really went to my head. At age twenty-five, I had convinced myself that the Yankees, Cubs, and Dodgers would all be lining up to secure the services of this Class A general manager with one good season behind him. The night the season ended, Mister R. E. and I sat in his car and talked. "It's been a great season, Coach," I said. "Thanks for all your help and encouragement."

Mister R. E. smiled knowingly. He could tell what I was thinking—and he knew I still had a lot to learn. "Patience is the key," he told me. "Pat, you have a right to be proud of what you've accomplished. But your job isn't done yet."

"Well," I said, "I've left the place in good shape for the next guy."

Mister R. E. sighed, and in his slow, calm way, he explained how the world works. "Pat, you think you're ready to move on because you've got one good year under your belt. I'm telling you it could have been an even better year. The real measure of success is how well you can build on what you've begun. There are a million salesmen out there who can sell for one year, but the real test is if you can sell yourself year after year. Stay here and prove yourself. Show the baseball world what you're *really* capable of. You can get all the experience you need right here in Spartanburg—and that's much better than to jump from team to team, trying to build a reputation for yourself at a lot of different whistle-stops. You can go to the big leagues right from here someday."

Well, that was hard advice for me to take—but I bought into it. After a few weeks had passed and my phone wasn't ringing with big-league offers, I figured Mister R. E. must have known what he was talking about. The following year, 1966, was even better. In a town of 45,000 people, we drew 173,000 to the ballpark. The team was a lot better, too—we even had a twenty-five-game winning streak at one point, and we won the pennant.

Looking back, I can see that one of the things Mr. Littlejohn liked in me was my drive, my eagerness to reach my goals. It's good to have young people in any organization because they love to make waves, charge ahead, challenge the status quo, and move up fast.

But it's also good to have older, wiser, more mature people who understand the need for patience. Mr. Littlejohn recognized my potential and enjoyed my enthusiasm. But he also wanted me to learn to temper that all-consuming drive with a healthy dose of maturity and patience. That is why he invested so much in me.

Mister R. E. learned patience dealing with business partner G. Leo Hughes—"Captain Leo"—a strong-willed, dominating personality with a big heart. Mr. Hughes would often get upset and make snap decisions. Then Mister R. E. would sit him down and calmly explain the facts. The 1964 season had been rough—the Phillies had sent a poor team to Spartanburg. Captain Leo went around complaining that the city needed a new affiliate. Finally Mister R. E. explained that there were no guarantees things would get better with another team and that the Phillies were doing their best to help us. As it turned out, we stayed with the Phillies and won championships in 1966 and 1967. I learned a lot about patience watching Mister R. E. handle that situation.

Coach John Wooden of UCLA was a wise and keen student of the human condition. He used to tell his players, "Be quick, but don't hurry," and he understood how different generations view patience:

> Most of us are impatient. As we get a bit older, we think we know more, and that things should happen faster. But patience is a virtue in preparing for any task of significance. It takes time to create excellence. If it could be done quickly, more people would do it. A meal you order at a drive-through window may be cheap, it may be quick, it may even be tasty, but is it a great dining experience? That takes time.
>
> Good things always take time, and that requires patience. Competitive greatness requires patience. Excellence requires patience. Most of all, success requires patience.
>
> Youth is a time of impatience. Young people can't understand why the problems of society can't be solved *right now*. They haven't lived long enough to fully understand human nature, and they lack the patience that eventually brings an understanding of the relatively slow nature of change.
>
> On the other hand, older people often become set in their ways, fear change, and accept problems that should be addressed and resolved.

The young must remember that all good and worthwhile things take time (and that is exactly as it should be). Their elders must remember that, although not all change is progress, all progress is the result of change.

One of the greatest examples of patience in leadership was provided by Abraham Lincoln—a man who possessed a great capacity for enduring delay, a man who waited for just the right moment to act. Charles A. Dana, who was assistant secretary of war in Lincoln's administration, recalled, "President Lincoln was a man who was never in a hurry, and who never tried to hurry anybody else."

Lincoln scholar Eugene Griesman attributes the man's patience to his practical nature. "He had observed, as a lawyer and a politician, that forcing an issue often spoiled a desired outcome. He came to the conclusion that political and legal processes, like flowers and trees, followed a natural sequence of development. Lincoln observed: 'A man watches his pear tree, day after day, impatient for the ripening of the fruit. Let him attempt to force the process, and he may spoil both fruit and tree. But let him patiently wait, and the ripe pear, at length, falls into his lap.'"

It's true. I love living in Florida, with orange, grapefruit, lemon, and tangerine trees in our yard. My biggest problem is that I can hardly stand to wait until the fruit is ripe. In the morning there's nothing like a glass of juice from a freshly squeezed orange just minutes off the tree—but I've ruined more glasses of orange juice by impatiently pulling unripened fruit from the tree.

In wisdom, there is patience. In patience, there is success. I learned this from one of the wisest, most patient men I ever knew, R. E. Littlejohn. And I learned more from him—including the importance of keeping it simple.

NINE

Keep It Simple

"Our life is frittered away by detail. Simplify, simplify." Henry David Thoreau wrote those words at Walden Pond in 1854. A century later, Mister R. E. gave the same advice to his eager young baseball manager. "Don't make things complicated," he told me. "Most good things in life are very simple and practical." I never forgot that advice.

A few years later, when I moved to Philadelphia to work with the 76ers, the team's owner, Irv Kosloff, gave me the same advice. "Pat," he said, "every morning when you start your day, just ask yourself two simple questions: What am I doing to help the team win more games? And what am I doing to sell more tickets? Your job here is really no more complicated than that." I never forgot that advice, either.

Simple is better. Offer me a choice between two VCRs, the one with the control panel that looks like a space shuttle cockpit or the one with a few buttons—STOP, PLAY, FF, RW, EJECT—

and I'll take the simple one every time. Less to learn, less to break down, less likely to flash 12:00 A.M. day and night for the next few years.

Experts tell us that events such as the nuclear meltdowns in plants at Chernobyl and Three Mile Island and the chemical disaster in Bhopal, India, were not mere freak accidents—they were the predictable results of complexity overload. Humans, too, can break down due to complexity overload. If there is one universal characteristic of our age, it is that people feel overstressed by life's complexity. We complain as if we have no choice—but the reality is that the life we live is the life we *choose*. We maintain a high-stress, hypercomplicated life because it is familiar, and most of us choose familiarity over change, even if the familiar overloads us. It is the fear of change that prevents us from downshifting to a simpler, less stressful life.

A Lifestyle—or a Life?

The guru of the simplicity movement is Elaine St. James. "It takes time to make time," she says. "You can't figure out how to create time for the things you enjoy if you don't take time to rethink what you're doing now. Maintaining a complicated life is a great way to avoid changing it."

In 1990, Elaine St. James was a busy real-estate investor with properties on both coasts; she also authored a book and conducted seminars in real estate investing. But her life was spinning out of control. She worked twelve-hour days, lived in a huge home that required continuous upkeep, and was married to a man she rarely saw because his schedule was equally busy. For years, her life was a maze of full-throttle, hyperdrive stress because she couldn't imagine any other way of living.

Gradually, it dawned on her that she didn't have a life, she only had a lifestyle. She decided to make a change, committing herself to working one hour less per day. She divested herself of possessions that cluttered her house and her life. Then she and her husband moved into a smaller house just a few minutes from his office, eliminating his four-hour daily commute. In the process, she estimated that the couple had carved out an extra thirty hours a week. "It's hard to put a price tag on that much time," she concluded.

Eventually, her new way of life led Elaine St. James to a whole new career built around her passion for the simple life. She has sold nearly two million books with such titles as *Simplify Your Life: 100 Ways to Slow Down and Enjoy the Things That Really Matter; Inner Simplicity: 100 Ways to Regain Peace and Nourish Your Soul;* and *Simplifying Your Life with Kids: 100 Ways to Make Family Life Easier and More Fun.* "Simplifying your life is really about gaining control of your life—creating more time, on the job and at home, to do the things you want to do," she explains. "A Time/CNN poll found that 65 percent of people spend their leisure time doing things they'd prefer not to do. That's staggering! What's the point of leading a 'full life' if you don't have the time and energy to enjoy it?"[12]

Simplify Your Game Plan

All the great coaches and players, regardless of their sport, will tell you that one of the keys to winning is simplicity. Coach Vince Lombardi used to say, "I believe in simple things done with consistent excellence rather than complicated things done poorly." And Babe Ruth used to say that the secret of his hitting prowess was simple: "I don't let that little white thing cross the plate." The message is clear: Simplify!

Basketball is a game of subtleties and intricacies. In pressure situations, with mere seconds on the clock, with everything hinging on the next shot, with the crowd rocking the house and the players nearing exhaustion, who is the likeliest to win? The team whose coach can diagram the simplest play—simple to understand, simple to execute.

John Wooden was at his best when coaching in pressure situations. He would take a time-out, call his players to the bench, and give them the winning play, calmly and succinctly. It would always be a play that the players had endlessly gone over in practice, so that inbounding the ball and executing the elements of the play would be elementary—they could do it in their sleep. "It's a simple game," says Wooden, "and coaches tend to foul it up and complicate it. I wanted to keep it very simple."[13]

Some coaches take an even simpler approach. Charlie Spoonhour, former basketball coach at St. Louis University, recalls an incident when a high school team of his went up against a team whose coach would call a time-out—then say absolutely nothing to his players. The players would sit on the bench, staring at their shoelaces. The horn would sound—and the coach would call *another* time-out, keeping his players on the bench even longer. Still, he said nothing to them. No pep talks, no diagramming of plays on his clipboard. What was he trying to accomplish?

"He had them thinking about what they should be doing," explains Spoonhour. When the horn sounded again, those players came out and battled hard, executing everything they had learned in practice. They just needed to settle down and remember what they had learned in practice. Though that coach's methods may have been a little extreme, Spoonhour learned a lot from that game. "When I was a young coach," he explains, "I'd try to tell [my players] fifteen things. Now, I say one or two things and save my breath." Again, the message is clear: Simplify![14]

Defensive back Rod Woodson enjoyed a brilliant ten-year career with the Pittsburgh Steelers, earning a reputation as one of the elite defensive players in NFL history and assuring himself a place in the Pro Football Hall of Fame. He was also named to the NFL 75th Anniversary Team (he later went on to play for the San Francisco 49ers and the Baltimore Ravens). A quiet, contemplative man in a loud, brash, emotional sport, Woodson plays the game as much with his mind as with his finely sculptured musculature. Though fantastically tough, aggressive, and physical when he bumps and shadows his foe, Rod Woodson is truly a thinking man's cornerback. One of the keys to Woodson's greatness: simplicity itself.

"When I first came into the league," he recalls, "I didn't know how to study game film. I should have been making myself some popcorn. It was like I was in the movies, just seeing everything in a general way, seeing nothing specific. A coach would ask me what I saw and I would say, 'Well, ah—what should I have seen?'

"But [Steelers defensive coach] Rod Rust taught me how to watch film. . . . It was early in my career. He told me that offenses can only run so much stuff from so many different personnel packages and eventually they all run the same patterns. All we do when we study is to complicate things. Once I started seeing things as being more simple, my film study got better. You start thinking that way—simple—and you say, 'Oh, wow, is that all they are doing?' It clicked in. I can watch less film now and know more, because I retain more and see more."[15]

The message is clear: You want to be effective? Want to achieve your goals? Want to win? Simplify!

Simplify Your Business Life

In business, too, less is usually more. A young woman became interested in floral arrangement and entered some of her work in the local flower show. She thought her arrangements were beautiful, spectacular, eye-popping—but the judges didn't agree. At the end of the show, she had won no prizes—not even an honorable mention. So she asked one of the judges what she was doing wrong.

"Come back tomorrow," he told her, "and I will tell you what you should do."

So she returned the next day, and the judge handed her three envelopes. "The next time you do an arrangement," he said, "open the first envelope and follow the instructions. Then do the same with the second and third envelope."

So she did. She went home, created a new arrangement—then opened the first envelope and read, "Take out half the flowers, and rearrange the rest." She followed the instructions, reduced the arrangement by half, and arranged it beautifully.

Then she opened the second envelope. Again she read this message, "Take out half the flowers, and rearrange the rest." And again she followed the instructions, reducing the arrangement by half.

She opened the third envelope, found the same instructions, and followed them again, reducing the arrangement one more time. Then she entered the arrangement in another flower show—

And won first prize. Simplify!

Isn't the business world complicated enough? Why not find ways to simplify your career? If you are writing a business plan, a marketing report, or some other business document, and you cannot reduce it to simplicity, then you are in trouble. The best answers are the simplest answers. Complexity stifles thought. Simplicity stimulates thinking. As Walt Disney often said, "Keep it simple, so a child can understand it."

Rich DeVos is one of the great success stories of our time. I first met him in August 1990. The Orlando Magic's ownership group was in the running to bring a National League expansion baseball team to Orlando—but at a crucial juncture the ownership had collapsed. We had to get a new owner in place very quickly, so a friend of mine, Billy Zeoli, set up a meeting with his friend, Rich DeVos. I flew up to Grand Rapids, Michigan, to meet with him.

There was no time to prepare a market analysis or a feasibility study or any of the other charts and graphs one usually brings to such a meeting. All I had was one piece of paper torn from my notepad. On it, I had drawn a circle with some crisscross lines indicating percentages of the whole, like pieces of a pie. It didn't look anywhere near as presentable as a fourth-grader's homework, but it illustrated in simple terms the shares of each investor in the ownership group, including the portion of ownership we hoped DeVos would agree to purchase.

My meeting with DeVos lasted no more than forty minutes. I made my pitch and showed him my hand-drawn pie chart. He nodded, then said, "Excuse me—I'll be right back." He was gone for less than five minutes. Then he returned and said, "Tell the league we'll go forward with them." He had made a $95 million decision—just like that!

The baseball franchise never materialized, but that meeting led directly to Rich DeVos becoming the owner of the Orlando Magic—and a good friend of mine. I kept that piece of paper and framed it on the wall of my office, tangible proof that simplicity works.

Houston-based Consolidated Graphics is a commercial printing company with plants in major cities around the country. Founded in 1985, the company went public in 1994, saw a 500 percent increase in stock value over the next five years, and is now listed on the New York Stock Exchange (as cgx). The secret of Consolidated Graphics' success, according to founder-CEO Joe Davis, is simplicity. He works out all of his business deals with a wooden pencil and a single sheet of letter-size paper. Forget computer-generated spreadsheets, he says. If the transaction can't be reduced with a pencil to a single sheet of paper, then the deal is too complicated—and you probably don't understand it. In such cases, he advises, go back and do your homework.

"I'm noted for putting things in the simplest format possible," he says. "If a guy says we need a new printing press and can prove it, I don't need a twenty-three-page document to support it. Some of the best ideas are not yet written down in the form of a business plan. After all, my company was founded during a chat at a cocktail party."

Or take the story of billionaire Craig McCaw. When his father died in the early 1980s, McCaw was a sophomore in college. After Craig and his mother finished liquidating the estate to pay off the taxes and bills, there was nothing left but a tiny cable TV system of two thousand subscribers in Centralia, Washington. Craig took the helm, running the company from his dorm room at Stanford University two states away. He expanded the business and gradually moved the company into the new and untried field of cellular phone service. By the end of the '80s, his new company—Cellular One— was the top nationwide brand in the burgeoning cellular business. He sold Cellular One to AT&T for a cool $11.5 billion—then launched a new venture, Nextel. The Nextel concept is to provide a full range of communication services in a single package and offer an honest, simple, easy-to-understand billing system that charges by the second instead of rounding to the next minute.

McCaw says he owes his success to this philosophy: "Work hard to keep things simple. Simple solutions solve complex problems; complex solutions rarely accomplish anything."

Effective, successful entrepreneurs and leaders like McCaw possess an extraordinary ability to focus on the essentials and arrive at simple, understandable, even elegant solutions to complex problems. They are not simplistic or superficial people. Rather, these leaders know how to take the complex and make it clear and practical.

Another such leader is Dave Thomas, the founder and pitchman for Wendy's fast food restaurants. When one of his corporate lieutenants suggested that the franchise company add taco salads to the menu, Dave thought the idea was worth investigating. In most corporate cultures, that means you spend a few hundred thousand dollars for market research. Not Dave Thomas. Wendy's became large because Dave can think small. Instead of ordering expensive market research, he said, "Let's just introduce it on a small scale and see what happens." Simple.

Dave found that his restaurants already had everything needed to make taco salads except taco chips and a ladle to place a dollop of chili on the salad. So the company supplied a Wendy's restaurant with ladles and taco chips, then sent researchers to conduct customer surveys in the restaurant. Total cost of testing the product for three weeks: $751.17. Wendy's taco salads were a hit. Within weeks, all Wendy's restaurants were serving taco salads and rolling up big profits.

Intel Corporation, which makes a completely different kind of chip (silicon instead of corn), also knows the value of simplicity. Roger Whittier, director of corporate purchasing, wondered if the company really needed to make employees fill out a requisition, obtain a manager's signature, send it to the purchasing department to place the order, have the receiving department receive it and route it, and have accounts payable pay the bill. Wasn't there a better way—a *simpler* way? Whittier discovered that the vast bulk of Intel's bills were for amounts under one thousand dollars, and that these bills totaled just 1.7 percent of all expenditures.

The result: SPOC cards (for Small Purchase Order Charge cards). These cards were issued to all employees with specified spending limits, good only for purchases from approved retailers. As a result, Intel now writes a single check per month to each supplier instead of hundreds—and Intel workers get their supplies in one or two days instead of weeks.

But isn't there a risk, trusting all those employees with a corporate credit card and very little bureaucratic oversight? Not according to Roger Whittier. Though transactions number around ten thousand a month, Whittier says, "I am not aware of a single case of abuse of the system."[16]

Another Dave has climbed onto the simplicity bandwagon—David Anderson of Famous Dave's barbecue shack restaurants. "As long as people are eating three times a day, there is going to be a need for great food," he told an interviewer on the MSNBC cable network. "So where can you go? The answer is really simple. How many backyards in America have a barbecue grill? We are America's food. We are barbecue ribs, we are barbecue chicken, we are cole slaw, potato salads, honey-buttered cornbread. That's simple, but it's really good eating. . . .

"We have a very simple concept. We have a real simple menu. Our training is very intense, but it's simplified. It's a training we call 'Three Step Simple.' We built our whole training program around things that are simple. And so when we put this thing together to franchise across the street corners of America, we made a commitment to keep everything simple. We kept our menu simple, we kept our training simple, and we kept our focus simple. Because of that, customers like to eat here and investors know that Famous Dave's is a company that can grow, and it can go into any community because it's about great food and simplicity of operation.

"What we are doing is as old as barbecue. It's as old as fire. It's something that everybody enjoys."[17]

Another popular restaurant chain—Papa John's Pizzas—uses the same simple recipe for success. Founded in 1985, Papa John's has zoomed to megamozzarella status in an astonishingly short time. At the beginning of the twenty-first century, after only fifteen years in business, Papa John's has well over a thousand outlets and is number four in market share behind Pizza Hut, Domino's, and Little Caesars, all of which have been in operation for more than forty years. Papa John's secret ingredient: simplicity.

Let the other pizza chains offer stuffed crust, buffalo wings, chicken topping and barbecue sauce—Louisville-based Papa John's devotes itself to "keeping the main thing the main thing." Its simple menu: pizza, bread sticks, soda, and nothing else. John Schnatter, the young founder and CEO of Papa John's, says he owes everything to simplicity.

That approach enables Papa John's to focus on quality with a fierce and single-minded determination. The company has spent millions on water treatment at its plants merely to ensure consistent quality in its pizza dough, and also spends extra on its sauce, which is made from tomatoes that are processed the day they are picked. A simple recipe—and a successful one![18]

Clear Away the Clutter

One aspect of society that creates imbalance, complexity, and stress in our lives is affluence. We have so much stuff! And we are constantly spending money, digging ourselves deeper into debt, and buying ever more stuff. And we are renting storage space so we have a place to stuff our stuff. Then we have to work harder and longer, enjoying life less so we can afford the payments on all our stuff! We must learn to earn more than we yearn.

We live at a frantic pace, desperately seeking fulfillment in an existence filled to the bursting point with things that just don't matter. Then we wonder why we have no room for the things that *do* matter: time with family, time in solitude and fellowship with God, time to enjoy life and discover life's deepest meaning. If we want to experience rich and satisfying lives, we need to clear out the clutter and simplify!

Tammerie Spires of Dallas used to be a management consultant with the accountancy firm of Price Waterhouse. She enjoyed her work and she enjoyed the big money she was making. It was the American dream—or so she thought. But after giving birth to her second of two children, she realized that she actually preferred family life to corporate life. Though her company offered her a pay raise to stay, she decided to leave her job and become a full-time mom. Now her family lives on the single salary of her husband, an engineer.

After making this radical move toward simplicity, she discovered something fascinating about herself. "I realized I was passionate about camping," she says, "so I wrote a book called *A Guide to Happy Family Camping,* and it got published. My great dream of writing a book would never have come true if I hadn't stopped believing in what other people defined as success and started looking for what *I* defined as success."[19]

Tammerie Spires isn't alone in her quest for a simpler, more meaningful life. Many people in corporate America are opting out of the affluence-and-ambition rat race, foregoing the perks, the high pay, and the stress of the fast-track, corner-office world, settling into simpler, less complex lives. Money, they have discovered, isn't everything.

Many suburbanites are trading in their three-thousand-square-foot, high-upkeep quasi-mansions for a more low-maintenance lifestyle, a smaller house, a townhouse, or even an apartment that's closer to work. They are trading a two-hour commute for a simpler home within walking or biking distance. Some are even telecommuting.

Many families are shoveling the clutter out of their lives, holding a big yard sale or making a truckload-donation to the Salvation Army. As they clean out their homes, they are reducing the stress-load and workload of their lifestyle—and they are finding much more time to devote to family, faith, and the simple things in life that bring real joy and contentment.

The *Dallas Morning News* reports that a poll by the Center for a New American Dream discovered that one-third of Americans say they own 50 to 100 percent more stuff than they really need—and 55 percent said they would be willing to part with many of their possessions and even reduce their income to make available more time with family and reduce their stress.[20]

After all, why work yourself into an early grave, making money to acquire things you don't need and would be happier without? Does that make any sense? This relentless, mindless drive for consumption is a national sickness—and someone has given it a name: "affluenza." The writer of Ecclesiastes saw that such a life was meaningless. He called it "chasing after the wind" (Eccles. 4:4).

Suzanne DuBois, a corporate trainer in Minneapolis, loved her work. During a creativity session offered by her employer, she drew a picture—and rediscovered her love for artistic expression. Though she didn't quit her job, she decided to devote more time to her artistic side—her love of art, music, and travel. So she simplified her life. She and her husband, David, sold their tony four-bedroomer and bought a smaller house for half the price, cutting their mortgage payments by seven hundred dollars a month.

"I asked myself," she told a reporter for the *Minneapolis Star Tribune*, "'How did I get into this acquire, acquire, acquire?' Because that's not who I am. . . . I'm wasting a lot of time worrying about stuff that did not matter." Now she thinks about the things that do matter, the things she truly loves.[21]

Some are finding that the road to simplicity is a spiritual road— a road to a deeper connection with God. They are finding that simplicity is not just about what to do. It is about how to *be*. "We are Christians," said Diane Clark, "and I think simple living is kind of a natural growth toward spirituality. We can spend more time on what is important. Christians, of all people, should be less materialistic. Simplicity is not depriving yourself of things and activities; it's about having a richer life, enjoying what you already have and making do with what you have."

Diane Clark and her husband, Craig, live off a single salary— Craig's income as a public school teacher. But that doesn't mean they don't live an exciting, adventurous life. They take extended, exotic vacations that most of us only dream of—but they do it on a budget. "We back-packed through England, France, Spain and Italy with our biggest expense being a bargain airfare and rail pass," Craig Clark explains.[22]

These are just a few of the people who are discovering the truth that Thoreau talked about when he settled at the edge of Walden Pond to, as he put it, "live deep and suck all the marrow of life." As Thoreau wisely counseled on another occasion, "Go confidently in the direction of your dreams. Live the life you've imagined. As you simplify your life, the laws of the Universe will be simpler."

Simplify!

A Simplicity Checklist

Here's a checklist to get you started at simplifying your life (some are adapted from suggestions by Elaine St. James).

1. *Think of a time when you felt truly happy and contented.* I contend it was a time when your life was uncomplicated and when you were enjoying the simplest things life has to offer. Use those memories to give you a mental image of what happiness and contentment really look like. How does that image compare with your life right now? Most likely, your life today is too cluttered and complex. So clean it out! You may have to change jobs, downsize your home and possessions, change your habits, and even reduce your income. But think of the rewards: simplicity, peace, and contentment. Isn't that worth it?

2. *Order your priorities.* "No one can maintain more than three priorities," observes Elaine St. James. "If you have a job you care about, that's a priority. If you have a family, that's a priority. Which leaves one more. Maybe it's staying in shape, maybe it's volunteering at your church—but that's it. Most people understand this intuitively. But they keep overcommitting themselves and overcomplicating their lives."[23]

3. *Clear out clutter that doesn't contribute to your life.* Make room for the things that matter. If your house is full of mementos that are meaningful to you, don't throw them away—store them. Every ten years or so, pull out the old track medals and high school yearbooks, dust them off and look them over—then put them away again and get on with the things that really matter.

At least once a year (say, on Arbor Day or Groundhog Day or spring cleaning day or Saint Swithun's Day), go through your house and get rid of everything you haven't used in the last twelve months. Hold onto the keepsakes and mementos, but get rid of anything that doesn't add meaning and joy to your life. Keep only those things that are truly useful, significant, and valuable to well-ordered, simple living.

4. *Make thoughtful purchases.* Ask yourself, "Will this purchase make my life simpler—or more complicated?" Before you buy, figure out how many hours of work it will cost you to pay for it. Ask yourself, "Do I really need this—or will it just be cluttering my closet two weeks from now?" Elaine St. James suggests doing what she and her husband do: Make a thirty-day list of prospective purchases. If there's something you want to buy, put it on the list and

wait thirty days. At the end of that time, ask yourself if you still want it or need it. "More often than not," she says, "we can't remember why we were so excited in the first place."[24]

Another idea: When you buy clothes or a lamp, leave the tags on for a week and hang on to your receipts. See if you really want to keep your purchase. If not—take it back to the store.

5. *Put extra hours in your life.* Let your mind roam—you might come up with a dozen ways. Move closer to the office and cut your commuting time. If your company offers flexible work schedules, choose a travel time that avoids rush hour. If it's hard to think or meditate at home, arrive at work early and have your personal quiet time—or use that time to work on your novel or some other project. Other ideas: Get up earlier. Avoid long phone chats. Simplify meal preparation and streamline cleanup.

6. *Enlist kids in handling household chores.* Teach them responsibility while freeing up more time for yourself. Show your kids how to make their own lunches and get their clothes laid out the night before going to school.

7. *Unplug your TV.* Doing so will free up valuable time for the entire family.

8. *Learn to say no.* People will always want a piece of your life for some pet cause of theirs. If the cause is important to you, if it adds meaning and depth to your life, fine, volunteer. But if it's drudgery, if it's a drag on your life, if you are just saying yes to be polite and thought of as nice, then just say no. It's okay to say no to friends, it's okay to say no to charity fund drives, it's even okay to say no to your church. Face it, some people become unhealthy churchaholics, burning themselves out in service to the church—not because it's God's will for their lives, but simply because they don't know how to say no.

I confess that this is a real issue in my life—my natural tendency is to say yes to everything and everybody. But I'm learning that when people make demands on me or requests of my time, it's okay to say politely, "Sorry, I'm booked." I don't need to give a reason or an explanation. People should respect my firm, polite refusal—and if they don't, it's their problem, not mine. As playwright Jules Renard observed, "The truly free man is he who can decline an invitation without giving an excuse."

Simplicity is one of the true keys to peace, happiness, and success. One of the most successful people I know is speaker-author Zig Ziglar—and he is one of the world's leading advocates for simplicity. "There are only three pure colors," says Zig, "but look at what Michelangelo did with those three colors! There are only seven notes in the scale, but look at what Chopin, Beethoven, and Vivaldi did with those seven notes! Lincoln's Gettysburg Address contained only 262 words, and 202 of them were one-syllable words. But think of the impact those simple, direct words have had on our society! I know many of our problems are complex, but I believe a simple (not simplistic) approach, a direct approach, worded in simple, understandable terms, is the best and most effective way to get results."

It's true. The same thing I have learned from Zig Ziglar and from Thoreau and especially from R. E. Littlejohn, I pass on to you: Simplify!

And that's not all I learned from this simple yet wise man. He also taught me the importance of managing my personal life well.

TEN

Manage Your Personal Life Well

During my four years in Spartanburg, I spent many mealtimes in the Littlejohn home, dining with Mister R. E., his wife, Sam, and their daughters, Carolyn and Dixie. I could see that Mister R. E.'s family thought the sun rose and set on this man. His daughters, even though they were grown and had children of their own, continued to look upon him with a childlike affection and awe. He was their daddy, and when he was sitting in his favorite chair, they would sit on the arm of the chair, drape their arms around him, snuggle up to him, and look deeply, lovingly into his eyes. That kind of love, trust, and respect between a father and daughter doesn't just happen. It cannot be commanded or demanded. It can only be earned.

One time in late 1965, the Littlejohns and I drove down to Fort Lauderdale for the winter baseball meetings. Mister R. E. drove, Sam sat beside him, and I was in the back seat. It was a long drive, and I was feeling kind of goofy and giddy, so I kidded with Mrs. Little-john. "Sam," I said, "next time we stop, why don't you get in the back seat with me."

She laughed. "Oh, no," she said, "I'd never do that. I'm used to a *man!*"

Well, that just broke me up. For years afterward, that became her catchphrase—"I'm used to a *man!*"—and we always laughed about it. The way she emphasized *man* just spoke volumes. After all their years together, she was completely in love with Mister R. E. because he was a real man. The respect and love Sam had for Mister R. E. was something he had earned.

Your spouse and children are the people who know you best. They see you responding to pressure, conflict, and disappointments. They see you when you let your guard down, when you think no one is looking. They see whether you live what you believe or whether you are a phony and a hypocrite. They know whether your character matches your image and reputation—or if you are hollow inside. The people who knew Mister R. E. best had nothing but praise for him. In my book, that speaks volumes about the man.

As I began working on this book, I received a letter from Mister R. E.'s younger daughter, Dixie. She wrote:

> I always felt blessed by the Lord just to have known someone like Mister R. E., let alone have him as a father. I loved him and missed him so much that it has taken years for me to reach a point where I could speak of him without crying. I learned so many lessons from him, one lesson being the fact that when you love someone so much and have the kind of relationship I had with my father, it is very painful to lose that person and give that person back to the Lord. My daddy was very special.
>
> We recently studied the gifts of the Holy Spirit in Sunday school, and I realized that Daddy was given many spiritual gifts. He especially had the gift of giving. The Lord used his generosity to touch many lives, and nothing made Daddy happier than to give to others. Perhaps it was because he grew up with so little during the depression. When he and my mother married, they had nothing but $156 in the bank and a lot of love—but even then he was a totally generous and giving person. He always said, "It's amazing when you

give something away—perhaps even something you couldn't afford to give—how much comes back in return."

After Daddy passed away, we heard from scores of people whose lives he had changed over the years—people he had quietly helped and told no one about. There were people he helped start in business, people he gave money to when they were down and out, people he gave money to at Christmastime so their children could have presents under the tree. There were some he helped find jobs for. There were some young people who had no money, whose parents were not well-off, and he paid their way through college. My mother and sister and I had no idea how many people he helped—we found out after he passed away and these people called or wrote and told us how much Daddy had meant to them.

Daddy loved Christmas and enjoyed giving presents to so many people. His trademark gift was a delicious assortment of jellies that he had especially packaged up for customers, employees, and friends. Christmas wasn't Christmas until you got your box of "Littlejohn Jelly."

Daddy was the executor of numerous estates. He believed God's Word where it says, "Religion that God our Father accepts as pure and faultless is this: to look after orphans and widows in their distress and to keep oneself from being polluted by the world" (James 1:27). When a local businessman died, Daddy might help the widow sell the business or he would show her how to run it, or he would set up the estate so that the widow would have an annuity—and he never took a penny from them for his work.

I miss Daddy so much. I miss having someone of his great wisdom as my counselor. Whenever I had a question, I always knew he would give me the right answer. He was a quiet man, but when he spoke, everyone else was quiet, because whatever he had to say was worth listening to.

He always taught me never to make a serious decision until I'd had a serious talk with God. He always taught me that communicating meant listening as well as talking; that anything worth doing is worth doing well; that you are no better than anyone else, but at the same time, no one else is better than you. He always said that the way to settle a disagreement is not to find out *who* is right but to find out *what* is right. And he said that the greatest gift we can give another person is a good example—and his example is one of the many gifts he gave me.

One of my treasured memories of Daddy is really a very little thing: His love for figs and his love for God's creatures. I knew he loved figs so much, and then I would see the birds eating the figs on his tree. I would think it was terrible that the birds would get those figs instead of Daddy. But he would never try to keep the birds away from his tree. Instead, he would smile and say, "How wonderful it is that the Lord made figs to feed those birds."

Pat, did you know how much my Daddy took care of his parents in their older years? He moved them into the city and bought them a house. He even went to the grocery store for my grandmother each week. Can you see him doing that?

When my husband, Bobby, started working for Daddy's company, Daddy started him at the bottom with the welders and the painters, then let him advance on his own. He always said that to really know how something works, you have to learn it from the inside out. Throughout his own life, Daddy continued to learn his business from the inside out. He always made it a point to talk with his drivers, mechanics, and welders, because he said that you learn more about the trucks from the people who drive them and fix them than you do from the executives. Everyone was always comfortable talking to him, because he was such a humble, gracious man.

Daddy received many awards, yet he was always amazed that anyone would honor him that way. He was never even aware of his own greatness. I am not sure he was even aware of how many lives he touched by his daily living. Over the years, literally hundreds of people have told me how much they respect Mister R. E. and how much he impacted their lives. They saw him as an amazing, unusual, one-of-a-kind humanitarian; he saw himself as just a person doing what should be the normal thing to do—serving God and helping his neighbor.

What a tribute! I wept when I read it. The Bible says, "The righteous man leads a blameless life; blessed are his children after him" (Prov. 20:7). Well, as you can see, Mister R. E. was a righteous man, by the Bible's definition. And 1 Timothy 3:4–5 says that a Christian leader, such as Mister R. E., "must manage his own family well and see that his children obey him with proper respect. (If anyone does not know how to manage his own family, how can he take care of God's church?)" Here again, Mister R. E. really fits the bill. This great man, who was like a second father to me, became my example for how a man should manage his personal life.

Managing Your Financial Life

The great preacher Dr. Harry Ironside used to say, "Show me the stubs in a man's checkbook and I'll tell you about the man." It's true. The way we handle our finances reveals who we are, our beliefs, and our values. The importance of being a good personal money manager was drummed into me by a man who truly lived what he preached, R. E. Littlejohn. He used to tell me, "You've got to prove that you can manage your own finances well before anyone will trust you to manage a business."

I was pleased to see that my son Jimmy, who is now twenty-five, learned that lesson quite well at a very early age. When he was only an eighth-grader, in Orangewood Christian School near Orlando, the father of Jimmy's friend, Tim Seneff, talked to the class about money management. Tim's dad, James Seneff Jr. (the Warren Buffet of Orlando), is the head of CNL Group of Orlando, a major real estate development, finance, and investment firm, and Jimmy says that to this day he can vividly recall what Jim Seneff said to Jimmy's class.

"When you're through high school and college, when you're a young person just entering the workforce, remember this: Save as much as you can. Spend as little as you can. Invest as much money as you can. As a single young person with few expenses and obligations, you have a wonderful opportunity to put away extra money and let that money work for you. Albert Einstein once said, 'Compounding is mankind's greatest invention because it allows for the reliable, systematic accumulation of wealth. The eighth wonder of the world is the miracle of compounding.'"

In case you're not familiar with "the miracle of compounding," here's how it works: When you make an investment that pays compound interest, the interest is computed not only on the original amount you invested, but also on the accumulated interest. A rule of thumb is used to determine how many years it takes for an investment to double in value through compounding—the Rule of

Seventy-Two. The formula is: $72 = R \times T$, where R is the annual rate of return on the investment (expressed in whole numbers) and T is the number of years it will take for the investment to double in value. The analysis assumes that the investor rolls over all dividends and other gains back into the investment.

If, for example, the investment earns 9 percent per year, R equals 9 (remember to use the whole number 9—not 0.09). The formula, then, reads $72 = 9 \times T$. To find out what T (the number of years) equals, divide 72 by R (which, in this case, is 9). We find that T equals 8 years. So it takes 8 years at 9 percent interest to double your investment by compounding.

Here's what that means in dollar terms: Suppose you invest $10,000 at 9 percent interest and never add another cent to the pot—you just let it earn compound interest. Here's your return over time:

On day 1, you have:	$10,000.
After 8 years, you have:	$20,000.
After 16 years, you have:	$40,000.
After 24 years, you have:	$80,000.
After 32 years, you have:	$160,000.
After 40 years, you have:	$320,000.
After 48 years, you have:	$640,000.
After 56 years, you have:	$1,280,000.
After 64 years, you have:	$2,560,000.

All of that—from just $10,000! And imagine how much more you would have by adding to the principal week by week.

Let's look at some other investing scenarios. Instead of compounding interest on an initial lump sum, let's add to the principal on a regular basis.

Say that Mom and Dad have a baby girl and decide to put away $10 every workday from the birth of that child. Assuming they invest it in the stock market and realize the historical average 12 percent return, they would have $150,000 by the time their daughter is eighteen and ready to begin college. If their daughter is brilliant and hard-working and gets a full scholarship, Mom and Dad can keep investing their money at the same rate, $10 every workday, and after thirty-three years at the same rate, they would have $1 million. After sixty-five years, they would have $2.35 million—enough to kick off a cool $200,000 per year in retirement income without touching principal.

How should the money be invested? Stocks? Bonds? Cash in the form of low-risk, interest-bearing bank accounts or money-market funds? The stock market has an excellent track record: Between January 1, 1926, and December 31, 1996 (a period that includes the Crash of '29 and the Great Depression), the market returned an average of 10.7 percent per year (including dividends), as measured by the Standard and Poors 500 stock index. Some examples of stock performance: A $1,000 investment in Coca-Cola in 1981, with reinvested dividends, would have been worth $62,000 in 1997. A $1,000 investment in Dell Computers, purchased at Dell's initial public offering in 1988, would have returned $104,700 in 1997. And if you had purchased 100 shares of McDonald's stock in 1966 for $2,250, it would have compounded to 37,180 shares—valued at $1.7 million—by 1997.

But remember, the market is volatile, and it's wise to balance stock investments with bonds and cash holdings. I leave it to you to do your own homework. The point is that compounding works with all kinds of investments—stocks, bonds, funds, and bank accounts. Some investments are more aggressive (and riskier) than others. But even safe, conservative forms of investment return rich rewards if held patiently over the long term. That's the miracle of compounding.

Well, when Jim Seneff revealed this miracle to that class of eighth graders, my son Jimmy bought into the concept in a big way. To this day, he is grateful for that igniting of his enthusiasm for saving and investing. As a twenty-five-year-old, he is already invested in real estate and the stock market, as well as other investment vehicles. I recently asked him, "Jimmy, what is your net worth right now?" He grinned. "Well, Dad," he said evasively, "it's in six figures." That's all he would say. But he said enough.

Not everyone gets that message. Some of my other kids spend every nickel they have, week after week, chasing the latest fads and having nothing to show for it later. That's true of much of the world. So I worry a little about some of my kids—but I don't worry about Jimmy. He knows how to manage his finances.

I believe that finance is, ultimately, a spiritual issue. Many Christians are surprised to learn that about two-thirds of the parables of Jesus deal with finances. He constantly warned against greed, pride, and coveting what others possess, because these are areas of life where Satan can get a foothold. "Watch out!" Jesus said. "Be on your guard against all kinds of greed; a man's life does not consist in the abundance of his possessions" (Luke 12:15).

Is it greedy to build financial stability and security for your family with wise investments? No. That is being responsible. The Bible tells us, "If anyone does not provide for his relatives, and especially for his immediate family, he has denied the faith and is worse than an unbeliever" (1 Tim. 5:8). I think greed truly reveals itself in our society when people go into deep debt, especially credit-card debt, to acquire things they can't afford and haven't earned.

Here are some clear warning signs that indicate when you are failing to manage responsibly your personal and family finances.

- Inability to pay monthly bills.
- Inability to save on a weekly or monthly basis.
- Reaching maximum limits and making only minimum payments on credit cards.
- Attempting to borrow your way out of debt with refinancing and bill-consolidation loans.
- Arguments in the marriage about money and spending.

If you recognize one or more of these warning signs, get help from a nonprofit credit counseling service or from a Christian financial counseling ministry, such Larry Burkett's Christian Financial Concepts (http://www.cfcministry.org/) or Crown Ministries (http://www.crown.org/). Your local church likely will have information about these organizations, which can help you to build wisdom and discipline into your financial life. Goals for healthy management of personal finances include:

- A family budget plan.
- A regularly balanced bank account.
- A weekly or monthly savings plan.
- A strong sense of financial partnership and teamwork with one's spouse.
- Zero revolving debt (credit-card balances paid in full every month).
- An emergency fund of at least one thousand dollars.
- Adequate life insurance.
- A legal last will and testament, prepared by a competent attorney, providing for the financial needs and education of minor children. (Even though you can get forms from the stationery store, this is not do-it-yourself time.)

Avoid get-rich-quick schemes, which are designed to appeal to your greed and impatience. As the Bible tells us, "The plans of the diligent lead to profit as surely as haste leads to poverty" (Prov. 21:5). So plan your financial future carefully, thoughtfully, and patiently. Get good advice from competent financial experts—not just people who want to sell you something. Read up on the financial world (*Money* magazine, the *Wall Street Journal*, *Investor's Business Daily*). Become knowledgeable and wise.

Neither a Borrower nor a Lender Be

I learned a valuable financial lesson from Mister R. E. my first season in Spartanburg in 1965. An old baseball friend in Miami called and explained he was in financial straights and needed to borrow a thousand dollars immediately, a large sum for a young guy starting his career. He said, "Pat, if you rush a check to me, I'll reimburse you in a few days. It's just a short-term problem, and I'll pay you back right away." I would have walked on coals to help him, and I was confident I'd get a check the next week. Well, the next week came, and no check—and another week and another. A month went by and I had not heard from my good friend.

After a week of calling him, I finally got through and awkwardly asked for the money. He apologized and said he was still in financial trouble but would pay me soon. What could I say? A few weeks went by and my friend called. He was having more difficulty. I broke off the conversation and raced to Mister R. E.'s office in turmoil.

Mister R. E. listened, aware of how upset I was, and then calmly said, "Pat, call your friend and tell him you are not in a position to mail him another check and firmly explain you want to be repaid. But Pat, don't be surprised if you never see that money again. In all likelihood, you've probably lost a friend. Please remember this for the rest of your life. If you want to give money as a gift, that's one thing, but the minute you start lending money, it will cause you nothing but grief."

As it turned out, I never got the money back, and I never saw my friend again. We may have talked a time or two on the phone, but it was never the same. In the fall of 1968, after I had joined the 76ers, I picked up the paper one day and read that my friend had died of a heart attack. I was sad, but through that experience, I learned an important lesson. As William Shakespeare wrote, "Neither a borrower nor a lender be."

The Ultimate Financial Secret

And one more piece of financial advice: Don't forget to invest in God's work. The Lord has his own investment plan that pays big dividends—eternal dividends. Mister R. E. would be the first to tell you that the best investment is giving to God. He will use your gift in a mighty way, and he will bless you because of your faithfulness. The Bible calls giving to God "tithing," from the word *tithe,* which means "a tenth." In other words, the first tenth of the fruit of our labors belongs to God. Leviticus 27:30 tells us, "A tithe of everything from the land, whether grain from the soil or fruit from the trees, belongs to the LORD; it is holy to the LORD."

There is no doubt in my mind that Mr. Littlejohn gave far more than 10 percent of his income to God, in the form of donations to his church, Christian missions and charities, and in the form of gifts in Jesus' name to individuals who were doing God's work or who were in need. Mister R. E. gave to God in an attitude of exuberance and excitement about what he believed God would do with his gift. He exemplified the words of 2 Corinthians 9:7—"Each man should give what he has decided in his heart to give, not reluctantly or under compulsion, for God loves a cheerful giver."

You may think, "But I can't afford to tithe—it would cost too much." Dr. Peter Marshall, when he was chaplain of the United States Senate, had an answer for that problem. A man once came to him and said, "Dr. Marshall, I used to tithe regularly, but I was recently promoted and I now earn $500,000 a year. Obviously, I can't afford to give away a tenth of $500,000 every year—that's $50,000!"

"Ah!" said Marshall, nodding gravely. "I see your problem. Let's pray about it." So they bowed their heads and Marshall prayed, "Lord, I pray that you would reduce this man's salary to a level where he can afford to tithe once more."

The man's eyes widened and his jaw dropped. "Oh, no! Don't pray that! I'll tithe! I'll tithe!"

Thanks to the example I had in Mister R. E., I have tithed ever since I came into a personal relationship with Jesus Christ. There have been times when tithing wasn't easy, especially with the size of our family. For obvious reasons, our family requires more housing, transportation, food, energy, and clothing than the average American household. There are months when I can't write a check to my church or a mission organization because of the huge financial commitments I have. I used to feel guilty about that.

Then one day, I felt God saying to me, "Pat, I want you to know that you are tithing, even if you aren't sending 10 percent of your paycheck to the church this month. I know you can't send money to the mission field right now, but you have brought the mission field into your home. Those fourteen children you adopted from around the world are your mission field, and your additional expenses in providing for them are your tithe this month." The day I sensed God speaking those words to my heart, it was as if a great burden was lifted from my shoulders.

There are times when I wonder how I'm going to pay all those bills—but God always comes through. As Malachi 3:10 promises,

"'Bring the whole tithe into the storehouse, that there may be food in my house. Test me in this,' says the LORD Almighty, 'and see if I will not throw open the floodgates of heaven and pour out so much blessing that you will not have room enough for it.'" We have taken the Lord at his word. We have tested him and found him faithful. His floodgates are open, and his blessings are still pouring into our lives. So my advice to you is to give generously to God. Invest in his eternal plan. Of all the investments you will ever make, that is the soundest one of all.

Learning to Manage Family Relationships

When I was born in 1940, my proud Scotch-Irish father wanted to cram as many Scotch-Irish names onto my birth certificate as would fit, so he named me Patrick Livingston Murphy Williams. I was three years old when he left home to go to war, so my earliest memories are of living in a house without a dad until he returned home in '45. I have a dim memory of standing in the Wilmington, Deleware, train station at age five as a stranger stepped off the train and ran to us. That stranger, of course, was my father.

So I really only had a father from the time I was five until I was twenty-two, when he was killed in an automobile accident. Dad taught and coached at Tower Hill School, a private school in Wilmington with an elite clientele. Some of my earliest memories revolve around being with Dad in the school locker room or on the bench by the field. He always stressed to me the importance of working hard. I had a paper route for six years, and he always got up with me at six in the morning to drive me around the neighborhood while I threw the papers.

Did my father ever tell me he loved me? He may have, though I don't recall. In those days, fathers weren't expected to show much affection and emotion toward their children—just a strong, firm, guiding hand. That was simply the cultural norm then. But even though I don't remember ever hearing Dad say, "I love you," I knew that he did, and that he was very proud of me.

My dad was not a perfect man, but he was a kind, caring man. He taught me a lot about treating others with kindness and respect, and that it's the content of one's character that matters, not the color of one's skin. He was a good man with strong family values, and he loved me very much. And yet I never had the sense that I knew him well—in part because I didn't know him in my preschool years, in part because he left this earth when I was a young man, and certainly in part because, for much of the time I was with him, I was a self-absorbed adolescent who didn't have the sense to sit down with my dad and ask him questions about himself and about life.

When Dad and I talked, it was about baseball or my schoolwork or getting my chores done. Looking back, I realize that a lot of what I know about managing a family and about managing my personal life I learned from Mister R. E. I learned it from talking with him and from watching how he interacted with his wife and daughters. I knew that, when I had a family of my own, I wanted to have that kind of love in my family—and I hoped to receive that kind of love in return. I hoped to be the kind of wise, instructive, guiding father that Mister R. E. was.

After I left Spartanburg and moved on to Philadelphia and then Chicago, I got married and started a family of my own. I set a goal to become the best husband and father I could possibly be. For that reason, I felt an incredible sense of loss and personal failure when my first marriage ended in divorce in 1996.[25] But after I met Ruth, I got a second chance to succeed in marriage. And of course, I still had a house full of kids to parent! The challenge of fatherhood is tough—and over the years, with each new birth or adoption, I have multiplied that challenge. But it is also the most enjoyable and satisfying challenge any man could undertake. To this day, being a dad is still the richest, most rewarding calling I can imagine.

From Mr. Littlejohn I have learned some valuable principles that I've tried to carry over (however imperfectly) into my own family relationships, including the following.

1. *Talk with your children.* Talk about values. Faith. Sports. Television. Movies. Current events. School. Drugs. Smoking. Drinking. Dating. Sex. Marriage. Decision-making. Career choices. Goals. Dreams. Life. Share stories from your own experience and childhood. Even if your children groan and give you a hard time, they really like to hear your experiences and compare their own lives with

yours. To encourage honest, wide-ranging discussions, ask open-ended rather than yes-no questions. Give nonverbal feedback when your children talk—a smile, a nod, and a lot of eye contact. Enjoy being with your youngsters, and they will enjoy being with you.

2. Be a patient listener. A good parent must be a good listener, and that takes patience. I have to confess: listening doesn't come easily for me. I'm a great talker. I've had to *learn* to sharpen my listening skills over the years, because every day there's a child in the Williams family who has something to express, something I need to hear. It's a daily discipline for me, trying to tune into the messages and moods of my family. The need to be heard may be demonstrated not in words, but in sulkiness or even silence. My job as a father is to look beyond the outward behavior and see a child who may feel neglected, misunderstood, or lost in the crowd.

3. Praise in public, criticize in private. Public praise inspires a child and builds his or her self-confidence. Criticism before others destroys a child's spirit and generates resentment. Mark Twain once observed, "Most of us can run pretty well all day long on one good compliment." I've learned that encouragement and affirmation are as vital to the soul as water, food, and air are vital to the body. When young people do well, let them know you are proud of them. Nothing improves one's hearing as much as a word of praise.

When my son Bobby was a high school senior and a catcher on the school baseball team, he had one particularly great game—he got two hits, blocked the plate well, threw out a runner, and made a great tag for an out at the plate. Later, as we walked toward the car, I asked him, "Bobby, what are you going to remember most about this game?"

"I'm going to remember," he said, "that Coach Barton shook my hand and told me what a great job I did." *Wow*, I thought, *if a coach's praise means that much to a boy, how much more the praise of a parent!* And I've tried to carry that lesson over into all my interactions with all my kids.

4. Give your family the gift of your time. Avoid bringing home paperwork and office problems. Family time is sacred time, and you should guard it like a bulldog against intrusions from the office. Demonstrate to the members of your family that you really value them and want to be with them, that you regard their needs as priority one. Even if you have a hectic schedule, deadlines, business trips, and crises at the office, make sure you spend evenings and weekends with your family—and don't neglect to build warm memories and lasting traditions with family vacations. Don't just *say* you love your spouse and children. *Prove* it with the gift of your time.

5. *Cultivate a healthy sense of humor.* Nothing undermines good family spirit and harmony more than a parent who is a grim, gray, humorless stiff. Well-known author and speaker Herm Albright once said, "Laughing a hundred times a day yields the same cardiovascular workout as ten minutes of rowing. During a good belly-laugh, your heart rate can top 120 beats a minute. So laugh it up! It's good for you." A good sense of humor can reduce tension, defuse conflict, create positive memories, and enhance the feeling of warmth and love in a family.

Most of the laughs in our family come from Thomas Williams. He is one of our twins from South Korea (his brother is Stephen). Thomas is a wonderful student and a hard worker—we've never had a minute of trouble from him. But Thomas is absentminded—to put it mildly. (Thomas once told me, "I know a lot, I just can't remember it.") He's been a good soccer player since he was just a small boy. In one of his games, when he was seven or eight, I was watching him on the field and noticed he was having a difficult time. He just wasn't playing up to his usual level. After the game, I found out why: When leaving the house, he had taken his sister Sarah's shoes, which were three sizes too small for him. He played the whole game in them! On another occasion he played an entire game in two left shoes. I'll never forget that amazing sight!

Thomas' absentmindedness didn't improve as he got older. Now a teenager, he recently threw our family into a crisis for an entire weekend. We were sure that someone had stolen the family van from our driveway one Friday night. We called the police and reported it stolen—but on the following Monday we discovered Thomas had forgotten he had driven the van to school Friday and had ridden home from the soccer game with friends. He had absolutely no memory of having taken the van—so it had sat in the school parking lot all weekend.

Once the crisis passed and the van was safely home, our whole family had a huge laugh. Best of all, we had one more Thomas story to add to the Williams family lore, to be told and retold in future years. Every family ought to have a Thomas. He brings the gift of joy and laughter to our home in a big way.

6. *Know what your kids are listening to and watching.* Watch and listen with them and know what they are exposed to on the radio, TV, recordings, and computers. Discuss with your children the things they see—especially scenes, behavior, and ideas which violate your family's faith and values. Give them a moral framework for dealing with a world that is largely hostile to good values and good behavior. Young people need values, limits, guidance, and love.

7. *Be a model of integrity.* You can fake a reputation, but you can't fake character and integrity. "Do as I say, not as I do" doesn't wash with youth. They are watching our lives all the time, and patterning themselves after the way they see their parents live. So our words and actions had better match—or our children will soon be veering off in some other direction.

To be a person of integrity is to be the same person in private as in public—to always tell the truth, to always keep your word, to always live an upright and moral life, even when no one is looking. As basketball star A. C. Green says in *Victory: The Principles of Championship Living,* "We reap what we sow. Whatever we do in private, or don't do, will come to light in public. . . . To be a champion you need a firm foundation [or] cracks will eventually show up."[26]

8. *Work hard at your marriage.* The best thing a parent can do for a child is to focus on the marriage and truly love and honor his or her marriage partner. The family is the child's entire world, and when the marriage breaks up, the child's world is split in half. A great deal of the pain and failure I felt when my first marriage ended in 1996 was a recognition of how much hurt it was causing our children. That is also the reason I fought the divorce so hard, and why I am working so hard at my present marriage.

There are two partners in a marriage, and both have to be 100 percent committed to keeping a marriage healthy and whole. Not 50 percent. It's not good enough to say, "Marriage is 50-50—I'm doing my half and that's all." That mindset leads many couples to draw a line down the middle of their relationship, then bicker endlessly about who's keeping up his half or overstepping her half. When you divide a marriage in half, you're halfway to divorce.

When you take full ownership, you become more willing to persevere through the internal stresses and the external problems that buffet a relationship. Pressing on through hard times takes a lot of love—not the mushy feeling most people think of as love. No, I'm talking about a love that is a *decision,* a deliberate, hard-headed *choice* to do what is best and right for everyone in the family, even when we don't feel like it. Marriages collapse when people act out of their emotions instead of their decisions and commitments. If you truly *love* your spouse and children, you will choose to do those things you don't *feel* like doing in order to give them the things they need for their growth, security, and emotional well-being. You'll go in for counseling, you'll swallow pride and admit wrongs, you'll stay up until three in the morning to talk things out, you'll do *anything* to keep the lines of communication open.

Live faithfully and morally with your spouse. People who often travel on business have more opportunities to be unfaithful, so don't put yourself in compromising or tempting situations. Evangelist Billy Graham was so careful in this matter that he avoided even the slightest appearance of impropriety. He had a rule that he would not even be alone in an elevator with a woman who was not his wife. If Billy Graham felt a need to be so careful about appearances and avoiding temptation, then how much more careful should the rest of us be! If you truly love your family, don't risk hurting or destroying your family with even one incident of unfaithfulness. Make your marriage your priority. Always be faithful.

9. Pray. As earthly parents, trying to love and guide our children, we need to rely on our Heavenly Parent to show us what to do. So we need to spend time in prayer, not only talking to God but listening to God, getting to know him better, drawing on his strength, and building his character into our lives so that we can better exemplify his love to our own children. We should pray *for* our children and *with* our children. And just between you and me, one of the most profoundly rewarding experiences any parent can have is to see a child learning from parental example and to hear the child's honest conversations with God.

Living Proof

Over my thirty-odd years in the NBA, I have made a rather grim and troubling observation. I have seen hundreds of African-American players pass through the teams I've been associated with, yet I can name on one hand the number of African-American players I've met who come from intact, two-parent families. I don't know what the cultural and historical reasons for this might be; I only know that, in a statistical sense, the African-American family has been through very hard times these past few decades.

In 1976, when I was general manager of the Philadelphia 76ers, we signed a 6´ 9″ forward by the name of Joe "Jelly Bean" Bryant. And I have to say that Joe Bryant comes from one of the strongest families I have ever seen. His mom, dad, and grandparents were always at his games, always completely wrapped up in his life, always available to him and supporting him. Joe Bryant got a great start in life, surrounded by the love of an intact, two-parent home, and he and his wife have carried that on to the next generation.

Two years after he joined the 76ers, Joe and his wife Pam had a son, named (according to Joe) after the Kobe Steak House in King of Prussia, Pennsylvania. Little Kobe Bryant was destined to grow up around the game of basketball. Joe moved from Philadelphia to the San Diego Clippers and the Houston Rockets, and finally retired from the NBA in 1984. He then moved to Italy where he played for eight years in the European leagues.

Joe and Pam Bryant found Italy to be a great place to play basketball—and a great place to raise a family. The Italian fans were passionate, waving team colors at the games and treating Joe Bryant as a cult figure, chanting his name as if he were Michael Jordan and Dr. J rolled into one. After a big win, the town would hold a huge festival, and the jubilant fans would buy him breakfast, lunch, and dinner for the rest of the week. The Italian streets were safe and crime-free, even at night, and Joe and his family enjoyed cafe life in the mild Mediterranean evenings.

During the season, young Kobe would watch his dad play, then spend hours after school, trying out new moves and improving his shots. Joe often took his son to practice with him. During team workouts, Kobe would find an unused backboard and practice layups. During halftime at his dad's games, Kobe would run onto the court and shoot baskets while the crowd roared its approval. He developed toughness from playing one-on-one against his dad (who showed the boy no mercy—unless Kobe's mother was watching). Kobe's entire life revolved around the game of basketball.

Kobe's grandparents in the States would tape NBA games and send the tapes to Italy, where Kobe would watch them again and again. He would study the players and their moves, and the various formations and strategies of the game. He learned his fadeaway jumper from watching Hakeem Olajuwon, his baseline jumper from Oscar Robertson, his juke moves from Earl "The Pearl" Monroe, and he acquired a sense of the pure joy of the game from his number one hero, Magic Johnson.

But Joe and Pam Bryant were diligent to build more into their son than a love of basketball. They wanted him to grow up to be a person of wisdom, values, and class, so they were careful to shape his mind and character as he grew up. "My wife and I used to pre-screen movies before we'd let the kids see them," Joe Bryant told *Sports Illustrated*. "We used to push the kids under the seat when the actors would start kissing." Joe and Pam were still screening Kobe's movies into his teens, just before he signed with the Los Angeles Lakers in '96 at age eighteen. Remarking on one of the most youthful players ever to play in the NBA, Jerry West, Lakers executive vice president, said, "Kobe is at least as mature as any player we have now, and you cannot discount his family's contribution to that."

After just one year with the Lakers, the superlatives were flying hot and heavy. Kobe Bryant was being compared in a single breath with the greatest legends of the game: He jumps like Michael Jordan—and demonstrates Jordanesque hang time, too. He slashes to the hole like Julius Erving. He creates his own shots like Magic Johnson. Where did Kobe's brilliance on the court come from—natural talent or hard work? Those who know Kobe best will tell you that this is a young man who works fiercely at his game. Even in the off-season, he spends five or six hours a day in rigorous conditioning—half in the weight room, half on the practice court.

As much as he loves the game of basketball, nothing is more important to Kobe than family. Even after he became a rising megastar in the NBA, he was content to live in his own bedroom in his parents' home. Noting that Kobe Bryant has been "completely unaffected by fame," the *Sports Illustrated* story concludes that he "didn't even have to leave home to make his dream come true."[27]

Knowing Joe and Pam Bryant from our days together in Philly, I'm not surprised that Kobe has turned out to be successful not only at his game but as a human being—a young man with his head screwed on straight, his values firmly in place, a good dose of wisdom, and a genuine sense of class and splendid humility. If Kobe has the sense to hang onto the virtues and wisdom his parents have instilled in him (and I suspect he has) then he's a young man who could go a long way, not only as a basketball star but as a hero and a role model to the generation that follows him. Joe and Pam Bryant know how to manage their personal lives well—and the living proof is their amazing son, Kobe.

Building Trust

One of the most important jobs in managing personal and family life is to build an atmosphere of trust and security in the home. Writer John Croyle relates the true story of a father who once took his two grade-school-age children for a river ride on a pontoon boat. The father's attention was focused downriver when suddenly the motor chugged to a stop. Turning, he was struck with horror—his daughter was not in the boat. He leaned over the stern and looked down in the water—and there was his daughter's red sweater tangled in the propeller. Just then, the man's son screamed, "Look, Dad! Sherry's in the water! She's right there!"

The father saw her face, six inches beneath the water, her eyes open and pleading, looking straight into his. Her cheeks were puffed out as she held her breath. With her sweater fouled in the propeller, she couldn't get to the surface.

The father went over the side and tried to shove the motor up, but it wouldn't budge. All the while, he could see his daughter watching him, waiting for him to do something, depending on him for her life. He took a gulp of air, then put his face under the water, pressing his lips to hers—and he blew. His daughter breathed the air into her lungs and held it. Three more times he did this, blowing his breath into his daughter's lungs while straining to free her from the tangled sweater, all to no avail.

Suddenly, an idea. He broke the surface and shouted, "Son, get the knife! The one we clean fish with!"

An eternity of seconds passed. Finally, the boy appeared with the knife. The father took it from the boy's trembling fingers, then slipped under the water and slashed at the red sweater, cutting the girl free. As he lifted her into the boat, he saw that she was cut and bruised from the propeller—but she was alive.

Hours later, at the hospital where she was recovering, someone asked the girl, "You must have been so scared! How did you keep from panicking?"

"Daddy always taught me never to panic," she said. "I knew he would figure out something. He always does." That's *trust*. And that's our goal as parents—to become worthy of our children's complete and confident trust.

From talking to Mr. Littlejohn and watching his life, I learned that the only truly successful person is one who can manage his personal life well, maintain a stable financial life and family life, and preserve relationships of absolute trust. By the measure of the love and trust his family had in him, Mr. Littlejohn was the most successful man I've ever known. He taught me so much about the importance of managing my personal life well.

But that's not all. He also taught me the importance of caring for the people you work with.

ELEVEN

Care about the People You Work With

One winter, when I was working for Mr. Littlejohn, I caught a respiratory bug, and it lingered for a long time. I was coughing for weeks, and the stubborn thing just refused to clear up. I was young and considered myself indestructible, so I never bothered going to the doctor.

Mister R. E. called me at my office one day. "Pat," he said, "let's get together for lunch. There are some things I want to talk over with you." So we met at Mabry's, a country restaurant on the edge of town, and we exchanged conversation about the coming season. I began to wonder why he had called me. There was nothing urgent or pressing on his mind—we were just shooting the breeze.

After lunch, I started to head for my car, but he pulled me aside and said, "Get in the car with me. Let's go for a ride."

Well, something was up—but I couldn't figure out what it was. As we drove along, Mister R. E. didn't say a word. But when he pulled the car over and parked, I instantly understood. We were in front of his doctor's office. "Come on in, Pat," he said. "Dr. Abel's expecting you."

So I went in and received a good going-over from Doc Abel. He prescribed an antibiotic, and in a week or so, my cough was all cleared up.

That was the kind of man Mister R. E. was. He cared about the people who worked for him—not just about their job performance, but about their lives and their health. He didn't just suggest I go to the doctor. He didn't even send me to the doctor. He *took* me to the doctor—because he knew I'd never go on my own. Mister R. E. *cared*.

And he kept caring long after I left Spartanburg in 1968 and went into the NBA. In October 1972 while the general manager of the Chicago Bulls, I got married at the Wheaton, Illinois, Bible Church. While standing at the front of the church during the ceremony, my knees were shaking so hard Mister R. E. noticed it from his pew in the sanctuary. After the service he came up and told me, "If your knees had started shaking any harder, I was coming up there to get you." And knowing Mister R. E., he would have too!

I believe that this very personal level of caring was one of the true keys to R. E. Littlejohn's success. To truly succeed, an owner, executive, or manager must recruit the best people, then do everything in his or her power to make those people feel appreciated, supported, empowered, and equipped to succeed in their jobs. You can't assemble and maintain a highly energized and motivated team without a high degree of personal caring.

When I think of success and personal caring in a single human package, I think of Bill Cosby. In January 1989, when we opened the brand-new Orlando Arena to the public for the first time, we brought in Bill Cosby to perform a one-man show. The Orlando Magic had not yet played its first game, but we were already rolling out our promotional merchandise, including an Orlando Magic sweatshirt bearing the team logo. Before the Cos went out to perform, we gave him one of our new Magic sweatshirts, and he wore it during his performance.

A little over ten years later, in April 1999, I traveled with the team to my old stomping grounds, Philadelphia, for a big televised game between the Magic and the 76ers. It was great being back in Philly, and as I was on the floor at halftime, I looked in the front row and who should I see but the Cos himself! He's a big NBA fan. I went up to him and reintroduced myself. "Bill," I said, "Pat Williams with the Orlando Magic."

His first words as he shook my hand: "Hey, man! I love my sweatshirt! It's my favorite. I still wear it." Then he gave me that sly Cosby grin and asked, "Hey, man, what's wrong with your team?"

Well, Cos had a point. We had started that game with four turnovers in the first six minutes, and were down 17 points at halftime. We would eventually finish that game with a 103-86 loss—our fifth in a row. But Bill Cosby took some of the sting out of that afternoon for me with a touch of class and personal caring, remembering a sweatshirt we had given him ten years earlier.

You might expect a person of his accomplishments to be too egotistical to be involved with other people; you might expect a person who has been through some of the difficult and tragic experiences he's been through to be aloof and withdrawn—but no, Bill Cosby is a captivating, thoroughly delightful person who is focused on other people and takes a personal interest in them.

Caring is a key to the success of the Cos, a key to the success of R. E. Littlejohn—and a key to your success and mine.

People: The Linchpin of Your Success

Whether you are in professional sports, business, government, the military, or religious service, your effectiveness depends on your ability to direct the best efforts of talented, motivated people. One successful business leader who understands this principle is Fletcher Byrom, former CEO of Koppers Company, a major chemical and manufacturing company. A frequent public speaker, Byrom often listened to elaborate introductions listing all of his achievements—but he realized that his greatest accomplishments were the result of a group effort involving all the people in his company. After a generous introduction, he usually would get up and, with disarming humility, respond, "When you see a turtle on top of a fence post, you know he didn't get up there all by himself."

Studies show that the average manager or executive spends at least 75 percent of his or her working day dealing with people. The single largest expense item in the budgets of most businesses is personnel—that is, people. The most valuable asset any company has is its people. Every decision, plan, marketing strategy, and sales effort a company undertakes must be implemented by people. When a company's plan falls flat on its face, it is usually because of some breakdown or failure on the part of its people.

Because people are such an integral part of the success or failure of every business, it is crucial that we learn to take good care of the people who work with us and for us. "As the manager of a football organization," observed Ron Wolf of the Green Bay Packers, "I can't play quarterback, and I can't coach. If I don't have strong people in those positions, we'll never be on top." President Woodrow Wilson had a saying: "I use not only all the brains I have but all I can borrow." And Bill Veeck often put it to me in his own folksy way: "Hire good people and let 'em do their jobs. Otherwise, why hire 'em?" It's true: The higher you go, the more you need to depend on people for your success. So you'd better learn how to care for them, how to support and affirm and motivate them—because they are the linchpin of your success.

A Tale of Two Managers

In the early 1970s, Gene Cattabiani took over as general manager of the Westinghouse Steam Turbine Division in Philadelphia. Those were turbulent days for Westinghouse—a time of falling profits and serious labor problems, including several ugly, violent strikes. Westinghouse management saw the labor union leaders as selfish, grasping troublemakers leading a workforce that had grown fat and lazy. Union leaders, however, charged that Westinghouse managers were contemptuous and unfeeling toward the working man. Cattabiani knew he had to find some way to bring labor and management together in a cooperative arrangement so the company and its workers could move forward.

Cattabiani concluded there was only one thing to do: He would go before the workers, explain the company's financial straits, and seek the trust and support of the Westinghouse workforce for the austerity measures that were required. He decided that, after years of distrust and management stonewalling, the key to gaining union cooperation was to treat the workers with respect and honesty.

Against the recommendation of advisers, Cattabiani held a series of meetings with the workers, showing them graphics and charts. He closed each meeting with an extended question-and-answer session so that workers could voice their opinions and ask questions. The first few presentations were raucous and contentious. Workers greeted Cattabiani with jeers, catcalls, name-calling, and threats. Cattabiani's colleagues begged him to call off the rest of the meetings—but he carried on. "I have to get them to listen," he said, "and I have to show them that management is willing to listen. We can't stay in business without trust between labor and management."

Gene Cattabiani worried about the process and about his own safety—and with good reason. But he courageously mastered his fears, exposing himself to a daily ritual of insults and taunts. He began a new practice of going out onto the factory floor and into the shops—something none of the previous managers had ever done. He talked one-on-one with the men, and as the days passed, a new mood began to take hold. Some who had attacked Cattabiani gave grudging respect. They would nod to him—and a few would even shake his hand. Sure, they would argue—but they would also listen. He was no longer an enemy to them, but a guy trying to do his job, just as they were trying to do theirs. In the process, Gene Cattabiani gained credibility and trust—and he learned a lot from his talks with the workers.

In the weeks that followed, labor-management relations took a slow but noticeable turn for the better. A good listener, Cattabiani responded to the criticisms of labor—and he instituted changes. He introduced ideas for greater flexibility in schedules and procedures and made changes resulting in higher quality and productivity standards. Sometimes, with deep reluctance, he laid off workers. Each change was a struggle, and there was plenty of anger and conflict in the process. But the workers had learned to trust that Gene Cattabiani was trying to do the right thing for the company and the workers, even if they didn't agree with him. The changes took place without strikes, without violence, and the profitability of Cattabiani's division improved. The division was saved—along with hundreds of jobs.

One of Cattabiani's young assistant managers during that time was William Peace. A few years later, in the early 1980s, Peace became general manager of the Synthetic Fuels Division at Westinghouse. William Peace faced a similar problem to the one Cattabiani had faced in the previous decade: Declining oil prices meant declining profits, and the division was facing liquidation unless the situation could be turned around. But that meant paring jobs—a prospect that Peace's unionized workforce was unlikely to accept without a fight.

Looking over the personnel records of the division, Peace saw that his workers were largely well-motivated people with excellent records. The thought of severing them after years of service made him sick at heart—but he knew what had to be done. He sat down with his department heads and, in a stormy, emotional meeting, they came up with a list of fifteen people who would have to be let go. Remembering Gene Cattabiani's courageous decision to handle tough chores personally, Peace decided to hold all the meetings himself, face-to-face. By doing so, he could scotch any rumors about wholesale firings. Besides, he believed he owed these people the courtesy of a personal explanation from the man in charge.

The meetings were painful. Some workers became angry; others wept openly; some merely stared at the floor. Peace explained the reasons for the layoffs and underscored the fact that the layoffs were based on economic needs, not dissatisfaction with performance. Some argued or accused him of ingratitude; Peace absorbed their anger and maintained his composure.

After several months, the Synthetic Fuels Division was restored to solvency. Westinghouse found a buyer for the division, and the new corporate owners retained Peace as general manager. The market for synthetic fuels picked up, and the new owners decided to expand the division. Suddenly, Peace found that he was in a position to rehire many of the laid-off employees. When he offered them their old jobs back, they accepted—every one of them, even those who had gotten jobs elsewhere. Instead of having to hire and train new people, he was able to bring back his experienced and valued workforce.

From Gene Cattabiani, William Peace had learned a valuable lesson: Even when you have a tough job to do, always demonstrate a personal touch. Always show you care. Always handle matters face-to-face, person-to-person. Caring pays off in worker loyalty and respect. Caring pays off in *success*.[28]

I saw this same truth lived out in the example of R. E. Littlejohn. Here are some principles I've gleaned from his life—principles about how to be an effective, successful, *caring* leader.

1. Get the Best People, Then Get the Best out of Your People

I have had the pleasure of sharing a podium with the gracious and megasuccessful Debbi Fields, founder of Mrs. Fields Cookies. Her recipe for a successful business is simple, practical, and profound: "Love what you're doing. Believe in your product. Select good people."

Other highly successful people agree. Billionaire presidential hopeful H. Ross Perot built his computer company by hiring the best people he could find. He compared quality employees to eagles. "Eagles don't flock," he explains. "You have to find them one at a time." And another old business and political campaigner, Adlai E. Stevenson, said that you can't build a strong organization on a foundation of weak people—you have to get the best people—then get the best out of those people. "There are only three rules of sound administrators," Stevenson explained. "Pick good people, tell them not to cut corners, and back them to the limit. Picking good people is the most important." Israeli military and political leader Moshe Dayan put it this way: "I am not supposed to be an expert in every field. I am supposed to be an expert in picking experts."

The most successful entrepreneurs, executives, and managers are those who hire the best assistants—and know how to get the best from them. A great leader is confident and secure enough to hire people who know more than she does, who have stronger skills than she does, who can carry out tasks even better than she can. An effective leader is not threatened by the knowledge, skills, and talents of others, because she knows that *her* skill is one of overall coordination, of bringing good people together and forging them into an effective machine. She knows that the more she delegates to competent people, the more she is free to work on the big picture and the big dreams.

A successful boss or leader gets the most out of his or her people in several ways.

1. *By sharing knowledge and skills.* The more people know, the more tasks they are able to handle. The better trained and equipped they are, the more effectively they can deal with new situations and problems and emergencies without your intervention. So teach and train your people. Give them opportunities to increase their knowledge and skill levels. Keep them in the information loop. Most people want to improve themselves and make themselves more useful to the organization. They also like working for bosses who can mentor them—that's the kind of leader they can respect. But they will lose respect for an insecure, ineffectual leader who refuses to share knowledge and skills with them.

2. *By providing challenging opportunities.* Bernard Haldane of Bernard Haldane Associates, a leading career management firm, put it this way: "If you want to get the best out of people, you must use the best that is in them." The more responsibility you give people, the more likely they are to rise to the occasion. The more often you give people the ball, the more often they will run with it—and you will be surprised by how often they will score. Sure, there may be an occasional fumble along the way. That's okay—allow room for mistakes. Give people a chance to learn from their mistakes—after all, isn't that how *you* got so smart?

3. *By providing the environment, tools, and material resources for success.* Make sure your people work in an environment that reeks of success—a bright, well-designed office with plenty of light, the latest equipment, beautiful decor and artwork, and tasteful furnishings. If they tell you they need this piece of equipment or that

kind of software, listen to them. They are closest to the situation and they probably are right.

True story: John, the head of graphic design at a major printing company, was constantly trying to get supplies and equipment needed for his department to do its job. The owners of the company continually turned down John's requests. Meanwhile, they remodeled the entire front office complex—all except John's art department office, which was in a shabby, poorly lit corner of the building. The owners also spent more than $900,000 on new press and camera equipment while turning down John's request for three thousand dollars to buy a new computer, scanner, and software to upgrade and streamline the company's graphic capabilities.

The last straw came when John requisitioned an electric pencil sharpener so the artists wouldn't have to walk halfway across the plant just to sharpen their pencils. Cost: $29.95. When even that modest request was turned down, John began looking for another job. He was soon hired by an arch-rival printing company a few blocks away. Within two months, three other artists defected to the competitor. Soon, many of the company's customers defected, too.

What a contrast between John's situation and my experience with R. E. Littlejohn! Mister R. E. always made sure I had everything I needed to do the job—including a nice new car every year. One of the hot cars at the time was the Olds Toronado, so he took me over to Glover Oldsmobile and introduced me to the manager, Earl Baker. We picked out a beautiful big Toronado—then Mister R. E. opened negotiations. The man just loved to wheel and deal—he called it horse trading. Mister R. E. didn't play golf or tennis. His favorite pastime was negotiating. It was a lot of fun for me to watch these two southerners—Mister R. E., the southern gentleman, and Baker, the slick, good ol' boy salesman—dicker it out. In the end, Baker would hand me the keys and I would drive off the lot in a brand-new Toronado.

There is a great sense of satisfaction that comes from helping people to develop and grow—not merely as employees or team members but as whole human beings. Eventually, the things you do for your people will return to you in greater recognition of your effectiveness as a leader—and economic rewards will come, as well.

2. Appreciate, Affirm, and Recognize Your People

Mr. Littlejohn was proud of me—and he constantly found ways to show it. Publicly, he always bragged about me and cheered for me. Privately, he often clapped me on the back and told me what a great job I was doing, saying, "You're mah boy!" in his rich Carolina drawl. When someone does that for you, there's nothing you can't do! When your mentor and role model is your number one fan, you feel you can take on the world—and you want to make sure you never disappoint him.

To be recognized and affirmed is a basic human need—almost as basic as the need for food, air, or sleep. A wise leader understands the boost that comes to people's morale and performance when their accomplishments and contributions are recognized. Studies have shown that most workers crave recognition even more than a raise. When they pull off a major sales coup or conceive a great idea, they want other people to know it. They want a handshake and a pat on the back and a word of "Well done!" from the people they respect and admire. That's just human nature.

Unfortunately, many bosses don't seem to recognize this. They are stingy with praise and commendation—possibly because they are a little jealous and fear that a subordinate's achievements might overshadow their own. Or they like to portray an image of a tough-minded, hard-to-please boss. Or they think, *If I say, "Good job," he'll hit me up for a raise.* Or they worry that if an employee gets too high an opinion of his own worth, he might go looking for a better job. All of these are self-defeating reasons for stinting on praise. Praise is valuable because it is scarce.

If you want people to be happy to work for you, happy with their salaries and benefits, and happy where they are, give them the praise and recognition they have earned. If you want to be respected, don't seek respect through fear, but through gratitude. Let your people know you're on their side, you want them to get ahead, and you recognize their efforts and contributions. Wise leaders don't fear giving praise; they are eager to dispense recognition at every opportunity.

After all, what motivates you? Is it just the money—or is it a desire to contribute, to feel valued and respected, to be appreciated and recognized for your accomplishments? The same human drives motivate the people who work for you. So let your people shine—and their light will reflect brilliantly on you.

3. Nurture Good Ideas

Every company, team, and church runs on ideas. Any organization that has run out of creativity is doomed to extinction. We must nurture the creative ideas of everyone in the organization. As businessman Charles Brower once observed, "A new idea is delicate. It can be killed by a sneer or a yawn; or it can be stabbed to death by a quip or worried to death by a frown."

Too proud or insecure to accept good ideas from subordinates? One of the great generals and presidents of our time wasn't. Here's what Dwight Eisenhower had to say: "A man begins to grow when he stops worrying about putting his own ideas over and keeps his mind open for the best ideas, no matter whose they are."

When you nurture good ideas, you nourish the spirits and enthusiasm of your workers. When you shut down their ideas, you shut down their motivation and their ability to contribute to your success. If an employee offers an idea or suggestion that won't work, avoid making him or her feel foolish for offering it. Instead of saying "That'll never work" or "That's a dumb idea," say, "That's a step in the right direction. Let's keep mulling it over and see if we can find the perfect solution." B. C. Forbes put it this way: "When you have to reject the suggestion of a subordinate, make sure you reject only the idea and not the person."

4. Build a Bond of Trust with Your People

The Packers' Ron Wolf understood the importance of a bond between leaders and followers. "A leader," he said, "creates a bond that encourages people to believe in him so much that they're willing to buy into his words." That bond of trust is the key to getting your people to move in the direction of your goals.

Thomas J. Watson, former CEO of IBM, once observed, "My most important contribution to IBM was my ability to pick strong and intelligent people and then hold them together by persuasion, by apologies, by financial incentives, by speeches, by chatting with their spouses, by thoughtfulness when they were sick or involved in accidents, and using every tool at my command to let them know I was a decent guy. I knew I couldn't match all of them intellectually, but I thought that if I fully used every capability I had, I could stay even with them.

"I never hesitated to promote someone I didn't like. The comfortable assistant, the nice guy you like to go on fishing trips with, is a great pitfall. Instead I looked for those sharp, scratchy, harsh, almost unpleasant guys who see and tell you about things as they really are. If you can get enough of them around you and have patience enough to hear them out, there is no limit to where you can go."

5. Be Aware of Problems in Team Chemistry and Team Relationships

In 1965, my first year with the Spartanburg Phillies, we didn't have a great team—but I enjoyed every minute of the season. Our team manager that year was Moose Johnson—a short, gregarious teddy bear of a man. He later went on to become a major league scout in Toronto. He was terrific—any outrageous thing I wanted to do, he'd say, "Let's give it a whirl."

The following year, we brought a new manager aboard—Bob Wellman, who had played briefly with the Philadelphia Athletics. We also brought in a new trainer, a friend of Wellman's named Red Zipeto. That year, we had a terrific ballclub and an outstanding season. We had future major leaguers Denny Doyle at second base and Larry Bowa at shortstop. We also played against some excellent talent (including the great Nolan Ryan, who was pitching at the time for the Greenville Mets).

Despite the fact that we were having a magical season, I was miserable. All the people around me—my secretary and the staff—could see how unhappy I was, and they worried about me. I had no energy, no pep, no appetite. Finally, Mr. Littlejohn took me to lunch and made me talk about what was bothering me.

To make a long story short, I was feeling crushed by Bob Wellman. He was an intimidating presence physically at 6′ 4″ and 270 pounds, but I found him even more intimidating to work with. He was a terrific manager but a negative person, and he griped about everything—the condition of the playing field, the talent on the team, the conditions on the bus, the promotions we were running—nothing seemed good enough to suit him. Here I was, so proud of this franchise and all we had accomplished in two short years—yet Wellman was telling me I couldn't do anything right. And to top things off, his sidekick, Zipeto, would second every gripe. My spirit was just getting hammered into the ground.

The day after Mister R. E. got me to talk about it, he brought Bob Wellman out to his office for a heart-to-heart. After that, things got better. I don't think Bob even realized what all that negativity was doing to me. He never intended to make me miserable; he just had a negative approach to getting things done. From then on, Bob was a lot more positive and cooperative—and my job became fun again.

A good leader or manager needs to care about how his people fit together, relate to each other, and get along with each other. In other words, he has to care about an elusive quality called *chemistry*. Most employers and managers, when they hire new people, look primarily for talent and experience. But I think chemistry is often more important than ability.

The chemistry of an organization is really a combination of ingredients, including personality and emotional makeup, values and beliefs, goals and ambitions, and people skills. Chemistry is not easy to assess until you actually put the organization together under real-world conditions and see how the members react to one another and work together. Getting just the right chemistry is a continual balancing act in which you add a person here, move a person there, let that person go, talk to this person, schmooze the other person. You're always testing and tweaking to achieve just the right blend.

When everyone is in sync, the organization purrs like a well-oiled machine. But when people are in conflict, it's as if someone has tossed a handful of sand into the machinery. The result: friction, heat, a lot of screeching noise, and seriously degraded performance. A wise manager or employer stays on top of the chemistry and relationships in his organization, faces problems and conflicts squarely, and makes sure issues are resolved promptly and fairly. As Red Auerbach, the legendary coach of the Boston Celtics, once observed, "They used to tell me you have to use your five best players, but I've found that you win with the five who fit together best."

Good chemistry is mysterious and elusive. You know when you've got it, you know when you've lost it, but you don't always know why. The best way to achieve it is to seek a balance of personality types—some aggressive go-getters, some motivators and cheerleaders, some leaders, some followers. Most of all, build an organization out of people with mature personalities—people who treat others with respect. If you can achieve a well-blended chemistry, you'll be a winner every time.

6. Oversee but Don't Interfere

An obsessive-compulsive manager once handed a task to a subordinate and asked, "When do you think you'll have this done?"

"In a couple of hours," was the reply.

"Good," said the manager, taking a seat near the subordinate's desk. "Mind if I watch?"

"You're going to watch?" the subordinate asked. "In that case, it'll take a couple of days."

One of the most important skills any leader or manager needs to develop is the art of overseeing without interfering. Granted, you need to hold people accountable for getting their work done within a reasonable time and up to expectations—but you also have to give people room to breathe and space to think. A good leader or manager delegates, trusts people to get the job done on their own, and monitors progress at key points along the way.

"When you find a man who knows his job and is self-motivated," said attorney Thomas Dreier of the Max Planck Institute, "keep out of his way and don't bother him with unnecessary supervision. What you think is cooperation is nothing but interference." President

Theodore Roosevelt observed, "The best executive is the one who has the sense enough to pick good men to do what he wants done, and self-restraint enough to keep from meddling while they do it."

The key to effective delegating and management is balance: Do not undercontrol; do not overcontrol. Keep in touch—but make it a *light* touch.

7. Be Patient with Mistakes

Financier John D. Rockefeller credited his success largely to his ability to work with people. On one occasion, one of Rockefeller's partners lost a million dollars on a bad investment. A lot of high-powered executives would have blown a gasket over such a loss—but Rockefeller took it in stride. What's more, he openly praised the partner for keeping the company's losses to "only" a million dollars. "The loss could have been much worse," he said, adding that the partner salvaged 60 percent of the original investment.

When Tom Watson headed IBM, one of his junior executives spent $12 million of the company's money on a project that failed miserably. After the debacle, the young executive trudged into Watson's office and plunked a letter down on his desk.

"What's this?" asked Watson.

"My resignation. I thought I'd save you the trouble of firing me."

"I'm not letting you go," said Watson. "I just invested $12 million in your education! Get back to work."

The most successful leaders care enough to be patient with mistakes.

Forget Ego

A final word of caution: You'll be more successful if you learn to keep your ego out of the way. As Ken Blanchard notes, ego is nothing but an acronym for Edging God Out.

In 1949, accordion-playing bandleader Lawrence Welk hired Myron Floren to play in his orchestra. Welk considered Floren the finest accordionist in the world. But when Welk informed his business manager, Mr. Karzas, of his decision, Karzas was furious.

"Welk, you've gotta be kidding," he retorted. "You've already got one accordion player—you. What are you gonna do with two? Fire him!"

But Welk held his ground. "This orchestra *needs* Myron Floren."

A few nights later, Karzas was in the audience when Floren made his debut with the Welk orchestra. At intermission, Karzas made his way across the crowded floor to the bandstand and beckoned to Welk. "Well," said Welk, "what do you think of my new accordionist?"

Grudgingly, Karzas replied, "He's a better accordionist than you."

Welk smiled. "Mr. Karzas," he replied, "that's the only kind of musician I hire."

Some people would rather massage their own egos than hire the best. But as Mark McCormack observes, "It takes a very confident person to be a good manager—confidence in the people who work for you and enough confidence in yourself to overcome these ego problems. It is human nature to want to see the fruits of your labor, to feel the dirt between your fingers, to perform tasks which not only produce tangible results but which are themselves tangible. Managers must seek a different kind of satisfaction. They have got to be able to build up people and give them responsibilities, to find ego gratification in training, directing, and overseeing others."

I encourage you to do what R. E. Littlejohn always did: Forget ego. Forget self. Take care of the people who work for you—and they will take care of you.

And that's not all. Here's the next success principle I learned from Mr. Littlejohn: the importance of facing problems squarely and courageously.

TWELVE

Don't Run from Problems

In 1965, just as we were starting our season in Spartanburg, it became painfully apparent to me that the parent organization, the Philadelphia Phillies, had a huge problem with a key employee. Talking to other managers in the minor-league system, I could tell that everybody in the system was as aware of the problem as I was. In fact, the buzz around the Phillies' farm clubs was that if the problem wasn't solved, it was going to wreck the organization.

I was concerned—not only because of the way this problem could affect my job as general manager of a club, but because of the fact that Phillies owner Bob Carpenter and his son Ruly were longtime friends. I sat down with Mr. Littlejohn and laid it all out for him. He said, "Pat, in fairness to your friend Bob Carpenter, you need to fly to Philadelphia and talk to him about the situation."

"You really think I should?"

"The only way to deal with a problem," he said, "is to face it squarely. Problems don't go away when you ignore them. They just get worse."

So I took Mr. Littlejohn's advice. I flew to Philadelphia. Even though Bob Carpenter was an old friend of my father, he was also the top man in the organization in which I worked. It was intimidating for me, as the new kid on the management block, to walk into the boss's office and lay out a major flaw in his organization—but I did it. After I explained to Mr. Carpenter what was happening and who was responsible, he said, "Thanks for coming all this way to tell me, Pat." Then he let out a deep breath and said, "Why am I always the last one to know?" Even though the problem was going on right in his own building, under his own nose, he didn't have a clue. If I hadn't told him, he might never have known until it was too late.

I returned to Spartanburg, reflecting on the valuable lesson I had learned from Mr. Littlejohn. As the poet Robert Frost observed, "The best way *out* is always *through*." Never run from problems. Face problems squarely. Solve them, beat them—then get on with your life.

Houston, We've Had a Problem

The Saturn V rocket—the most powerful machine ever built—lifted off on April 11, 1970. Atop the rocket was a space capsule carrying three men—Commander James Lovell, Command Module Pilot Jim Swigert Jr., and Lunar Module Pilot Fred Haise Jr. Only eight months earlier, their colleague, Neil Armstrong, had become the first man to walk on the moon. By this time, the public already considered moon shots to be routine. The flight of Apollo 13, however, would be anything but routine.

Two days later, on April 13, Jim Lovell matter of factly radioed to Earth, "Houston, we've had a problem."

That was an astronaut's typical understatement. Lovell and crew had more than a problem—they had a crisis. An oxygen tank had exploded, ripping out a section of the spacecraft, leaving the ship crippled. Precious oxygen was bleeding into the void. Power levels were dropping. Warning lights were flashing. The onboard computer was failing. The ship had gone into a slow, out-of-control tumble. No one, either on the ground or in space, knew the cause of these problems—and no one had any solutions.

For months prior to launch, the crew had practiced in simulators for every conceivable kind of emergency. But this emergency was unlike anything conceived. Never in simulation had so many things gone wrong at once. This was a problem for which no one had trained.

At Mission Control in Houston, flight director Gene Kranz assembled a team of controllers to figure out what had gone wrong. Kranz knew the mission already had failed. The ship was dying, and the astronauts would die as well if a solution wasn't found—soon. Lovell and his crew were over two hundred thousand miles from earth and moving farther away with every passing second. The spacecraft was off-course for the so-called free return trajectory, a loop around the moon that would bring the ship back to Earth. Kranz's top priority: Move Apollo 13 back into a free return trajectory or the ship would miss Earth by three thousand miles and sail on forever.

The crew worked feverishly to shut down systems and conserve oxygen and power. Once that was done, Lovell and Haise tried to maneuver the ship into the return trajectory—but the crippled ship was sluggish and wobbly. The controls handled strangely. Lovell found it was like learning how to fly all over again. Finally, he got the craft oriented, then fired the engine for thirty-one seconds. Soon Apollo 13 was back on trajectory—but the problems were far from over.

Electrical power was critically low, as were supplies of water and air. Because the life-support system of the command module had been seriously damaged, Lovell, Haise, and Swigert moved into the lunar module. It had been designed to keep two men alive for forty-five hours; somehow, it would have to sustain three for twice that long.

As Apollo 13 approached the shadow of the moon, a second firing was needed to position the ship for the return to Earth—and that's when a new problem arose. The astronauts needed to align the ship precisely for the firing by sighting stars with a telescope. But the ship was shedding many tiny, sparkling fragments of debris that obscured the stars. Houston scientist Ken Russell came up with the solution. He proposed sighting on a star that was sure to be visible: the sun. It wouldn't be pinpoint accurate, but it would be close enough to work. Lovell shifted the attitude of the craft while Haise looked through the telescope's protective filter, finding the bright disk of the sun. The maneuver worked.

As the ship swung around the far side of the moon, the astronauts were cut off from radio contact with the earth. Through the lander's triangular windows, they saw the moon sailing past. Swigert pondered a grim irony: he had joined the Apollo 13 crew just the day before the launch. The original pilot, Ken Mattingly, had been dropped after being exposed to measles (doctors were concerned he might get sick during the mission; as it turned out, he never came down with the illness). Swigert also pondered the fact that, to get home, the crew would have to leave the lunar module, return to the dead command module, and reactivate its damaged systems. No one knew if the systems *could* be reactivated—it had never been done before.

As Apollo 13 emerged from the lunar shadow, Lovell and Haise executed another four-minute rocket burn. Then, to conserve energy, they shut down all power, including the computer and guidance systems. But as Lovell, Haise, and Swigert drifted in the dark toward home, another problem arose: carbon dioxide was building up. The lithium hydroxide canisters used to scrub the air in the lunar module were nearly spent. There were fresh canisters aboard the dead command module—but those canisters were square, not round like the ones in the lunar module. Since they didn't fit, they wouldn't work—and if the carbon dioxide levels could not be controlled, the astronauts would suffocate before the ship reached Earth.

Flight director Kranz demanded a solution from his troubleshooters. "Failure," he said, "is not an option." Again Mission Control found a solution to a seemingly insolvable problem. Houston engineers rigged up a makeshift system for filtering out carbon dioxide using only items the astronauts had onboard: a plastic storage bag, a plastic notebook cover, and duct tape. Mission Control told Haise how to cobble together this system. Haise built it and installed it—and the carbon dioxide levels began to edge downward. It worked. The solution wasn't elegant, it wasn't by the book, but it saved three lives. By that measure alone, the solution was a masterpiece.

There were still more problems to come. Because of the power-saving measures, the temperature inside Apollo 13 dropped to thirty-eight degrees. Moisture condensed on the walls and instruments. It was impossible to sleep. Swigert's feet, drenched by a leaking water dispenser, became numb with cold. Exhaustion set in, clouding judgment and fraying tempers. Lovell, normally calm and professional, lost patience as Houston worked to invent new landing procedures. "We just can't wait around up here," he snapped.

Four days after the explosion, Lovell, Haise, and Swigert saw the earth looming ahead of them. Lovell checked the ship's position. They were off-course for reentry, approaching at too shallow an angle. If they didn't correct the course, Apollo 13 would skim across the atmosphere and rebound into space. But if they overcorrected and came in too steeply, the ship would burn up like a meteor. This was the most critical juncture of their journey—yet the astronauts were exhausted and half-frozen, and Haise was sick with an infection.

Swigert and Haise climbed into the command module. With a silent prayer they attempted to restart the ship's power and computer systems. The systems flickered—then came on. Swigert considered it a miracle. According to the book, the ship should have been beyond resuscitation. Lovell soon joined his fellow astronauts in the command module, sealed the hatch, and separated the lunar module. The section of spacecraft that had saved their lives tumbled away.

Swigert nudged the controls of the command module, positioning the craft for reentry. *Not too much,* he told himself, *and not too little.* Apollo 13 became a streak in the sky, leaving a trail of superheated gases and vaporized heat shield. Communications between the ship and Houston blacked out. When the time came for the radio blackout to end, Mission Control tried to raise the astronauts—but there was no answer. Fifteen seconds passed, then half a minute, then a full minute. Hope battled despair throughout Mission Control.

Then Jack Swigert's voice crackled over the speakers. Apollo 13 had come home.

Some say that NASA's finest moment was when Neil Armstrong stepped upon the moon and said, "That's one small step for a man. . . ." But I think NASA's finest hour was when everything went wrong aboard Apollo 13, when problem after problem beset the mission, yet the NASA scientists, engineers, and astronauts rose to every challenge, went outside of the rule book for answers, attacked the problem from every conceivable angle, found solutions where there were none, and brought three heroes back alive.

The Difficult Way Is the Easiest

If you want to be successful, you can't run from problems. You have to face them squarely and solve them. This principle is as true of an entire civilization as it is of individuals. Our society has so many problems to solve to survive and thrive—problems of race relations, poverty, pollution, international tensions, terrorism, the nuclear threat, political corruption, and on and on. People we elect to solve these problems seem to spend most of their time ducking responsibility for them or blaming them on the other political party.

Everyone is aware of how the global celebration of the new millennium was somewhat soured by a potential time bomb called the millennium bug, often referred to as Y2K. During the 1990s, the media were all buzzing about an insidious little computer problem set to trigger on January 1, 2000, when the two-digit calendars of many computer systems would mistake two zeros for the year 1900. This nasty little bug was well-known among computer experts for decades—but no one wanted to think about it. No one wanted to talk about it. And certainly no one wanted to spend the money to fix the problem—until it became a matter of near-panic.

Suddenly, everyone was fretting about how Y2K was going to cause bank computers, government computers, electric company power grids, trucking and railroad transportation systems, and much more to grind to a halt—right in the middle of our Happy New Millennium party. Thousands became convinced that the end of the world was at hand, and began stockpiling freeze-dried food and canned goods so they could ride out the apocalypse in their basements. I ask you: What could be a more dramatic example of the need to face problems squarely than the panic over Y2K?

Writer Henry Miller put it well: "In this age, which believes that there is a shortcut to everything, the greatest lesson to be learned is that the most difficult way is, in the long run, the easiest." Why, then, do we avoid facing our problems? Why do so many of us choose to run from life's challenges rather than facing them and defeating them? The number one reason, I believe, is fear. We naturally have an aversion to unpleasant experiences—so we procrastinate. Or we live in denial, pretending not to notice the elephant in the living room. Or we try to shift the blame onto someone else. Or we retreat into escapist entertainment, alcohol, or drugs. The result: The problems don't go away. They get worse.

"Problems," observed M. Scott Peck in *The Road Less Traveled*, "call forth our courage and our wisdom; indeed, they create our courage and our wisdom. It is only because of problems that we grow mentally and spiritually. . . . It is through the pain of confronting and resolving problems that we learn." Effective people look at life's problems as opportunities to explore the limits of their endurance. "A man of character," observed Charles de Gaulle, "finds a special attractiveness in difficulty, since it is only by coming to grips with difficulty that he can realize his potentialities." And the Roman poet Horace exulted, "It is courage, courage, courage, that raises the blood of life to crimson splendor. Live bravely and present a brave front to adversity."

Here, then, are some principles to keep in mind whenever you are called upon to face a problem.

1. Accept Your Problems as an Exciting Challenge

"All the fun," said sculptor Claes Oldenburg, "is locking horns with impossibilities." It's true. Life would be boring without problems to solve and challenges to test ourselves against. A sweet sense of exhilaration comes with defeating a problem, braving an adventure, winning over obstacles and opposition, and reaching a goal we thought was beyond our reach. Facing problems may not be fun at the moment of deepest pain and frustration, but a sense of satisfaction comes when we have proven ourselves in a business crisis, or when we have come back from a twenty-point deficit to win the game, or when we've beaten cancer.

You may be facing a tough problem right now. I know you'd rather be on a beach in the Caribbean or skiing at Aspen than going through such a trial. But your present problem will be much easier to bear if you will look at it not as a burden but as an adventure. Anyone can steer a ship when the waters are calm—but to bring a ship safely to port through a howling storm, now that's an accomplishment! Battling adversity makes us feel truly alive and engaged with the adventure of living.

2. Accept Personal Responsibility for Dealing with Your Problems

The comic-strip character Pogo once said, "Everywhere I go, there I am again." It's true. You can't run away from yourself. Everywhere your problems are, there you are, too. So the wise thing to do is to accept responsibility for solving your own problems. Whining and blaming others doesn't solve anything. It just keeps us stuck where we are.

In *The Confidence Course: Sevens Steps to Self-Fulfillment,* Walter Anderson makes this wise and practical observation: "I am responsible. Although I may not be able to prevent the worst from happening, I am responsible for my attitude toward the inevitable misfortunes that darken life. Bad things do happen; how I respond to them defines my character and the quality of my life.

"I can choose to sit in perpetual sadness, immobilized by the gravity of my loss, or I can choose to rise from the pain and treasure the most precious gift I have—life itself."

The problem that confronts you may be a marketing plan you must design for your never-satisfied boss, or a paper you must write under an impossible deadline, or a person you can't get along with, or a mountain you must climb, or a novel you've been struggling to write for three years. Whatever you face, understand that the real battle is not "out there" somewhere. The real battle is not in your office or in that pile of paper or in that other person or up on that mountain. The real battle is *within you.*

The enemy you must conquer is your own fear, your own self-doubt, your own weariness and exhaustion. The enemy you have to beat is the voice inside you that wants to whine or complain or give up. If you can master the enemy within, you can master your problems, you can beat your circumstances, you can finish that novel or reach that summit. You can *win!* It all begins the moment you accept responsibility for solving your problems.

3. Think Outside the Box

Be creative. Seek original ways of approaching your problem. Here's a riddle: What can you sit on, sleep on, and brush your teeth with? To find the answer to this riddle, you have to think outside the box. You have to be creative in your approach to the problem.

Psychological researcher Abraham Maslow once said, "If the only tool you have is a hammer, you tend to see every problem as a nail." The more varied tools you keep in the toolbox of your mind, the more innovative ways you will possess to solve your problems.

What do I mean by tools? Here are some examples.

Imagination—the ability to envision what is not yet real or present; the ability to see beyond what is to what could be. "Imagination," said Einstein, "is more important than knowledge." Imagination is the strongest nation on earth. A person of imagination does not need a manual to solve problems; he or she envisions potential solutions that can't be found in any book. Such a person believes that in an infinite universe there are an infinite number of ways to solve a problem. Those ways are just waiting to be found and tried. Imagination is the highest flying kite one can fly.

Resourcefulness—the ability to apply imaginative solutions to difficult problems; the ability to combine existing materials and components in new ways, to produce new solutions. A great example of resourcefulness occurred when Gene Kranz's Mission Control engineers concocted the makeshift life-support system out of a plastic storage bag, a plastic notebook cover, and duct tape to save the lives of the Apollo 13 astronauts.

Creativity—the ability to think outside the box, in ways that are not dictated by restrictions, or by the belief that "this is the way we've always done it," or by a self-censoring assumption that "this is how I ought to think." A creative mind is uninhibited and free.

Remember the riddle I asked a few paragraphs ago—What can you sit on, sleep on, and brush your teeth with? The answer is so simple most people miss it: A chair, a bed, and a toothbrush. The natural tendency is to assume that the riddle asks for one answer, because that's the way riddles usually work. The creative mind wonders, "Why does it have to be *one* answer? Why not *three?*" Once we have gone outside the box of our assumptions, the problem is easy to solve: You sit on a chair, you sleep on a bed, you brush your teeth with a toothbrush. "Creativity can solve almost any problem," said the famed advertising art director George Lois of Papert, Koenig, and Lois in New York. "The creative act, the defeat of habit by originality, overcomes everything."

Insight—the capacity to see beyond appearances to the true nature of a problem or situation. Insight can't be taught—but it can be learned from experience. It is the ability to develop keen, accurate hunches, based on fragmentary information that the mind processes at an unconscious level. It is the ability to grasp and appreciate reality by opening one's mind to multiple impressions and multisensory input. It is the ability to find solutions to problems that defy analysis or that offer too little hard data to be solved in a purely rational, mechanical way.

Sometimes you just don't have enough information to solve a problem cognitively. You have to go with your gut. You have to use insight. Sometimes, you try to apply your intellect to a situation, you draw up your list of pros and cons, you see that your cons far outnumber your pros—yet you feel your gut telling you to go with the pros. That's insight. "Some problems," observed Jerome Wiesner, "are just too complicated for rational, logical solutions. They admit of insights, not answers."

Humor—the ability to maintain perspective about problems by not taking them too seriously; the ability to substitute a smile or a laugh for tension and frustration. Face it: problems cause us to tense up, and they can even paralyze us. A good sense of humor keeps our minds lubricated so we don't freeze under the pressure of problems. The ability to laugh in tough situations can be a huge asset for resolving those situations. In his book *Jump Start Your Brain*, author Doug Hall notes, "You can increase your brain power three- to five-fold simply by laughing and having fun before working on a problem."

Obliquity—the ability to view a problem from an oblique angle, from a new and divergent perspective. Sometimes, to solve a problem, you have to stop banging your head against it and simply pull back. A writer friend of mine says that he gets some of his best ideas by stepping away from his word processor and taking a walk or a jog or a shower or a rest on the couch. "Sometimes," he says, "you just get too close to the problem to solve it. Step away for five minutes, get a new perspective, let your subconscious roll it around for a while. Give your cerebral cortex a break—and suddenly the answer just comes to you out of the blue, like a snap of the fingers."

Experienced stargazers know that you cannot see faint stars in the night sky by viewing them directly. This is because of a small depression near the center of the retina of the eye called the fovea centralis. Weak light does not register on this area. So to see a faint star, you have to look slightly to the right or left of it—you have to view it obliquely.

It is the same with problems. Sometimes it seems there is a fovea centralis of the mind—if you stare directly at a problem, the solution is invisible. You must move off-center and view it from a different angle. As French novelist Andre Gide observed, "It is not always by plugging away at a difficulty and sticking to it that one overcomes it; often it is by working on the one next to it. Some things and some people have to be approached obliquely, at an angle."

4. Break Your Problem Down into Its Parts

Many problems that loom large and insolvable become manageable when broken down and dealt with a piece at a time. Sometimes, the solution is not one big answer but a lot of little ones. The Greek philosopher Heraclitus said, "Men who wish to know about the world must learn about it in its particular details." And Picasso observed that a single individual component of one of his paintings was often the key to the entire composition. "One does a whole painting for one peach and people think just the opposite—that that particular peach is but a detail." So learn to see the importance of those details, the individual parts of the problem—and soon you will find the solution.

5. Be Confident

Bruce Barton was an advertising executive and author of *The Man Nobody Knows*, which explored the life of Jesus Christ as a prototype for effective living in the business world. Barton once said, "Nothing splendid has ever been achieved except by those who dared believe that something inside them was superior to circumstance."

Most of us have God-given talents, abilities, and capacities which we have never even begun to tap and utilize. Former IBM chief Tom Watson put it this way: "Within us all there are wells of thought and dynamos of energy which are not suspected until emergencies arise. Then oftentimes we find that it is comparatively simple to double or treble our former capacities and amaze ourselves by the results achieved." And psychologist William James said, "Great emergencies and crises show us how much greater our vital resources are than we had supposed."

There are always people around us who will try to blunt our confidence with negativity. Oh, they won't call it that. They will say, "Hey, I'm only being practical," or, "I'm only being realistic," or, "I'm only trying to get your head out of the clouds and bring you down to earth." Don't let anyone tell you that the solution to your problems is out of reach or impossible. As Elbert Hubbard once said, "The world is moving so fast these days that the man who says it can't be done is generally interrupted by someone doing it." So be that lone, daring person who confidently does the impossible, regardless of what people around you say.

When faced with problems, focus confidently on God's ability and on the ability he has given you to find the solution to your problems. It's a natural human tendency to focus negatively on the problem—but we choose to focus on the solution! The great guru of positive thinking, Norman Vincent Peale, said, "Go forward confidently, energetically attacking problems, expecting favorable outcomes."

6. Maintain a Positive Attitude

"I've never seen a monument erected to a pessimist," observed radio commentator Paul Harvey. And you know, he's right. I've never seen one either—have you?

To solve problems and overcome obstacles, you've got to maintain a positive attitude. When nineteen months old, Helen Keller was struck blind and deaf by a severe illness. Without any sensory input from the society around her, she grew up more like a wild animal than a human being. When Helen was seven, Anne Sullivan of the Perkins Institute for the Blind taught her to read Braille. As Helen turned ten, Anne decided to teach her to speak; though deaf, Helen learned to speak after only a month of instruction. At twenty-four, Helen Keller graduated with honors from Radcliffe College, and went on to be an author and a lecturer, writing six books over a fifty-year period.

Despite her disabilities, Helen Keller learned the power of a positive attitude in overcoming the obstacles of life. "Be of good cheer," Helen Keller once said. "Do not think of today's failures, but of the success that may come tomorrow. You will succeed if you persevere, and you will find joy in overcoming obstacles. Remember, no effort that we make to attain something beautiful is ever lost." Or as another blind motivational speaker, Craig McFarlane, put it, "We all have inconveniences of one kind or another. How you deal with them ultimately determines how successful you are."

Your problems are outside of you. What is inside—your spirit, your soul, your attitude—is what counts. As someone once observed, "All the water in the world cannot drown you—unless it gets inside."

Another key to a positive attitude is to maintain enthusiasm. To have enthusiasm literally is to have a God-inspired joy for living. That word *enthusiasm* comes from a Greek root word *entheos*, from *en-* (to be in or possessed by) and *theos* (God). "Enthusiasm releases the drive to carry you over obstacles and adds significance to all you do," wrote Norman Vincent Peale, one of the most enthusiastic people who ever lived. "One way to become enthusiastic is to look for the plus sign. To make progress in any difficult situation, you have to start with what's right about it and build on that."

So be filled with God and with godly enthusiasm as you tackle your problems. As someone once said, problems are only opportunities in work clothes.

7. Persevere

In the 1960s, Martin Luther King Jr. confronted a massive problem—centuries of racial injustice in America. It was a problem he knew would not yield to simplistic solutions. It would take courage and fortitude. It would take patience and persistence. Before the fight was over, it would even take his life. But he was not deterred. "We must accept finite disappointment," he said, "but we must never lose infinite hope."

Perseverance is especially crucial to problem-solving when your problems involve *people*—those who oppose you, who criticize you, who (sometimes with the best of intentions) tell you to give up and accept defeat. "Whatever course you decide upon," said the poet Emerson, "there is always someone to tell you that you are wrong. There are always difficulties arising which tempt you to believe that your critics are right. To map out a course of action and follow it to an end requires courage."

Don't yield to circumstances. Don't yield to opponents. Don't yield to critics. Endure—and outlast them all. Remember, the anvil lasts longer than the hammer. Let people and circumstances hammer you as much as they like. You are an anvil and you cannot be broken or shaken.

8. Accept Reality: Problems Are Inevitable

Life is a never-ending exercise in problem-solving. The sooner we accept this truth, the sooner we can get on with the business of living. In *The Road Less Traveled*, author Peck put it this way: "Life is difficult."

This is a great truth, one of the greatest truths. It is a great truth because once we truly see this truth, we transcend it. Once we truly know that life is difficult—once we truly understand and accept it—then life is no longer difficult. Because once it is accepted, the fact that life is difficult no longer matters.

Ultimately, we cannot run away from life and its problems. Sure, we would love to escape from our problems, especially when they reach the boiling point, the point that seems beyond human endurance. In *The Ideal Problem Solver,* authors John D. Bransford and Barry S. Stein observe, "It is not uncommon to find oneself thinking such thoughts as 'I can't stand this' or 'If only I didn't have to do this.' As psychologist Albert Ellis notes, such thoughts frequently involve whining. In essence, we are acting like babies and whining about things 'not being fair.' . . . It is usually more efficient to simply accept the fact that life is not always a bowl of cherries, stop whining, and get on with the task."

I would urge you to courageously live by the precepts that have been articulated by so many wise souls.

- Death and dying researcher Elisabeth Kubler-Ross: "Should you shield the valleys from the windstorms, you would never see the beauty of their canyons."
- Walter Anderson, author of *The Confidence Course:* "True hope dwells on the possible, even when life seems to be a plot written by someone who wants to see how much adversity we can overcome. True hope responds to the real world, to real life; it is an active effort."
- Former vice president Dan Quayle: "The question in life is not whether you get knocked down. You will. The question is, 'Are you ready to get back up and fight for what you believe in?'"

- Cherokee leader Big Elk: "Misfortunes do not flourish particularly in our path. They grow everywhere."
- MacRina Wiederkehr, author of *A Tree Full of Angels*: "Gather up the joys and sorrows, the struggles, the beauty, love, dreams and hopes of every hour that they may be consecrated at the altar of daily life."
- Norman Vincent Peale: "You can be greater than anything that can happen to you."
- Advice columnist Ann Landers: "Expect trouble as an inevitable part of life and repeat to yourself the most comforting words of all: 'This, too, shall pass.'"

So accept the reality: Problems are inevitable. But problems are also temporary. The satisfaction of meeting life's challenges is lasting and profound.

9. Recognize That Problems Benefit Us

Surmounting problems gives us character strength, wisdom, beauty, and self-understanding. When this is our perspective, we can face our problems knowing that, even if we are unable to change them, we can still allow problems to change *us*, to make us stronger and better human beings.

Mr. Littlejohn understood this very well. He always seemed happiest when I had a problem to solve. I don't mean he took sadistic delight in my misfortunes. But whenever some situation came along that needed a solution, he was definitely pleased. He *enjoyed* watching me wrestle with a problem because he knew I needed problems in order to learn and grow. I can still hear his voice in my mind. He would say, "Pat, this is going to do you good. This problem will give you a wonderful opportunity to sell yourself." In other words, an opportunity to learn, to grow, and to show others what you can do.

It can be annoying when someone else is so cheerful about your problems, but in retrospect I can see that Mr. Littlejohn was right. Solving problems *was* good for me—and those experiences did give me opportunities to prove myself and sell myself. And he wasn't the only one who took that cheerful attitude toward my problems.

Some years later, when I was in Chicago, I was having lunch with my pastor, Dr. Warren Wiersbe. I was pouring out some problems I was wrestling with, and I suppose I expected some sort of sympathy from him. No way! Instead I got more Littlejohn-style cheeriness: "Now, Pat," he said, "don't waste your sufferings. Life is full of problems, so you might as well put them to good use."

I still don't like problems any more than I did when I was in my twenties, but I can see all the growth and maturity I've gained from problems, and I wouldn't trade those experiences for the world. Problems are good for us. Problems force us to stretch and grow. And they really do give us a chance to prove to ourselves and others what we can do.

Botanists tell us there is a sound and positive purpose behind the strong winds that blow every March. Trees need those powerful winds to flex their trunks and bend their branches, so that the nourishing sap can be drawn up into the developing leaves. This is an apt metaphor describing the gale-force winds that often blow through our lives. We may dislike those winds while the storm is raging, yet when we look back months or years later, we can see how that blustery opposition actually nourished our character, making us stronger, wiser, and more resilient.

I do not believe that any of us was put on this earth merely to mark time or experience endless bliss and tranquility. We were put on this earth to learn and to grow—and that means we were put here to experience struggles and pain and problems. Times of difficulty and problem-solving reveal our substance. Samuel Johnson once said, "He knows not his own strength who hath not met adversity. To strive with difficulties, and to conquer them, is the highest human felicity." Or as country singer Dolly Parton put it, "If you want the rainbow, you gotta put up with the rain."

This wisdom is as old as the Bible. In the New Testament book of James, we read, "When all kinds of trials and temptations crowd into your lives, my brothers, don't resent them as intruders, but welcome them as friends! Realize that they come to test your faith and to produce in you the quality of endurance. But let the process go on until that endurance is fully developed, and you will find you have become men of mature character" (James 1:2–4, PHILLIPS).

Aimee Mulins has learned this lesson in a big way. She was born without a fibula—a major weight-bearing bone—in either leg. Both legs were amputated just below the knee when she was one year old. Doctors expected Aimee to spend her life in a wheelchair. At age two, she learned to walk using prosthetic legs made of wood. Once, when dancing at school with other second graders, one of her wooden legs snapped in half. Aimee wasn't hurt, but the sight of her leg breaking off sent her classmates screaming. "I decided at an early age," Aimee said, "to transform my setbacks into strengths, and to tackle them head-on."

As a teenager, she became so comfortable with her prosthetic legs that she swam, skied, played soccer, and delivered newspapers on her bike. She has even worked as a fashion model. In her twenties, she became a Paralympic runner, and she now holds two world records for disabled athletes. This double-amputee sprints faster and exhibits greater endurance than many able-bodied athletes. After winning a full academic scholarship, she attended Georgetown University's School of Foreign Service, graduating in May 1998. Reflecting on circumstances that many might consider unfair disadvantages and cruel problems, Aimee is upbeat, positive, and even grateful. "The truth is," she says, "I'm sort of lucky to have this body, because it forced me to find my strength and beauty within."[29]

So instead of resisting, resenting, or complaining about problems, accept them as gifts to enable you to develop greater character strength, wisdom, beauty, happiness, and self-understanding. Decide to learn the lessons brought by problems and difficulties. As Benjamin Franklin said, "Those things that hurt, instruct." So don't waste your sufferings, my friend. Wring all the benefits you can from your problems.

Solving Problems in the Air

Greg Brenneman is a professional problem-solver. As a partner at Dallas-based Bain and Company, his specialty was engineering corporate turnarounds—turning failing companies into success stories. Writing in the *Harvard Business Review,* he told about his first Dallas-to-Houston flight aboard then-failing Continental Airlines:

> It was a hot, humid day in May 1993. . . . I was seated in the last row of an unattractive and dirty DC-9. The airplane's interior had seven different color schemes, which I later found out was not uncommon. After all, Continental was the product of mergers among seven airlines; when a seat needed to be replaced, the company used whatever was in stock. Worse, no one had hooked up the plane's air-conditioning. Departure time came and went, and people continued to trickle on board for another 40 minutes. I found this remarkable given that the flight time was only 36 minutes. There were no announcements about our delay, and none of the crew seemed particularly concerned.
>
> Finally, probably to prevent a riot, the captain turned on the DC-9's auxiliary power unit. This cooled down the airplane all right, but it also caused condensation to build up on the inside roof of the aircraft. When we took off at last—50 minutes late—the accumulated condensation flowed like a waterfall along the top of the baggage bins to the back of the airplane. It came pouring out above the center seat in the last row of coach—directly onto my head. My best suit and I were soaked.

Soon afterward, Greg Brenneman was handed the seemingly impossible job of turning this failing airline around. Continental was, at that time, the most dysfunctional company he had ever seen. Having gone through ten presidents in ten years, its management was paralyzed by fear and uncertainty. Employee morale was in the tank. Ranked tenth out of ten U.S. airlines in customer service by the Department of Transportation, Continental had just emerged from bankruptcy and hadn't been profitable since 1978. If Brenneman didn't find a way to turn Continental around, forty thousand employees would be out of a job.

Brenneman knew that to save the company, he had to find ways to cut costs while improving the quality of Continental's product. Continental had to start doing what it had not been doing in years: getting customers and their luggage to their destinations on time in clean, attractive airplanes. Though it seems like a simple goal, the entire Continental corporate structure seemed diabolically contrived to sabotage this goal. Brenneman knew he had to make drastic changes—right away and all at once.

His first step in attacking the problem was to form a partnership with Gordon Bethune, Continental's forward-looking chairman and CEO, who had just come aboard after a successful stint in the upper echelons of Boeing. Both men saw that Continental was hemorrhaging cash, alienating customers, and drifting toward yet another bankruptcy—one which would result not in protection from creditors but in final liquidation. They sat down together over dinner and wrote down everything that was wrong with the company—"a very long list," Brenneman later recalled. Then they came up with something they called the Go Forward Plan. "We named it that," said Brenneman, "because we knew our history was not going to help us. Did you know that there are no rearview mirrors on an airplane? The runway behind is irrelevant."

Brenneman quickly applied a clamp to Continental's financial hemorrhage. When he learned that almost a fifth of the company's routes were money-losers, he asked pointed questions.

"Why are we flying empty planes between Greensboro and Greenville six times a day?"

The reply: "It's a strategic route."

"Does it make money?"

"No."

"Did it ever make money?"

"No."

"Then how 'strategic' can it be? Cut it."

Monitoring the company's cash flow, Brenneman made a shocking discovery in November 1994. In about eight weeks, the company no longer would be able to make payroll. No one else even had a clue of the impending disaster. How could such a problem go undetected? "Some of the finance people," Brenneman explained, "had regularly been inflating our profit projections by plugging in overoptimistic revenue estimates. . . . To this day, I can't understand why anyone would try to hide an impending cash shortage. . . . Hiding the fact that you are about to run out of money is like resetting the fuel gauge when you're low on gas."

Acting quietly to avoid scaring stockholders and customers, Brenneman called a meeting with Continental's number one creditor, which held $3.5 billion of the company's $5 billion in debt. He explained the situation and the need for restructuring the debt— and the creditors hit the roof. Seeing that the meeting was going nowhere, Brenneman got up and walked toward the door.

"Where are you going?" the creditors shouted.

"Home," said Brenneman.

"You can't dump this on us and walk away!"

Brenneman responded, "Do you know what the first step in problem solving is?" Brenneman answered his own question: "The first step is to ask yourself, 'Who's got the problem?' Measured by the share price of this company's stock, Continental is worth about $175 million, and you are holding the bag for $3.5 billion. Looks like it's your problem, not mine. You run the company. I'm going home." And he left.

Brenneman got no farther than his office when the creditors caught up with him and begged him to return to the meeting. So the meeting resumed and the parties worked out a plan for restructuring the debt. The crisis passed.

Brenneman and Bethune proceeded to clean house from top to bottom. Brenneman recalled concluding that members of Continental's existing management team were not up to the challenge of turning the company around. "They were too busy trying to knock each other off. In fact, for fifteen years, the way to get ahead at Continental was to torpedo someone and then take his or her job." Within his first few months on the job, Brenneman had removed fifty of sixty-one company officers, replacing them with just twenty new hires, cutting both cost and bureaucracy. All new hires were proven team players, the best and brightest he could recruit. One of his techniques for acquiring top talent was to hire away the number two people from departments at other airlines and make them number one in their department at Continental, with vastly increased authority to get things done. He also offered them stock options, so that if the shareholders won, the executives would win, too. Within weeks, Continental had become a completely different company.

Brenneman and Bethune sold the workforce on the plan to upgrade service, and the results showed up in Department of Transportation tracking statistics of Continental's increased on-time arrivals, decreased incidences of mishandled baggage, and reduced consumer complaints. Brenneman also turned up shortsighted "cost-cutting" measures that actually were costing money. For years, Continental had been shaving costs, skimping on quality, and driving customers away—a false economy that would spell disaster if not corrected.

An example cited by Brenneman: Continental pilots were paid bonuses for reducing fuel consumption. The pilots cut fuel consumption and earned their bonuses—but the problem was in how they accomplished those reductions. For one thing, the pilots reduced their cruising speed, which caused passengers to arrive late and be angry over missed connections. The company paid out many times more for accommodating customers and putting them on rival airlines than it saved on costs of fuel. Pilots also skimped on air-conditioning, making cabin conditions steamy and unbearable. The result: Customers fled to other airlines. Other self-defeating "cost reduction" measures eroded Continental's bottom line. As soon as Brenneman and Bethune uncovered them, those policies were scrapped.

Other steps Brenneman took included such obvious actions as upgrading the quality of in-flight food service and such innovative measures as having Continental's top brass make personal phone calls to customers and travel agents who had written letters of complaint. These personal apologies went a long way toward restoring consumer confidence in the company.

Brenneman also launched a campaign to "retire the meatball"— that is, to replace the ugly, red Continental logo with a blue globe featuring gold lettering. When the maintenance department told him it would take a minimum of four years to repaint the fleet's exteriors, redecorate the interiors, and recarpet the airport terminals, Brenneman replied, "You have six months."

"We can't do it in six months," came the reply.

"Then I'll find someone who can."

The job got done in six months. Brenneman recalls, "Our customers loved Continental's new look. Who wouldn't after flying on the old Continental? In March 1995, I boarded a 737-100, which at 27 years was the oldest airplane in our fleet. The gentleman sitting next to me looked at me and said, 'Isn't it great that Continental is getting all these new airplanes?' I just smiled. . . . One of our MD-80 captains called me and said, 'Greg, I knew we would be a good airline again once our airplanes were the same color.'"

Six months after Greg Brenneman arrived to retool a terminally ill airline, Continental was flying shiny, clean, comfortable planes, taking off and arriving on time, with hardly any lost or misdirected baggage. Employees who once ripped the company logo off their uniforms in shame were proud of Continental once more. Every Valentine's Day, all Continental employees received profit-sharing checks equal to roughly 7 percent of their annual paycheck. Morale was high—and so were ridership, customer satisfaction, cash flow, and stock values.[30]

The lesson of Greg Brenneman's experience is clear: Never run from a problem. Always face it squarely, assess it honestly, attack it forcefully, solve it decisively—and win. That is the lesson not only of Continental Airlines, but the lesson of Apollo 13, the lesson of Helen Keller and Aimee Mulins—and a lesson instilled in me every day I worked with Mister R. E. in Spartanburg, South Carolina. Another lesson he taught me: Surround yourself with greatness.

THIRTEEN

Surround Yourself with Greatness

Mister R. E. often told of the advantages he had as a young businessman. "I was fortunate," he said, "to be surrounded by older and wiser businessmen who shared with me the secrets of the business world." He made a deliberate decision, early in life, to surround himself with greatness. As he sought out role models of greatness—older mentors and successful businessmen such as D. W. Royster, L. A. Odom, and Mr. Littlejohn's business partner, Leo Hughes—some of their greatness rubbed off on Mister R. E. It was the poet Longfellow who wrote in his "Psalm of Life,"

Lives of great men all remind us
We can make our lives sublime,
And, departing, leave behind us
Footprints on the sands of time.

What these other models of greatness were in the life of Mr. Littlejohn, he was to me—a great man who left footprints on the sands of my life. I looked at the example of this man, and I thought, *If a man like Mister R. E. needs to surround himself with greatness, how much more do I!* Even as a boy, I was attracted to greatness. It wasn't enough for me merely to be a spectator in the stands—I wanted to get close to my sports idols. I wanted to shake their hands, get their autographs, exchange a few words with them, soak up some of their glory. So I went to the ballpark and hung around the Phillies locker room and met all my baseball heroes—men whose greatness in baseball I hoped to one day emulate.

As a young man, I went out of my way to meet and talk to great people, not only people who had achieved greatness in my chosen field of endeavor, but also people who had achieved greatness in other areas. I reached out to people of accomplishment in the sports world—Bill Durney, Bill Veeck, Bob Carpenter, and many others. I cultivated friendships with people who were clearly success-oriented and ambitious, even though they hadn't arrived yet—people like baseball manager Sparky Anderson, broadcaster Larry King, pitcher Ferguson Jenkins, broadcaster Billy Packer, shortstop Larry Bowa, and more. These people had a tremendous impact on my life over the years and have contributed enormously to my success in life and my growth as a person.

But, of course, the greatest of all influences was Mister R. E. I wasn't the only one who recognized his greatness. Every Christmas day, Phillies owner Bob Carpenter would call Mister R. E. from his home near Wilmington, Delaware, just to pay him respect. And often, when Carpenter had a big decision or a problem, he would call Mister R. E. for counsel and advice. I often thought, *Wow! Here is a big-league owner calling the owner of a Class A affiliate to get the benefit of his wisdom!* That spoke volumes to me about the greatness of this humble and self-effacing man, R. E. Littlejohn.

Several times each season, Carpenter's son Ruly would visit us in Spartanburg and spend time with Mister R. E. Ruly would always learn something from him. I remember one discussion centered around the Phillies' leasing or buying automobiles for their scouts. Mister R. E. advised Ruly to lease them, which the Phillies did for a number of years.

In 1965, Mister R. E. and I drove together from Spartanburg to Florence, South Carolina, to meet with a ballplayer, Elmo Lam. Elmo had played baseball at Clemson University, then signed with the Phillies, played a few years, and retired. We needed some help in Spartanburg, so we asked Elmo to return to give us an infusion of experience and star quality. He agreed to play in Spartanburg for the rest of the season.

Mister R. E. and I returned from that trip a little past midnight, and there was a message waiting for him at his home: "Please call John Quinn! Urgent!" Quinn was the general manager of the Philadelphia Phillies, and he had a major personnel decision to make at the front office level—a decision that would affect the future of the ballclub in a big way. Quinn didn't want to make such a momentous decision until he had input from Mister R. E. *Incredible!* I thought. *Even the Phillies' general manager doesn't make a major move without talking to Mister R. E.!*

If Bob and Ruly Carpenter and John Quinn thought that much of Mister R. E., I knew that this was a man I needed to listen to. So throughout my brief time in Spartanburg, and long after I left in 1968, I never let more than a few weeks go by without talking to him. In any big decision, I always sought his observations and counsel. Throughout my NBA years, from Philly to Chicago to Atlanta to Philly again and right up to the moment I made my move to Orlando, I never made a major personal or career decision without discussing it with Mr. Littlejohn.

In October 1986, shortly after I moved to Orlando, and when Mister R. E. was very ill and coming to the end of his life, a community luncheon was held in Spartanburg to honor him. I was invited to speak at the testimonial, and it brought our long relationship to a fitting culmination. I had the honor of paying tribute to him in his presence, in front of his friends and his community. It was a special experience for me—a bittersweet occasion, because he was extremely weak by that time and I knew he would not be with us much longer (he died three months later). I became teary-eyed and there was a catch in my throat several times as I spoke of the love I had for this great man, and of all he had meant to my life.

A poet once described my feelings for R. E. Littlejohn—"sighing that God formed but one such man, and then broke the mold." I don't expect to meet another man like him—a man of such humility and such greatness.

What Is Greatness?

Open the pages of *People* magazine and you will find many famous people, many celebrities—but you will find very few great people, very few authentic heroes. As historian Daniel J. Boorstin observed in *The Image,* "Celebrity-worship and hero-worship should not be confused. Yet we confuse them every day, and by doing so we come dangerously close to depriving ourselves of all real models. We lose sight of the men and women who do not simply seem great because they are famous but are famous because they are great."

Living and working in the professional sports world, I see it all the time: children, young people, and people old enough to know better mistaking the rich and famous, the sports heroes and entertainers, for people of greatness. Having seen so many of these so-called heroes when they are off the court, behind the scenes, and away from the glare of the spotlight, I can tell you that there are few—some, yes, but few—that I would call *great* human beings, people to be emulated. The real role models are those who work hard at what they do, who work patiently and honestly, who display wisdom, values, and class, and who can explain to others how to rise from the mire of mediocrity to the zenith of success.

Near the end of his life, Mickey Mantle sadly summed it all up at a press conference at Baylor University Medical Center. Having been ill with hepatitis, cirrhosis, and cancer—the result of years of drinking and abusing his body—"The Mick" had just received a desperately needed liver transplant. Seated beside his doctors and flanked by poster-size pictures of himself from his glory days with the New York Yankees, Mantle looked frail and tired, and his face was filled with regret. "I would like to say to the kids out there," he said, "take a good look. This is not a role model. Don't be like me. God gave me a body, the ability to play baseball, and that's what I wanted to do. But I just—" He choked up and couldn't finish the sentence. Recovering his voice, he said, "I was given so much. But it's just wasted."

The liver transplant only prolonged his life a short time. His message was clear and poignant: great athletic ability does not make a person a great role model. True greatness comes from something much deeper than physical prowess and athletic skill. It comes from a source much more profound than mere fame or wealth.

Greatness is the result of *character*.

Another baseball hero, home-run champ Mark McGwire knows the difference between a great baseball player and the kind of greatness that qualifies a person to be a hero and a role model. His own hero is his father, John McGwire—a man who continues to inspire Mark to this day. When he was a boy, John McGwire suffered an illness that left him with one leg shorter than the other, preventing him from pursuing a career in professional sports. Still, John was passionate about sports, and as an amateur boxer he pursued his passion with all the intensity of a pro and with constant preparation and training. One of Mark's earliest memories is the sound of his father pounding away at a boxing bag in the garage.

Mark McGwire never forgot who his own hero was, or why. Once, while driving in city traffic, he was cut off by a BMW that swerved in front of him. The driver of the other car rolled down the window and held out a baseball card. "Mark McGwire!" the man called. "You've gotta sign this for my son! You're his hero!"

McGwire climbed out of his car, scowling and jabbing a finger at the other driver. "You're his parent!" he growled. "You should be your son's hero, not me!" But, nice guy that he is, McGwire signed the card.

McGwire is a rare breed in this celebrity-crazed world. He is family-focused. He is generous. Unlike many players, he never charges to sign autographs (unless the money goes to charity). He is deeply involved in crusading for victims of child abuse. Humble and unselfish, he always takes time for his fans—but he rejects the notion that anyone should look to him or other sports figures as heroes. "You may have a favorite baseball player," he says, "but how can that person be your hero? You don't even know him. That really bothers me. Your hero should be your father, or your mother, or an aunt, or an uncle. Look to your family, to people around you."[31]

Surround Yourself with Great People

Sandra Bullock's exotic beauty and quirky personality have made her a box-office hit in such films as *Speed*, *The Net*, *Hope Floats*, and *While You Were Sleeping*. When *USA Today*'s Claudia Puig asked her about the source of her success as an actress, Sandra Bullock replied that she had achieved success by surrounding herself with greatness. "I've learned that success comes in a very prickly package," the actress explained. "Whether you choose to accept it or not is up to you. It's what you choose to do with it, the people you choose to surround yourself with. Always choose people who are better than you. Always choose people who challenge you and are smarter than you. Always be the student."[32]

Great people inspire us, lift us up, and carry us on their shoulders to heights we never imagined we could reach on our own. Their greatness moves us to reach for greatness ourselves. "Great men are rarely isolated mountain-peaks," wrote clergyman Thomas Wentworth Higginson. "They are the summits of ranges." This is true whether the greatness we aspire to is in the arts, in sports, in ministry, or in business.

Howard Schultz, the CEO of the Starbucks coffee chain, came from unlikely beginnings. Born into the bleak conditions of Brooklyn's Bayview Projects, Schultz earned a degree in communications, sold copy machines for Xerox, and became vice president of U.S. operations for a Swedish manufacturing company that made, among other things, drip coffeemakers. When a Seattle retailer ordered a large number of coffeemakers from his company, Schultz was intrigued. He visited one of the retailer's four coffee shops—and discovered the unique flavor of Starbucks coffee. Impressed, he met with the company's owners and was hired as director of Starbucks' marketing operations. He quickly ascended to the top post in the company. Under his leadership, Starbucks expanded from four Seattle outlets in 1981 to more than 1,500 outlets nationwide today.

Employing more than 25,000 people, the company has annual revenues in excess of a billion dollars.

In an interview with a writer for *Entrepreneur Magazine,* Howard Schultz explained one of the reasons for Starbucks' success—and his own: "The ability to recognize limitations in yourself is what determines whether you have a great idea that can become a great business. . . . Surround yourself with great people and get out of the way."[33]

Miles S. Nadal is founder, president, CEO and controlling shareholder of MDC Communications Corporation, a company specializing in secure electronic transactions (checks, credit, debit, telephone, and smartcards), postage and excise stamps, event tickets, transportation tickets, corporate payables, and more. Though Nadal founded the company with five hundred dollars (charged to his VISA card) and two employees (his parents), MDC is now a $400 million company that conducts business throughout North America and the Pacific Rim. "We went public," Nadal recalls, "on Friday, October 16, 1987, the day before Black Monday, so our evolution as a public company has been an interesting one, to say the least. The true test of character is adversity, so we have certainly established a great deal of character!"

The secret to the success of Miles Nadal and MDC Communications? He has surrounded himself with greatness! "It has been said," he told an interviewer for the *Wall Street Corporate Reporter,* "that if you want to build a team of giants, you have to surround yourself with people who are winners and give them the incentive and motivation to continue their success."[34]

I once heard a great speaker tell a television interviewer what he believes is an indispensable success secret—both for himself and for anyone else who wishes to succeed:

> If there's one thing I'd say to people out there who want to change their life, it's this: Above all else, who you spend time with is who you become. Whoever you spend time with, you begin to adopt some of their values. For most of us as human beings, our lives are really a direct reflection of the expectations of our peer group. If your peer group is about changing the world, making a difference, contributing, working at the homeless shelter, you're going to probably find

yourself spending time there. If your peer group is about making money, you're there. If your peer group is about settling for mediocrity, then even if you start to go for it, they're going to say, "Come on, don't try so hard! Why are you so pumped up? Relax!"

So I'm saying, seek out people who will challenge you! If you want to be great in tennis you don't play against somebody who's worse than you or at your level. The only way you get stronger is to get someone who's better. . . . The same thing is true with the people you surround yourself with and that's one of the reasons people go to [motivational] seminars. It's not just to hear people like me, but to meet the people who go to these programs—people who are driven and want to achieve and experience more for their life and contribute more.[35]

Randy Smith was twenty-nine when he took the job as general manager of the San Diego Padres in 1993—the youngest general manager in major league baseball history. Today, he runs the Detroit Tigers organization. "I never thought twice about my age," he says, explaining the key to his success in baseball. "The biggest thing is to surround yourself with quality people. Digest all the information they can give you."[36] In baseball as in business, surrounding yourself with greatness is the key.

The same is true of Jackie Joyner-Kersee, world-renowned athlete and humanitarian. Named for Jacqueline Kennedy, she grew up poor in East Saint Louis, Illinois, in a neighborhood infested with drugs and crime. Having friends who died from drugs, alcohol, and violence convinced her there had to be a better way of life. At age nine, she committed herself to excelling in sports. She was named to the all-state basketball team while in high school and was Amateur Athletic Union Junior Olympics pentathlon champion. Graduating from UCLA in 1985, she went on to set several Olympic records, winning six Olympic medals in the process.

Joyner-Kersee's success secret: "I try to surround myself with winners. When Gail Devers is out there being successful, then I'm going to be out there being successful, because we train together and we know how to get it done. That's what you want. Find people out there who say, 'You can do it. I'll help you get it done.' Surround yourself with that kind of people."[37]

In one field of endeavor after another, one truth comes through again and again: To be successful, to be a great human being, surround yourself with greatness.

Study the Lives of Great People

Another way to surround yourself with greatness is to study the lives of great people. Their stories inspire us to greatness. Their dreams and goals elevate our own. The struggles of great people teach us not to give up. So study greatness—examine not just the lives of great people in your chosen field but the lives of great people in every endeavor.

Study the life of Abraham Lincoln, certainly one of the greatest souls who ever lived. Born in the Kentucky backwoods, a rail-splitter, boatman, storekeeper, surveyor, and lawyer before entering public service, he was elected the sixteenth president of the United States at a time when the states were anything but united: seven states already had seceded from the Union, and four more followed after his election. He guided America through its darkest years, pulling the fragmented nation back together, ending slavery, and delivering one of the most moving speeches of all time, the Gettysburg Address, drafted on the back of an envelope. "I don't think much of a man," he once said, "who is not wiser today than he was yesterday." This is a life worth learning from and emulating.

Study the life of Joe DiMaggio, an athlete whose place in the public memory transcends baseball, assuming the proportions of legend. He was the quintessential gentleman—self-controlled, self-possessed, elegant, dignified, understated. He was so different from the brash, trash-talking sports "heroes" of our own era. Once married to Marilyn Monroe, he was a celebrity, no question—but he was more than a mere celebrity. DiMaggio exemplified *class*—and I think it was this more than his prodigious athletic prowess that gave him his mystique and legendary status. I once had the privilege of sharing a limousine with Joltin' Joe—and I can tell you there was definitely something special about this man, an aura of greatness. After DiMaggio's death, George Will observed, "We judge a great person the way we judge a great ship, by displacement. The Yankee Clipper still takes up a lot of space in the nation's memory."[38]

Or study the life of Golda Meir, one of the founders of the state of Israel, and prime minister of that nation from 1969 to 1974. Meir was a tireless worker for peace and for diplomatic solutions to Arab-Israeli conflicts. "You cannot shake hands with a clenched fist," was her motto, and she once observed, "We do not rejoice in military victories. We rejoice when strawberries bloom in Israel." She was a great peacemaker—and a great lady.

Study the life of Sir Winston Churchill, who led England through the dark and fiery trial of World War II. With his "We shall never surrender" speech, he galvanized the unbreakable spirit of England. A brilliant mediator and negotiator, he helped maintain a fragile wartime alliance between the U.S., England, and the Soviet Union. He foresaw the emergence of the Cold War and coined the term Iron Curtain to symbolize Soviet oppression of eastern Europe. In 1953, he received the Nobel Prize for literature for his book *The Second World War*. The following year, in an address to Parliament, he displayed one of the true keys to the Churchillian greatness: his humility. In that speech, he averred, "I have never accepted what many people have kindly said—namely that I inspired the nation. Their will was resolute and remorseless, and as it proved, unconquerable. It fell to me to express it." The humble words of a great man.

Study the life of Sojourner Truth, black evangelist, abolitionist, and women's rights advocate. Born into slavery in 1797 with the name Isabella Baumfree, she was beaten and abused by several slave-masters during her childhood. The youngest of her own five children was illegally sold into slavery in the South; she won him back after a lengthy court battle. She told of experiencing numerous visions from God and felt him calling her to "travel up and down the land" in his name, singing and preaching. This led her to change her name to Sojourner Truth in 1843. She went from town to town, preaching the Christian gospel, advocating love and the brotherhood of all humanity, attacking slavery, and fighting for equality for women. During the Civil War, she helped supply black volunteer regiments for the Union forces, and was honored at the White House by President Lincoln. After the War, she helped resettle freed slaves and worked for integration. She was a great lady who devoted her life to a great cause—the cause of human freedom.

Study the life of Vince Lombardi, who exemplified all the excitement, dedication, hard work, and sacrifice that go into excelling at the game of football. He was a man of unparalleled drive and determination, with an unquenchable thirst for winning—and he instilled these passions in his players. Under his direction, the Green Bay Packers dominated professional football during the 1960s and won five NFL championships, including the first two Super Bowls. His often-quoted football wisdom transcends the sport, serving as a guidepost for living. "Football is like life," he once said. "It requires perseverance, self-denial, hard work, sacrifice, dedication and respect for authority."

Study the life of Albert Einstein, the greatest theoretical physicist of the twentieth century. His theory of relativity completely revised our understanding of matter, energy, and physical reality, earning him the Nobel Prize in physics in 1922. He fled Nazi persecution in 1933, accepting a position at the Institute for Advanced Studies at Princeton University. An ardent pacifist, he worked as passionately for peace as he worked to understand the laws of physics. Though he worried about the long-term implications of the atomic bomb, he convinced President Roosevelt to pursue the development of the bomb which hastened the end of World War II. Einstein believed in surrounding himself with greatness and immersing himself in the thinking of great minds. "If I've been able to see far," he once observed, "it's because I've stood on the shoulders of giants." He also had a formula for success—not as famous as $E=MC^2$, perhaps, but important in its own way. He said, "If A equals success, then the formula is A equals X plus Y plus Z. X is work. Y is play. Z is keep your mouth shut."

Study the life of Emily Dickinson of Amherst, Massachusetts— a woman who published only seven poems in her lifetime, yet became one of the greatest poets of all time. She did not write to become rich or famous, and when she lay dying in 1886, she asked her sister to burn all of her unpublished poems. Her sister, wanting to preserve the poems while honoring Emily's last request, came up with an ingenious solution. First she published the poems, then she burned the originals. Thanks to Emily's sister, the world has been enriched and inspired by such exquisite words as these:

> There is no Frigate like a Book
> To take us Lands away
> Nor any Coursers like a Page
> Of prancing Poetry.

Study the life of Martin Luther King Jr.—preacher, activist, humanitarian. Through eloquent words and nonviolent demonstrations, he taught a divided nation that all men are brothers. His life's mission culminated in the 1963 March on Washington, in which two hundred thousand people of all races raised hands and voices for change. In 1964, he became history's youngest recipient of a Nobel Peace Prize. "The ultimate measure of a man," he once said, "is not where he stands in moments of comfort and convenience, but where he stands at times of challenge and controversy." The words of a great man.

No study of great lives would be complete without an in-depth study of the greatest life ever lived, the life of Jesus Christ. Some years ago, an American minister, Dr. James Allan Francis, preached a sermon on the life of Christ, and a portion of that message has become famous under the title "One Solitary Life." He observed:

> A child was born in an obscure village. He grew up in another obscure village, where He worked in a carpenter shop until He was thirty. Then for three years He was an itinerant preacher.
>
> He never wrote a book. He never held an office. He never owned a home. He never had a family. He never went to college. He never set foot inside a big city. He never traveled two hundred miles from the place where He was born. He never did one of the things that usually accompany greatness. He had no credentials but Himself. He had nothing to do with this world except the naked power of His divine manhood.
>
> While still a young man, the tide of public opinion turned against Him. His friends ran away. One of them denied Him. He was turned over to His enemies. He went through the mockery of a trial. He was nailed to a cross between two thieves. His executioners gambled for the only piece of property He had on earth while He was dying—

and that was his robe. When he was dead He was taken down and laid in a borrowed grave through the pity of a friend.

Nineteen wide centuries have come and gone, and today He is the centerpiece of the human race and the leader of the column of progress. I am far within the mark when I say that all the armies that ever marched, and all the navies that ever were built, and all the parliaments that ever sat, all the kings that ever reigned, put together have not affected the life of man upon this earth as powerfully as has that One Solitary Life.

Incredible greatness—and a life truly worthy of our study, our emulation, and our awe. The genius of the greatness of Christ is that he made a decision to bestow his greatness upon all his followers. "I tell you the truth," he said, "anyone who has faith in me will do what I have been doing. He will do even greater things than these, because I am going to the Father" (John 14:12). Amazing— *his* greatness can be *ours!*

And the list goes on and on—Theodore Roosevelt, Mother Teresa, Henry Ford, Benjamin Franklin, Jackie Robinson, Dale Carnegie, George Washington, John Wooden, Norman Schwartzkopf, Margaret Thatcher, Thomas Edison, Franklin D. Roosevelt, Christopher Columbus, Ronald Reagan, Robert Frost, Billy Graham, the apostle Paul, Shakespeare—so many great souls, great minds, great achievers, and great lives after which to pattern our own lives. Surround yourself with the greatness of the ages. Study great lives.

Surround Yourself with Great Books

I once saw a sign in a library that read, "Books are not lumps of lifeless paper, but minds alive on the shelves." The power of a book is nothing short of astounding. Pick up a book and you can engage in a dialogue with a great mind that lived a hundred or a thousand years ago. Through the written page, a person can set down experiences, feelings, thoughts, beliefs, values, hurts, and joys in lasting symbols. When you open a book, you open the life of another human being—and you are changed forever by the encounter.

One of the first books I ever read, *Pop Warner's Book for Boys,* made a profound impact on me. My father gave me that book when I was seven, and I treasured and reread it over the years. Written by Pop Warner, a great man who coached the immortal Jim Thorpe, it was filled with advice for young athletes about caring for your body, maintaining a winning attitude, and playing the game of football. The lessons of that book reverberate in my life to this day.

Another book that changed my life was Bill Veeck's autobiography, *Veeck as in Wreck,* published in 1962. I was fresh out of college at the time, embarking on a career (a very *brief* career, it turned out) as a pro baseball player. Veeck's book altered my life so dramatically that I made decisions about my future as I was reading it. I still read that book once a year as a refresher.

And then, of course, there is the Book of Books. In 1968, after becoming a Christian, I made a decision to get serious about digging everything I could out of the Bible. That book, which I believe is the inspired Word of God, has transformed my life as I have read it, studied it, and memorized passages from it.

And there are so many hundreds of other books that have influenced my life. I probably read two or three books a week, and I always keep good books around me wherever I am. I read the best books two, three, or more times—books on motivation and success, faith, sports, military and Civil War history, biographies, all sorts of books. My life has been shaped by books. Everything a person needs to know about great lives, and about living a life of greatness, can be found in books.

A nationally known speaker writes in one of his books, "Many people fear their own potentiality and consequently settle for much less than what is satisfying and meaningful for them. They are willing to accept being mediocre because they can't seem to muster the internal sense of pride and purpose which would allow them to be great. . . . All of us have a potential for greatness within ourselves. Most of us never allow ourselves to think about it."

Don't coast along with the mentality of mediocrity. Surround yourself with greatness—great people, great influences, great words contained in great books. Then have a great life!

The next important lesson I learned from R. E. Littlejohn: Be a good listener.

FOURTEEN

Be a Good Listener

Bill Campbell, a longtime sports announcer in the Philadelphia area, is a good friend of mine and an excellent play-by-play man. His distinctive broadcast voice is forever linked to one of the great moments in NBA history— when he called Wilt Chamberlain's 100-point game in 1962. But I think Bill's greatest talent as a broadcaster is his skill as an interviewer. Having a weekly sports radio show of my own in Orlando, I wanted to learn all I could about my craft, so I asked Bill, "What is the key to being a good interviewer?"

"Listen," he replied. "Listen to what your guest is saying. Too many people in this business just go down their list of questions and never hear the answers. When you listen, you don't just have an interview. You have a conversation." I've never forgotten that advice.

When I was gathering material for this book, I contacted dozens of people who knew Mister R. E., asking them for their impressions of him. All the people I contacted responded enthusi-astically, sending letters filled with love, praise, and appreciation. Common themes included: "He was the finest Christian busi-nessman I ever knew." "He was like a second father to me." "I never knew a wiser, more compassionate man than Mister R. E." But one theme seemed to recur more than any other: "He was a good listener."

Dr. M. B. Morrow Jr., of Gaffney, South Carolina, said, "He was the one I always went to for advice and counsel, and he never failed to help me. He always had time to listen."

Bill Jeffords of Woodruff, South Carolina, who served with Mis-ter R. E. on the board of Furman University, recalled, "He was a great listener! In a group or meeting, he would remain quiet, wait-ing for everyone else to voice their ideas and opinions, listening and assimilating everyone's input. Then, at just the right time, he would render his own wise influence. His ability to digest other people's thoughts and sift everyone's information through his keen judgment was truly amazing!"

His longtime secretary, Marilyn Scruggs, sent her observations of the man she called "The One-and-Only Original Mr. L." Among her many reminiscences: "He never had a superior attitude toward anyone—never! He was willing to listen to anyone who came to him. He was never in a hurry with people. The person he was lis-tening to was more important than anything that was waiting for him. He gave everyone his full attention."

Hub Blankenship, who succeeded me as general manager of the Spartanburg Phillies, said, "He always took time to listen. People came from all walks of life to seek his counsel, and he gave of his time and wisdom freely."

And Mister R. E.'s pastor, Rev. Alastair Walker, wrote:

> People would seek him out for his guidance. He had a natural gift of putting complicated situations into perspective, so I often sought his guidance.
>
> He participated in various decision-making committees in the church. I observed him, both in his role as a trustee of a great uni-versity and as a deacon in our church. He would always sit quietly, listening intently to the opinions of others. Inevitably, after consid-

erable discussion had taken place, the group would turn in his direction and ask, "What do you think, Mister R. E.?" And he would sum up his analysis of the situation. Invariably, the committee would follow his guidance.

Whenever a problem arose, such as a difficulty with a parishioner or a decision that might be misunderstood or controversial among some in the congregation, Mister R. E. would say to me, "Pastor Walker, let me handle this." And he would go to the people, talk to them, listen to them, and resolve the matter before it ever became a problem—nip it in the bud. He averted many potential controversies because everyone had such a deep respect for him, and he was such a good listener.

Mister R. E. was the best listener I've ever met. I knew I could always come to him with a problem, and his door was always open—and he always had some insight that would help me sort it out. I also saw him exercise his profound listening skills in so many group situations—in meetings with the ballclub, in his church, or in his tanker-trailer business. I saw how he listened to his employees, gathering information from his front-line troops so that he could make better decisions as a businessman.

From Mister R. E., I learned that a wise person isn't someone who knows everything—he or she is a person who is always learning, always listening for new ideas and new information. As well-informed and well-read as he was, Mr. Littlejohn always believed that other people had something to teach him, and he was always eager to hear what others had to say. He exemplified the adage, "It's what we learn after we know it all that counts." It takes maturity and humility to truly listen to other people, and to give them the gift of your time. It takes a recognition of the fact that, however much we may know, we still have much to learn. Former Secretary of State Dean Rusk once said, "One of the best ways to persuade others is with your ears—by listening to them."

Here, then, are some principles I've acquired over the years as I have tried to follow Mister R. E.'s advice and example, and become a better listener:

1. Learn from Subordinates and Invite Their Input

As I write, Chuck Daly has resigned as head coach of the Orlando Magic. Chuck has been a good friend ever since we were together in Philadelphia—when I was general manager of the 76ers and he was an assistant coach. Chuck is a good listener, and he recalls a lesson in listening when he was with the 76ers, coaching a high-powered collection of stars including Julius Erving, the renowned Dr. J.

"Julius came to me," says Chuck, "shortly after I came aboard as assistant, and he said, 'Do you know where every player on this team wants a shot from?' You see, a lot of coaches have a play designed, and they don't take into consideration whether or not a player likes to take a shot from that spot. Ever since Julius pointed that out to me, I make it a point to find out where each player feels most comfortable shooting from, and I try to get him a shot from that spot. Julius taught me that."

Baseball manager Sparky Anderson knows the value of learning from subordinates. "If a manager or a teacher or any kind of boss is smart," he observes, "he's going to learn as much from the people he's leading as they're going to learn from him. You learn how people act in certain situations; then, you make adjustments so that next time is always better than the last. If a person can't do one thing, maybe he can do something else—but you aren't going to know if you don't learn from those around you."

This same willingness to listen and learn from subordinates is just as important in business and industry as it is in the sports world. Some very bright people have it—and some don't. Those who don't may discover to their dismay that the inability to learn from subordinates is the Achilles' heel of their success. When Henry Ford began his car company in 1903, his right hand man was James Couzens. Ford was a masterful entrepreneur, whereas Couzens was a masterful administrator. It is a truism that good entrepreneurs make poor administrators and vice versa, and this was especially true in the case of Couzens and Ford. James Couzens provided what Ford lacked in day-to-day operating expertise. His ideas, though largely uncredited, contributed greatly to Ford's early success.

Couzens, unfortunately, became a victim of his own effectiveness—and the ego of his boss. He was so efficient as an administrator that Ford came to feel jealous of this man who was engineering Ford's long-term success. In 1917, the growing friction between Ford and Couzens came to a head during a heated dispute over the future of the Model T. Couzens contended that the car, which had been in continuous production since 1908, was obsolete. Car buyers, he believed, wanted new and improved models every year. Ford argued that people viewed the Model T as standard and reliable, and would continue buying the car long into the future. He forced Couzens out of the company and continued building his Model Ts for the next ten years. Only in 1927, when other car companies had nearly run him out of business with their aggressive marketing of ever new and improved models, did Ford realize that Couzens had been right all along—and he finally stopped production of the T.

If we have people working for us who are more knowledgeable than we are in some area—well, that's why we hired them. "Why must we act as if we're smarter than the folks beneath us?" asks management guru Tom Peters in *Success* magazine. "If the boss who promotes us is any kind of boss at all, we get promoted for just the opposite reason: because we're able to harvest the brains and energies of our subordinates; because we recognize that since they're the people who perform the frontline work, they must be the experts."

When I arrived in Orlando to help build the Magic, I had many encounters with people from the Disney organization. In August 1989, at a business dinner in one of the Disney hotels, I found myself seated next to Dick Nunis, head of Disney Attractions. Dick, a former football star for the University of Southern California, began with Disney in 1955 and worked alongside Walt Disney for years, overseeing the design of theme park attractions. Eager to gain some first-hand impressions of Disney the man, I asked Nunis, "What were the qualities that made Walt Disney so successful?"

I spread out a napkin and jotted down Dick's answer. "I think you can chalk up his success to nine character strengths." And Nunis listed them for me: Creativity, integrity, hard work, people skills, motivational skills, a willingness to take calculated risks, a commitment to excellence, a willingness to be challenged, and—

"And," Nunis concluded, "he *listened* well. Walt Disney was willing to learn from anyone, including his subordinates."

For example, whenever Walt Disney would begin a new animated feature, he would display the storyboards for the movie on one entire wall in his Burbank studio. Any Disney employee—from the animators and writers to the secretaries and custodians—could go to that wall and post suggestions for improving any aspect of the movie. Disney would read every idea, and many of the ideas were incorporated into the finished movie. In this way, Walt Disney drew upon the creativity and imagination of every person in his organization, and he utilized this collective brainpower to elevate the quality and success of his animated features.

Nunis was profoundly influenced by his close association with Disney, and he became as good a listener and learner as Walt. After Disney passed away, Nunis became one of the chief overseers of an unfulfilled Disney dream, Epcot Center at Walt Disney World. Some months before opening day, Nunis was driving around the Epcot property in a golf cart, inspecting progress at various attractions. Arriving at the Land Pavilion, which featured a large skylighted courtyard and restaurant complex, Nunis examined the great mobiles suspended from the ceiling. The mobiles, depicting springtime, growing time, and harvest, were designed to rise and fall slowly on suspension cables—but there was an unforeseen problem: The mobiles did not remain in alignment—instead, they twisted and bumped into each other.

Nunis and several of his top engineers stood gazing up in perplexity at the blundering mobiles. No one had a solution. Then a laborer, a man who was sweeping up sawdust with a broom and a dustpan, spoke up. "Years ago," he said, "I worked on an oil derrick. We had to hoist heavy stuff on cables, and we used some kind of cable that didn't twist. It had something to do with the way the cable was braided."

Nunis and his engineers looked at each other. Then Nunis said to one of them, "Call a company that does oil drilling. Check it out." The engineer took off. Nunis turned to the fellow with the broom, asked his name, and thanked him for the idea.

And that's how the problem was solved.

Dick Nunis is a listener and a learner—he doesn't care where an idea comes from. All he cares about is that it works. And he makes sure that people with good ideas get the credit.

The best and most successful leaders of business understand this lesson. Kenneth A. Hendricks, president of ABC Supply Company, put it this way: "If you really want to know what's going on in most companies, you talk to the guy who sweeps floors. Nine times out of ten, he knows more than the president of the company. So I make a point of knowing what my floor sweepers know, even if it means sweeping the floors myself." And John Kelly, CEO of Alaska Airlines, said, "Leading means listening. If you don't involve people in the process, you miss the thousands of other brains out there that know the job better than you do. There's no one that knows the job better than the person doing the job."

So find ways to encourage members of your workforce to come to you with ideas. It's not enough to simply be willing to listen to them—you must *invite* them, *encourage* them, and *urge* them to speak up. Many people are too shy to offer ideas until asked. So ask. Tell people you value their ideas. Praise them and reward them for their contributions. Foster an atmosphere of free-flowing communication, imagination, and creativity. You'll not only have a happier, more fun, more productive workplace—you'll also have a wealth of new ideas to make your organization more successful.

Listening to employees was part of the genius of the late Sam Walton, founder of Wal-Mart department stores. "Visiting the stores and listening to our folks," he observed, "was one of the most valuable uses of my time as an executive. The key to success is to get into the store and listen to what the associates have to say. Our best ideas come from clerks and stockboys."

Other successful companies have made the same discovery. IBM pays bonuses to employees who submit money-saving ideas. And 3M's Post-It Notes were the brainchild of an employee who sang in a church choir and wanted a better way to mark pages in the hymnbook. His suggestion that the company develop pads of small adhesive-backed papers led to one of the company's most successful product lines.

People feel empowered and significant when their opinions are valued. They want to know their work is meaningful, and that they make a significant contribution to their organization's goals. Let's face it: Most jobs are really not very glamorous and exciting. Operating a cash register or an acetylene torch, entering data on a computer or cutting and wrapping meat all day, asking customers, "Paper or plastic?"—these tasks are repetitive and boring and can lead to malaise on the job. But when you ask people to use their minds and contribute their thoughts, you raise the level of excitement and involvement in the organization's goals.

2. Be a Sponge for Ideas

A friend once complimented Thomas Edison on his genius as an inventor. "Oh, I'm not a great inventor," Edison demurred.

"How can you say that?" asked the friend. "You have over a thousand patents to your credit."

"Yes," said Edison, "but the only invention I can really claim as absolutely original is the phonograph."

"But all your other inventions—" the friend began.

"Were sparked by the ideas of others. You see," Edison said, "I'm a very good sponge. I absorb ideas from every source I can, then I put them to good use. I take promising ideas and improve them until they are of some practical value. The ideas I use are mostly the ideas of other people who never bothered to develop them themselves."

The late Konosuke Matsushita was called "the Henry Ford of Japan" due to his reputation for mass-marketing low-cost consumer products. He also was the most admired businessman in that country's history. Born in 1894, Konosuke was working ninety-hour work weeks by age nine, assembling charcoal heaters and earning about ten dollars a month.

In 1918, Matsushita, then twenty-four, invested fifty dollars to start a company that manufactured electrical adapter plugs. In time, he expanded the company's line of products to include all sorts of inexpensive, sometimes odd, but always practical electrical gadgets: a portable burglar alarm to protect women's purses, a battery-powered bicycle light, and electric pants to keep workers warm in unheated buildings. Shortly after the end of World War II, Matsushita introduced the first electric rice saucepan, a low-priced electrical appliance that revolutionized Japanese cooking. Another of Matsushita's contributions to Japanese society: the five-day workweek.

By the time he died in 1989, Matsushita was a national hero. Today, his company employs some 265,000 workers worldwide and is the world's tenth largest corporation with about $68 billion in annual revenues (roughly five times that of Microsoft).

Konosuke Matsushita was the first to admit that he was not the source of all the product ideas his company developed. His success was based on the fact that he was a sponge for ideas—and he knew how to turn ideas into practical realities. Many of those ideas came from his own workforce. "The core of management," he once said, "is the art of mobilizing the intellectual resources of all employees in the service of the firm."

Every time an idea is successfully marketed or effectively put into practice, the same idea already has been conceived ten, a hundred, or a thousand times before by people who somehow didn't have what it took to make them practical. So listen for new ideas—and let those ideas propel your success.

3. Be a Sponge for Vital Information

One universal trait of effective, successful people is that they have voracious minds. They continually extract information from people, books, magazines, newspapers, and broadcasts. They listen, they learn—and then they apply what they learn to ever-changing situations in business.

Abraham Lincoln was an information sponge. Though there were no public opinion polls or focus groups in his day, he kept in touch with what the common people were thinking and saying—more than any other political figure of his time. He came up with his own approach to gauging public opinion, which he called "public opinion baths." He would open the doors of the White House and invite people to come in off the street and voice their ideas and reactions to his policies. Though he was not a slave to public opinion, and he often went against public opinion when he felt he was right,

Lincoln was a good listener and always tuned in to the voice of the people before making a major decision or policy change.

Lincoln also invited people to send him their ideas and opinions by mail, and the response was overwhelming—hundreds of letters a month, more than any other president had ever received. He often shaped policy according to public sentiment, but even more often, he used the information he received from the American people to determine the best way to promote the policies in which he believed. His ability to listen to the people was one of the reasons he was so effective as president.

Harry Truman was another president who had the common touch and the gift of effective listening. He once observed,

> A president's performance depends a great deal on the information he has and the information he is able to get. I sought the background of every important question that confronted me. I talked with people interested in the welfare of the country, who could give me their viewpoint exactly as they thought and believed, no matter what they thought my opinion was on a particular subject. Frank opinions were hard to get. Too many people tried to find out what I wanted to hear, and then gave it to me. But the people I wanted around me did not do that.
>
> I made it my business as president to listen to people in all walks of life, and in all fields of endeavor and experience. I did not see only the people who ought to be seen—that is, those who were "well-connected." I always tried to be a good listener.

Bill Grimes, former president of the ESPN sports network, put it this way: "I've met a lot of people in business who are smarter than I am. I listen very closely to what people are saying, because there is a good chance they know something I don't." And Ralph Waldo Emerson felt the same way: "Shall I tell you the secret of the true scholar? It is this: Every man I meet is my master in some point, and in that I learn from him."

Eddie Robinson, who recently retired from Grambling State University as college football's winningest coach and head of a program that sent an unusually high number of its graduates into professional football, said, "You can never stop learning. When the pro scouts came through, I'd take them out to eat and pick their brains. I wanted to find out what was new in the NFL that I could use in my program."

Be a sponge for information. Listen—and learn.

4. Admit Your Ignorance and Ask Questions

"All you've got to do is own up to your ignorance," Walt Disney once said, "and you will find people are eager to fill your head with information." I've never understood why some people find it so hard to say, "I don't know." There's a lot that I don't know—and the more I learn, the more I find out just how much I don't know.

The best way to learn is to ask questions. Every day I keep in mind some instructive lines by Rudyard Kipling:

> I keep six honest serving men.
> They taught me all I knew:
> Their names are What and Why and When
> And How and Where and Who.

On my weekly radio show in Orlando, I talk to top sports people from across the country. I start every interview with a what, why, when, how, where, or who question, and does it bring out fascinating answers! The best interviewers have a knack for asking probing questions. As Larry King has said, "The most important word in the English language is why."

People who ask questions gain answers—and wisdom. Those who don't ask questions are afraid of learning. A Chinese proverb says, "To know the road ahead, ask those coming back." Ask people who have been where you are going—and you will save yourself a lot of costly detours. Asking questions is a sign of curiosity, humility, and maturity—all the hallmarks of a successful person. That is why Michael J. Gelb, author of *How to Think Like Leonardo Da Vinci,* observes, "Geniuses ask questions with the same intensity that kids do. They want to know how everything works, and they have a commitment to test knowledge through their experience. That leads them to pose more questions."

5. Be Curious about Everything

Shove your eye up against the keyhole of life! Explore the mysteries of the universe. Exercise your God-given faculties of curiosity and discover truths, facts, and ideas you never imagined before.

Ernest Hann, an enormously successful developer of major shopping malls, once said, "You have to have an innate curiosity about things and people. If you notice someone digging a hole, go over and see what it's for. If you don't understand, have the ability to converse with the ditchdigger who's doing it—even if you're out there in a suit and tie—and let him know that you're really curious and not talking down to him. That's the enjoyment and love of a fellow man. If you just enjoy people, your inventory of knowledge is endless. People tell you things. People educate you."

Adventures await those with the gift of curiosity. Mark Twain, in *The Innocents Abroad,* described what it feels like to live that adventure: "Discovery! To know that you are walking where none others have walked; that you are beholding what human eye has not seen before; that you are breathing a virgin atmosphere. To give birth to an idea, to discover a great thought—an intellectual nugget, right under the dust of a field that many a brain-plough had gone over before. To find a new planet, to invent a new hinge, to find a way to make the lightnings carry your messages. To be the first—that is the idea."

An avid curiosity—a thirst for the adventure of discovery—is a key component of a successful business or sports leader. "I'm certainly not an expert on many subjects," says the Green Bay Packers' Ron Wolf, "but I want to learn everything I can possibly absorb. If you don't ask, you can't learn. It's that simple. So I'm always probing for information."

6. Listen Carefully and Critically

Sift through everything you hear. Use what works; discard what doesn't. Not all ideas are equal. Some are better than others. Heed your internal reality-checker so that you can separate the gold from the fool's gold, the wheat from the chaff, the truth from the half-truth.

Some people flit from person to person, gathering conflicting bits and pieces of advice. They listen indiscriminately—and soon their heads are full of ricocheting ideas and confused opinions. Too lazy to think for themselves, they have tried to get everyone else to do their thinking for them—but it gets them nowhere.

Successful people listen to others, but know their own mind, their own values, their own direction in life. The most successful people are those who listen carefully, consider all input—then make up their minds, firmly and decisively. Miami's Don Shula—the winningest coach in NFL history (with a record of 347-173-6 over a thiry-three-year career)—put it this way: "Learn from everyone; copy no one." And Bill Dooley, who coached football at Virginia Tech, Wake Forest, and the University of North Carolina, said, "Borrow from other coaches. Pick and choose the things that work for you—but you have to coach to suit your own personality."

Listening critically also involves learning from the mistakes of others. Famed pool shark Minnesota Fats said, "You can learn a lot from idiots. Watch what they do—then don't do it." And UCLA's John Wooden observed, "My favorite American hero is Abraham Lincoln. He had alertness. He once said that he never met a person from whom he did not learn something, although most of the time, it was something *not* to do. That also is learning."

7. Listen to Your Inner Wisdom—and to God

Many people ask for information and advice when they already know the answer—but wish they didn't. Deep down, most of us have a pretty good idea of what we ought to do most of the time—we just don't want to do it. We are too lazy, or too complacent, or too much in denial to do the right thing—so we ask around, hoping someone will give us the advice we would *rather* hear so we can take the easy way out.

Sometimes the best advice we can get comes from within. It comes from listening to that still, small inner voice—the voice of common sense, the voice of conscience, or the voice of God trying to get through to us. To hear that voice, we need to stop and listen. In Psalm 46:10, God counsels us, "Be still, and know that I am God."

The most important listening we need to do each day is to stop, sit still, and listen to God. As someone once said, "I can be active and pray. I can work and pray. But I cannot be busy and pray."

Perhaps you've made the excuse, "I've got so much to do today; I don't have time to pray!" But Martin Luther used to say, "I have so much to do today, I need to spend an extra hour on my knees." It is amazing but true: Prayer actually adds time to busy schedules. Prayer—the act of not only talking to God but *listening* to him as well—helps to focus our minds and order our priorities. As the late Ray Stedman, longtime pastor of Peninsula Bible Church in Palo Alto, California, once observed, "Who better to consult for time management advice than the one who created time and space?"

But how do we listen to God? What is his "voice" like and how do we recognize it? Bill Glass, NFL star turned evangelist, offers this advice:

> Try praying, "Lord, I'm in this mess. I need wisdom. You said ask, so I'm asking." You are claiming James 1:5 (NAS), "But if any of you lacks wisdom, let him ask of God. . . ."
>
> One time when I was struggling with a problem, I remembered this verse and decided to claim it. Since that time, anytime and in any situation when I say, "Lord, I need wisdom about this problem or need," He gives me an impression in my heart. Whenever I follow it, everything always works out right.
>
> If you are puzzled by your problem and can't figure out what God is up to, just ask for His wisdom. He'll give you impressions about what to do, and you can be certain of His leading. When you claim God's wisdom and receive a clear, lasting impression consistent with the Bible, you can act in faith.

One of the most insightful writers and speakers of our time, Keith Miller, described his prayer life in a way that challenges us to rethink our response to God:

> I don't pray much for myself anymore. Mostly I just ask, "Please show me your will for me today." Then I sit quietly for a few minutes in a listening attitude. Next I think about what is already before me to do this day. And I get up and start doing it. I have found

that doing the job at hand is the best way for me to find the next thing God may have for me. . . .

I believe that the purpose of prayer is not to get things I want but, in fact, to get to know God and *his* way of doing and being. I have learned that his ways are often very different from mine and a lot better. I have become hesitant to pray for specific things. If I believe that God loves me and all people and can in fact take better care of us than we can take of ourselves, then my job is to learn to *hear* what he is saying to me.[39]

So tune your ears. Sharpen your listening skills. Seek out information and ideas. Don't hesitate to admit your ignorance—ask questions. Be curious about the world around you. Listen carefully and critically—and sift through everything you hear. Above all, listen to God, to his still, small voice within you. The wisdom of the ages is in that voice. Learn to hear it, and learn to follow it.

These are life lessons I learned from Mister R. E.—lessons that have always stood me in good stead in my personal and professional life. But we're not there yet—not quite. The next lesson he taught me was one of the most important: You've got to pay your dues.

FIFTEEN

Pay Your Dues

After my first season with the Spartanburg Phillies when I was named the league's Executive of the Year, I thought I was ready for the big leagues. Even as days passed and major-league offers never materialized, my hat size was still in desperate need of shrinking. I drove my big Toronado and wore my sharp clothes. I was a legend in my own mind, but I was back for another season. In 1966, Spartanburg had one of the best seasons ever enjoyed by a minor-league club. We packed in the fans every night, and we brought home a championship. Again, I was named Executive of the Year by the league. The people in the front office in Philly were watching, so in September I got a call from Bob Carpenter. At first, I thought he was calling to ask me to be general manager of his big-league franchise. Hey, I was ready!

But no, his plans for me were, to my immature thinking, strictly bush-league: He wanted me to start up a new double-A farm club in Reading, Pennsylvania. I groaned inwardly. Didn't he know who he was talking to? Didn't he realize what I had accomplished in two short years in Spartanburg? Why should I go from an established minor-league team to one I would have to build from scratch, even though it was a higher classification? Why go to Reading and start over again?

I should have been highly flattered by Mr. Carpenter's faith in me—but my swelled head got in the way. I agreed to meet with the Phillies' brass, but I was 99.9 percent sure I wasn't interested.

Bob Carpenter flew me up for the big meeting at the Philadelphia office. On the way, I thought about what an important guy I must be, being flown all the way to Philadelphia just so I could turn down their offer! I arrived at the big ballpark at the intersection of 21st and Lehigh (now renamed Connie Mack Stadium) and strode into the executive offices. Everyone was there: Bob Carpenter, general manager John Quinn, farm director Paul Owens, and Bob's son Ruly, who had recently graduated from Yale and was moving up the executive ladder.

Bob Carpenter did the talking. "Pat," he said, smiling broadly, "we're pleased with the progress you've made in Spartanburg. We want to offer you an opportunity to start a new ballclub in Reading as a sign of how much confidence we have in you." And he proceeded to lay out the plan.

I cringe to recall my arrogant response. "I just don't see how this would be a good career move for me," I said. "I'm getting ready to move up in baseball, and I'm not about to jeopardize my career by moving to Podunk, Pennsylvania. I mean, how do I know it's really a baseball town? Why risk everything I've accomplished over a pig-in-the-poke like this Reading deal?" And for the next half hour or so, I proceeded to dig a hole for myself with my mouth, telling the Phillies' brass what they could do with their offer.

As I talked, the smile faded from Carpenter's face. I could have easily given them a warm, gracious thanks-but-no-thanks. I could have told them I wanted to honor my commitment to Mister R. E. for the '67 season—but noooooo! I had to play the big shot. In my youthful arrogance, I gave my career a .38-caliber hotfoot. It was a miracle I still had a job to return home to.

Prior to that time, my paycheck had come from the front office in Philadelphia. As soon as I arrived back in Spartanburg, I was informed that the organization had cut off my salary and health benefits. Mister R. E.'s organization would write my paycheck from then on.

A few weeks later, Mr. Carpenter sent Ruly to see me. We sat down to talk and he said, "What was that performance all about? I've known you for years, and you were always such a level-headed guy. What in the world got into you, Pat?" I could only shrug and confess, "I don't know."

I had counted on winning the Minor League Executive of the Year award from the *Sporting News* that fall—but the award went to someone else. I couldn't believe it. Our promotions had drawn 173,000 fans in a town of 46,000—and they passed me over. But what I failed to consider was that the *Sporting News* might consult with the front office before making its selection. Looking back, I'm convinced that my behavior in that meeting cost me the award.

I went home to Wilmington, Delaware, for Christmas. While I was at my mother's home, Bob Carpenter called and invited me to his house for a meeting. I knew what was on his mind. Squadrons of butterflies fought dogfights in my stomach as I drove to his house. I had known him practically all my life. I had been in his home and eaten at his table many times. He had given me my start in baseball. But I had made a fool of myself in that September meeting.

I arrived at his palatial home and he ushered me into his study. He got right down to business. "Pat," he said, frowning, "tell me one thing."

"Yes, sir?" I said weakly.

"What have they been feeding you down there in Spartanburg?"

I gulped. "Sir?"

"You're not the same young man I sent down there two years ago. You used to be a bright, decent, well-mannered young man. That's not the young man I saw in Philadelphia four months ago."

"Mr. Carpenter," I stammered, "all I can say is—I'm sorry. Please forgive me for how I acted."

He accepted my apology—but that didn't change the fact that I probably had ruined my chances of advancing within the Phillies' organization. Still, I had learned a valuable lesson: Don't get cocky. Don't think, just because you've had a few victories, a few successes, that the world is going to beat a path to your door. Don't expect to run the world at age twenty-six. Pay your dues. If you just keep proving yourself, success will come to you when you're ready.

PHD Attitude: Poor, Hungry, Driven

My wife, Ruth, who teaches for Franklin Covey, maker of the Franklin Planner, spends eight hours a day teaching up to four seminars a week. She has been a great public speaker for as long as I've known her. (I met her when I attended one of her seminars in Orlando and was completely riveted by her presentation.) But as good as she is, Ruth is constantly improving. She is a better instructor and speaker today than she was a month ago. Why? Experience. Every time she gets up before a group, she acquires more skill at what she already does very well.

Experience, they say, is the best teacher. Even at my point in life, I believe there are two ways to get paid: with money and experience. I still say the best pay is experience. If you have the experience, the money will follow. In my own speaking career, I figure that every time I address an audience, even if I'm donating the talk to charity, I'm getting paid in experience. My weekly radio show will never pay the family bills, but when that red light goes on, when it's me, a guest, and a microphone, I love it! I feel my communication skills improving from the experience—and it's fun.

I look around at the young people in the Magic organization and in other organizations, and I see so many who spend their days thinking, "What's my next move? Where do I go next? How do I make it happen? Where's my shortcut to the corner office?" I tell them the same thing Mister R. E. would tell them: "You need experience, and you can get the experience you need right where you are. Don't be so impatient. Don't expect the world to beat a path to your door. Pay your dues."

I remember during our '67 season in Spartanburg, we had a specific amount budgeted for promotions—and I busted that budget like it wasn't even there. I paid out thousands to bring in stars like

NFL quarterback Bart Starr to draw big crowds to Duncan Park. Mister R. E. saw how far over budget I was going, but he never said a word about it. We had a great year, we drew well, and we should have cleared an enormous profit. I had an arrangement in my contract whereby Mister R. E. would pay me a percentage of the profit, which was an incentive for me to watch the bottom line. But I was so promotion-crazy, I completely forgot about the bottom line. My year-end bonus was $3,000—a nice piece of change, but nowhere near what I would have received if our promotional expenses hadn't been so high.

Why did Mister R. E. let me bust the budget? To give me *experience*. He knew what was coming—he was tracking the numbers—but he let it play out so I could learn. He knew an expensive practical lesson would teach me much more than any words he could say. And I learned my lesson. I paid my dues—and I paid them in real dollars.

"Good judgment," someone once said, "is usually the result of experience, and experience is usually the result of bad judgment. No mistakes, no experience; no experience, no wisdom." Sam Walton, founder of Wal-Mart department stores, once gave a speech before a group of students, followed by a question-and-answer session. One student asked Walton, "To what do you attribute your success?"

"Good decisions," Walton replied.

"Well," continued the student, "what does it take to make good decisions?"

"Experience," Walton replied.

Exasperated, the student followed up again. "Then how does a person gain experience?"

Walton's reply: "Bad decisions."

If you want to get ahead, you have to gain experience—*and you have to pay your dues.* But don't take my word for it. There are plenty of other highly effective, successful people who will tell you the same thing. One of the most respected coaches in professional hockey is Ted Nolan, who until recently was the head coach of the Buffalo Sabres. He was named National Hockey League Coach of the Year in 1997 (though he and Sabres general manager John Muckler were forced out the following year; some accounts say the owners felt threatened by Nolan's popularity with players and fans).

Ted Nolan is a full-blooded Ojibway of whom *USA Today* said, "His success is a profile in perseverance." Raised on the Garden River Reserve for native Americans in Ontario, Canada, one of a dozen children in a house without indoor plumbing, he recalls, "We didn't have much money, but we were rich in values. . . . I believe in hard work."

His NHL career began when he signed to play with the Detroit Red Wings—but he left his first training camp, taking the first bus back to the reserve because he was homesick. His tough-minded mother tossed him back onto the bus and sent him straight back to Detroit. With no place else to go, Ted Nolan decided he had better make something of himself in hockey.

Later, when an injury cut short his playing career, Nolan—a shy young man who had difficulty holding up his end of a conversation—enrolled at Lake Superior State College, taking classes in public speaking. He was determined to shed the handicap of shyness and become a coach in the pros. He worked his way up, coaching the minor-league Sault Sainte Marie Greyhounds and assisting the NHL's Hartford Whalers before being hired by John Muckler as head coach of the Sabres. "What impressed me the most about him," Muckler recalled, "is all that he went through to get where he is today. He's worked hard for everything he has. He's a very motivated man—a career coach who was willing to pay his dues. . . . When he was coaching in Sault Sainte Marie, I noticed his teams always overachieved."

Nolan never forgets his roots and annually returns to the reserve where he grew up, visiting the graves of his parents, who instilled in him the values of patience, hard work, and perseverance that made him such a respected coach. "I still practice the traditional ways," he says. "Family is important to us. My heritage is important. Hopefully, I can be an inspiration to other native youths." There has even been talk on the reserve of making him chief of the Ojibways. And why not? Ted Nolan has *paid his dues*.[40]

In a 1997 article in *USA Weekend,* Rick Pitino, then coach of the University of Kentucky Wildcats, was called "college basketball's best coach." In that article, Pitino set forth his "Ten Steps to Success."

1. *Thrive on pressure.* "Pressure," says Pitino, "is negative only when we are ill-prepared. Pressure can bring out extraordinary accomplishments."

2. *Establish good habits.* He recommends such habits as getting to work *early,* not just on time; taking responsibility instead of making excuses; being organized; tackling unpleasant tasks early instead of procrastinating so you are free to enjoy the rest of the day.

3. *Master the art of communicating.* "Listen more, talk less," he says.

4. *Build your self-esteem.* "The way to do that," observes Pitino, "is to *deserve success,* to establish a great work ethic and . . . discipline."

5. *Always be positive.* The more negative your circumstances, the more important a positive attitude becomes.

6. *Learn the lessons of adversity.* When you fail, step back, take a good, hard look at your failure, accept your share of the responsibility, then take those lessons into your next big challenge. Odds are that you won't make the same mistake—and you'll succeed.

7. *Learn from others.* Emulate the example of good role models—and learn from the failures and mistakes of bad role models.

8. *Set high goals.* Don't make excuses for your weaknesses—conquer them. Set high personal and professional standards—then put in the time, hard work, and discipline to achieve them.

9. *Don't let successes go to your head.* Discipline and focus often evaporate in the wake of a big win. "So never forget what you did right," says Pitino. "Write down your own secrets to success. Study them. If nothing else, they'll remind you it wasn't good fortune that caused your success, but an entire lifestyle of achievement."

10. *Pay your dues.* "The people who ultimately succeed," observes Pitino, "are the ones who understand that success is a long-term commitment. Look at writer Patricia Cornwell, who spent years at the typewriter before she sold her first mystery novel, but who kept doggedly working at her trade until she became one of the hottest writers in the country. You have to pay your dues. . . . Develop a 'PHD' attitude: poor, hungry, and driven, the kind of attitude that will drive you to learn more and be better."[41]

Overnight Success or Persistent Dues-Payer?

Some people have called country music star Randy Travis an overnight success—but that's just because they don't know the whole story. His "overnight success" only came after ten long, lean years of paying his dues. The road to success began when he won a talent show at a Charlotte, North Carolina, nightclub. Travis (his name was Randy Traywick in those days) won a little cash, a steak dinner, and a few free hours in a recording studio to cut a demo record. The manager of the nightclub, Lib Hatcher, liked his music and offered him a weekend job. Soon, she offered to manage his career—and sometime later, they got married.

Randy recorded two independent records, one as Randy Traywick, the other under the name of Randy Ray. Then Lib and Randy got into a car and drove all across the South, stopping at one radio station after another, trying to get his songs on the air. They spent four years in Nashville while Randy auditioned for every record producer in town. They all turned him down. Lib pawned jewelry to pay the rent while Randy worked at the Nashville Palace, singing on stage, then going backstage after his set to wash dishes and fry catfish and steaks on the grill.

One night in 1985, Bob Saporiti, promotions director for the Warner Brothers label, stopped by the Nashville Palace to catch the show, entering through the backstage door. "I ran into this guy in the kitchen peeling potatoes," Saporiti recalls. "So I tell him I want to meet the singer who was going on that night, and he says, 'That's me.' He went onstage and just blew us away, and afterward I go back again to say goodnight, and there he is washing pots. It's one of those great country music stories, and it's true."

Saporiti signed Randy to a contract, changed his last name to Travis, and by the following year, 1986, Randy's debut single, "On the Other Hand," had hit number one on the country charts. His second collection, *Always and Forever,* topped the charts for forty-three weeks and sold five million copies. After twelve years with Warner Brothers, Travis switched recording labels, becoming the first artist to sign with Steven Spielberg's new multimedia company,

DreamWorks SKG. He also branched out into acting, and has appeared on TV and in more than a dozen feature films.

Travis and Lib stayed focused on their dream. After a decade of paying their dues, the dream came true. "If you work at something long enough," he says, "and keep believing, sooner or later it will happen."[42]

And there are so many other dues-paying stories—the reality behind the myth of the overnight success. One of those stories involves celebrated comedian Bob Hope. An entertainment institution today, he came close to giving up on show business back in 1928 when he was broke, hungry, and unable to find work. "I was standing in front of the Woods Theater in Chicago," he recalls. "I couldn't get a booking and I was ready to chuck it all and go back home to Cleveland."

Just then, a friend from the vaudeville stage happened to meet him on the street. "How are things going?" asked the friend.

"I'm starving," Hope replied.

The friend started to laugh—then saw that Hope was serious. The man put an arm around Hope and walked him over to the office of agent Charlie Hogan. "Let me see your act," said Hogan.

So Hope auditioned—and Hogan liked what he saw. "Son," he said, "I can get you a fill-in booking at the West Englewood Theater. It's only one day, but it pays twenty-five bucks. What do you say?"

Hope, who had been making only ten dollars a show when he was working at all, jumped at the offer. "That," he later recalled, "was the booking that got my career rolling."

And then there's the story of Theodor Geisel. He wrote a children's book and submitted it for publication—and it was promptly rejected. So Geisel sent it to another publisher, and another, and another. The book was rejected by twenty-three publishers. The twenty-fourth publisher he sent it to published the book—and it sold six million copies. If you're thinking you've never heard of Theodor Geisel—think again. He's much better known by his pen name: Dr. Seuss. That first book—*And to Think That I Saw It on Mulberry Street,* published in 1937—was followed by many more best-selling children's classics such as *The Cat in the Hat, Horton Hears a Who,* and *Green Eggs and Ham.*

And what about Mary Kay Ash? When she started her cosmetics company in 1963, everyone around her predicted failure—and during her first few years in business, it seemed that the critics and doomsayers were right. Her accountant told her she was paying too high a commission to her salespeople. Her attorney tried to convince her to quit, showing her a list of cosmetics firms that already had gone bankrupt that year. A rival firm offered to buy her out for a fraction of what she had invested, predicting that if she didn't sell then, in a few months she'd be begging the company to buy her out for even less. She refused to give up on her dream.

"The odds were against me," she recalls, "but even back in 1963, I knew four things for certain: (1) People will support that which they help to create; (2) in this great country there is no limit to what an individual can accomplish; (3) if given the opportunity, women are capable of superior performance; (4) I was willing to work long, hard hours to implement my convictions." Mary Kay Ash persevered through the tough times, and today she presides over one of the largest cosmetics companies in America. "If you think you can, you can," she says. "And if you think you can't, you're right." She knows. She has paid her dues.

And then there's the experience of Abraham Lincoln. He spent most of his life paying his dues, surviving failure and defeat and frustration, never knowing any real measure of success until the last few years of his life. Born into poverty, Lincoln failed in business—twice. He lost eight elections. He even suffered a nervous breakdown. But persevering under enormous burdens, pushing his way through every obstacle and opponent, he ultimately became what many people consider to be the greatest of all American presidents. After his defeat in a race for the Senate in 1854, and just six years before his first triumph in being elected president of the United States, he wrote, "The path was worn and slippery. My foot slipped from under me, knocking the other out of the way, but I recovered and said to myself, 'It's a slip and not a fall.'" Those are the words of a man who has paid his dues.

Sam Walton, Ted Nolan, Rick Pitino, Randy Travis, Bob Hope, Dr. Seuss, Mary Kay Ash, Abraham Lincoln—that's an eclectic group of people. But they all have two things in common: They all succeeded in reaching their life goals, and they all paid their dues.

Tips for Dues-Payers

I am not Mr. Hi-Tech. In fact, in this computer age, I'm still trying to figure out how to use my Viewmaster. But I have a good friend, Dwight Bain, who is constantly flooding me with E-mails and Internet material. I recently got a beauty from him, which we have framed and hung in the bedroom of each of our children. I have no idea who wrote it, but I call it "Eleven Rules for Paying Your Dues."

1. Life is not fair; get used to it.
2. The world won't care about your self-esteem. The world will expect you to accomplish something *before* you feel good about yourself.
3. You will *not* make $50,000 a year right out of high school. Don't expect to be a corporate vice president with a car phone until you have earned both.
4. If you think your teacher is tough, wait till you get a boss. He doesn't have tenure.
5. Flipping burgers is not beneath your dignity. Your grandparents had a different word for burger flipping; they called it "opportunity."
6. If you mess up, it's not your parents' fault. So don't whine about your mistakes—*learn* from them.
7. Before you were born, your parents weren't as boring as they are now. They got that way from paying your bills, cleaning your clothes, and listening to you talk about how cool you are. So before you save the rain forest from the blood-sucking parasites of your parents' generation, try delousing the closet in your own room.
8. Your school may have done away with winners and losers, but life has not. In some schools they have abolished failing grades; they'll give you as many times as you want to get the

right answer. This, of course, doesn't bear the slightest re-
semblance to *anything* in real life.

9. Life is not divided into semesters. You don't get summers off,
   and very few employers are interested in helping you find
   yourself. Do that on your own time.
10. Television is *not* real life. In real life people actually have to
    leave the coffee shop and go to jobs.
11. Be nice to nerds. Chances are you'll end up working for one.

Writing in *Cosmopolitan,* women's issues writer Laura Ziv has
some advice for those who are getting tired of paying their dues.
"Life isn't going exactly as planned?" she writes. "Get over it! . . .
Get over the fact that you don't rule the world." She explains:

> *Your vision:* A corner office with a panoramic view, a six-figure salary,
> a fat expense account complete with a generous clothing allowance,
> and a gleaming limousine to ferry you to and from the office . . . all,
> of course, before you hit 30. *Your reality:* A cubicle the size of a bath-
> room stall, a paycheck that gets chuckles from the bank teller when
> you cash it, and a bus ride (with two transfers) to get you home . . .
> and the big three-oh is coming at you. . . . What happened?
>
> While there is nothing wrong with a good dose of ambition, bear
> in mind that "it is extremely rare to reach the apex of your career in
> your 20s or 30s," says Jan Yager, Ph.D., a sociologist and workplace
> expert and author of *Friendships* (Hannacroix Creek Books, 1997).
> "Every career has a path, and you should be aware of what yours is
> for your industry. Whatever field you're in, there is a certain amount
> of information you must absorb, both academically and experien-
> tially, before you reach the top. It's called *paying your dues.*"[43]

Here are some tips I've discovered to help you survive the dues-
paying experience, so that you can have a lifetime of success:

1. Pay your dues cheerfully. Maintain a positive, eager attitude.
Show the boss you are a team player. This does not mean you must
be content to stay in the same job forever out of misplaced loyalty
to an employer or fear of failing in a new job. Always be ready and
eager to move out, to move up—but while you are waiting, be productive and be positive.

2. Set clear goals for your life and career. Write down your goals, post them in a visible place, and review them often. If you stick your goals in a drawer and forget them, you may wake up someday and realize that instead of paying your dues, you've been sleep-walking through life.

3. Don't be complacent—be proactive and assertive. Opportunities come to those who reach for them; they rarely fall into your lap. Many times, young people have come to me and said, "I want to get ahead in the sports business. Here are my goals—how would you advise me to go about reaching them?" I've never felt that such a question was too pushy. I've always respected such a proactive attitude—and I've always tried to help young people who approached me that way.

4. Don't expect your dues-paying work to be glamorous and fulfilling. It won't be. That's what dues-paying is all about—doing the things you'd rather not do in order to work your way up to the things you really want to do. If your job isn't fulfilling right now, that's okay. It'll come. In the meantime, find fulfillment in outside interests—spiritual pursuits, leisure activities, hobbies, friendships, and relationships.

5. Be persistent. Adopt the long view of your career—don't expect shortcuts or lucky breaks. If you happen to get lucky or find a shortcut, fine. But most successful people make their own luck over time, persevering through obstacles and setbacks. The way to success is usually a ladder, not an elevator, so keep climbing—and you'll make it.

6. Be flexible. If you try to put your career on a rigid timetable, you're likely to become discouraged and frustrated. Life is full of detours and obstacles. No one's life moves in a straight line—you have to flex a little when life takes zigs and zags. Monitor your progress, remember your goals—but when things don't go the way you expect, don't let it throw you. Adjust to changing circumstances, and keep moving forward.

7. Hone your abilities. Keep learning. Keep finding ways to better yourself and become a more valuable employee. Read books, take courses, and develop new skills. Don't just run in place—keep moving forward.

8. Never slam a door shut behind you. Never do what I did with Bob Carpenter and the rest of the Phillies' brass. Don't get cocky. And never bad-mouth employers or fellow employees, even after you leave a place of employment. If your experience was negative, stay positive. Keep your words soft and sweet. You may have to eat them.

So that's my advice—the advice of a fellow dues-payer.

But wait. Turn the page. We have just one more lesson to be learned from Mr. Littlejohn—and this one is the most important of all.

SIXTEEN

Have Faith in God

From the time I was seven years old and saw my first big-league baseball game, I trained myself for success. I set my sights on a pro sports career, and pursued it for all I was worth. When I was in Spartanburg, working for Mr. Littlejohn, I felt I had arrived. Oh, I knew it wasn't Major League Baseball, and I still had plans for getting to the big leagues—but that was just a matter of time. Meanwhile, I was still in my twenties and already gaining a reputation for working wonders at Duncan Park. I felt I had achieved as much success as a person my age could ask for. I fully expected that, along with my success, I would experience a deep sense of contentment and satisfaction.

I was wrong.

Fact is, I felt restless, unfulfilled, and empty inside. It was baffling. I had gotten what I wanted—why wasn't I happy?

I had assumed that the key to happiness in life was to set goals, then achieve them. Knock down one goal and move on to a bigger and better one. I was sure that all you had to do was keep up your momentum, keep racheting up the excitement—and if that didn't make you happy, what would?

But I was living my dreams, and I still wasn't happy.

Though my mother had taken me and my sisters to Sunday school and church when we were small, I never associated my quest for fulfillment with God or faith. The only time I even thought about God was when I was with Mister R. E.—he was *always* talking about God. His faith permeated everything he did. I thought, *Well, it's nice that Mr. Littlejohn is so religious.* That's what I thought it was all about with Mr. Littlejohn—being religious.

I couldn't have been more wrong.

A Little Dose of Religion

My years with Mr. Littlejohn marked the first time I had ever experienced unconditional love from another man. It was something I didn't understand. I can see now that it wasn't so much Mister R. E's love for me, but the love of Jesus Christ flowing through him. It baffled me and intrigued me at the same time. I couldn't get a handle on what it was all about, why Mister R. E. should take such a profound interest in my growth and welfare.

During my few years in Spartanburg, Mister R. E. reached out to me many times and cared for me in a way I had never known before and have rarely known since. On several occasions I was so moved by his unconditional fatherly love for me that I broke down and wept while he wrapped his arms around me. That Christlike love of his would just flow over me like hot syrup on morning pancakes.

Mr. Littlejohn had heart problems during those years and eventually needed a bypass operation. I vividly remember one day hearing that he had experienced severe chest pains and was being taken to the hospital in Atlanta. I rushed over to the Littlejohns' home, but they were gone. "How long ago did they leave?" I asked the housekeeper, Azalee. "Just a few minutes ago," she said. So I jumped into my car and raced out onto the highway. I was so scared that I might never see him again.

I caught up with their car and motioned them to pull over. They did. Mr. Littlejohn and his wife were in the back of the car. I flung open the door, threw my arms around Mister R. E. and wept. He told me he loved me, and I had never heard that from another man. I don't remember my dad ever saying that to me, although he might have, and I certainly knew he did—but it was quite another thing to hear Mister R. E. actually say the words, "I love you, Pat." It was something he told me almost every time I was with him, and it always came straight from his heart.

I didn't understand that kind of Christlike, unconditional love—not yet. But I was about to.

My Transformation

One day in February 1968, I went to the Spartanburg gym-auditorium to watch a basketball game. The state women's basketball tournament was going on, and I had dated a woman who coached one of the teams. On the way into the gym, I was handed a flyer for a singing group, the New Folk, which was performing upstairs in the auditorium. I watched the first game, then went upstairs to check out the concert.

The New Folk was made up of eight young men and women performing the kind of folk music that was popular in the '60s. It was a mixture of traditional folk tunes and newer songs with a spiritual message. The members of the group talked between the songs—not about religion but about something they called a relationship with Jesus Christ. Until that day, I had always assumed that God graded human beings on a curve—and on that basis, I figured I was doing okay. I didn't have many vices, I was kind to my mother, I was a pretty good guy. But the New Folk described God's moral standards as being absolute, black and white—you're either in or you're out. That was a troubling thought, because I wasn't at all sure that I was in.

After the concert, I struck up a conversation with a pretty blonde in the group named Sandy Johnson. Frankly, I was interested in a date—but she deftly steered the conversation toward spiritual things. I could see that Sandy had something I really wanted—a radiance, a joy, that same elusive *something* I had seen in the life of Mister R. E. "Here," she said, handing me a little booklet, "let me leave this with you. I think it will help you a lot."

I went back to my apartment, flopped onto my bed, and began reading the booklet Sandy had given me. It was called *Have You Heard of the Four Spiritual Laws?* I opened it and read it in just a few minutes. Then I said to myself, "Is *that* the 'something' I see in Sandy and Mister R. E.? Is *that* why I have all this success but feel empty inside?" I had to know more.

I called Sandy at the motel and offered to buy her breakfast the next morning at the local pancake house. We met and she explained to me what it meant to have a relationship with Jesus Christ. It was all so simple—too simple, it seemed to me. Surely that couldn't be all there is to eternal life, could it? We talked until Sandy had to leave to drive to her next concert. After she left, my mind was still whirling with unanswered questions.

I couldn't concentrate that day. I was filled with a gnawing, unsettled feeling—and I wanted to settle it. By two o'clock, I finally decided I wasn't going to get anything done that day. I had to talk to someone. *Maybe Mr. Littlejohn can help,* I thought, and I drove to Mister R. E.'s office. We sat down and I told him everything I had been thinking about. As I talked, I saw his eyes glisten with joy. "Oh, that's wonderful," he said, "just wonderful! My wife and I have been praying for you ever since you came to Spartanburg. Pat, God has given you a wonderful platform in the sports world, and when you talk, people listen. You've got so much ability, and I just know that God wants to use you in a powerful way if you'll just let him. Are you ready to make that decision?"

The answer was suddenly clear: Yes, I was ready. It was as though everything had suddenly popped into focus. In an instant, I understood why all my successes and accomplishments had left me dissatisfied and empty. I realized that God loved me; that he had a plan to use my life and make it meaningful and full; that even though I was a sinner, Jesus Christ had taken all the punishment for my sin on himself. Most of all, I saw what I needed to do.

All my life, I had set my own agenda and my own goals for success. I had manipulated and maneuvered to be seen, noticed, applauded, and promoted. I had always tried to be in the right place at the right time. I had always felt the pressure and burden of doing everything right so I could be successful. Suddenly, as I stood at the brink of that decision, I felt all of that pressure sliding off my shoulders. What a feeling!

I instantly knew my sins were forgiven—but even more, I felt a huge sense of relief that I didn't have to run my own life anymore. I had been running, running, running ever since I was seven years old, racing after something that was always in view but just out of reach. Finally, I didn't have to run anymore. I could surrender it all to God.

So as Mr. Littlejohn led me, I dropped to my knees, opened my heart to God, and said, "God, I admit that I'm a sinner. I believe that Jesus died for my sins and is alive today. Please forgive me and give me the gift of eternal life, and I promise to follow you as the Lord of my life. In Jesus' name—"

And instantly, I felt completely changed.

I felt an incredible sense of being *clean* inside for the first time in my life. The joy and peace that had always eluded me, even in my moments of triumph and success, suddenly flooded into my being while I was on my knees in Mr. Littlejohn's office. I was so overcome with gratitude for what Jesus Christ had done for me that I just broke down and wept while Mr. Littlejohn wrapped me in his arms.

A Relationship, Not Religion

The time and date of my transformation are forever etched in my mind: February 22, 1968, at 4:00 P.M. sharp. From that moment forward, I felt an urgent impulse to do something for God. It wasn't the kind of compulsion that comes from fear: "Oh, I hope I'm doing enough to please God so he'll accept me!" No, this was a healthy, joyful compulsion that comes from love and gratitude: "After what God has done for me, I can't wait to do something for him, just to say, 'Thank you!'"

After years of running in place, trying like mad to generate my own success, I finally had a sense of peace and security. I just knew that life was going to work out a whole lot better in the coming months and years. And I also knew that God was going to give me opportunities to do something for him. I didn't have to wait long.

The first place I spoke publicly about my newfound faith was at an adult Sunday school at First Baptist Church in Gaffney, South Carolina. I found out that I enjoyed promoting Christ even more than promoting baseball! A few weeks later, when Paul Owens from the Philadelphia Phillies organization canceled a speaking engagement, I was asked to fill in at a meeting of the Spartanburg Lions Club. There I told the hundred or so most influential men in town about my new relationship with Jesus Christ.

Then Mr. Littlejohn's pastor, Rev. Alastair Walker, asked me to tell my story from his pulpit at a televised Youth Sunday event. People all across the state saw that broadcast, and soon my speaking schedule was packed. I was asked to speak in places I'd never heard of. As a new Christian, I was able to communicate what had happened in my life without a lot of Christian jargon—and that seemed to connect with a lot of people.

Rev. Walker and Mr. Littlejohn stressed the importance of daily Bible study, prayer, and regular fellowship with other Christians. They warned me that the emotional high I was feeling would wear off, and that I probably would wonder about the validity of my relationship with Christ—and they were right. They warned me that my new faith would not insulate me against problems and would actually present me with a new set of problems and temptations—and they were right. They warned me that I would slip back into old habits and old attitudes from time to time—and they were right.

But they also told me that if I persevered in Bible study, prayer, and worship with other believers, I would continue growing and maturing in my faith. So I did what they said—and they were right. What I had found one February day in Mr. Littlejohn's office was not religion. It was a *relationship* with the living Christ. I discovered I could really talk to God—and he listened. Daily prayer and Bible study kept me going long after the emotional high wore off.

Ready to Move Up

During my first couple of years in Spartanburg, people around town would question Mr. Littlejohn: "How long is Pat going to stay here? Certainly after the seasons he's had, some big-league team is going to snatch him up someday. When is he moving up?"

Mister R. E. would always say, "Pat will move up when he's ready. He's not ready yet."

I think Mr. Littlejohn had some sort of sixth sense, a *spiritual* sense that enabled him to tune in to God's timetable. When he said I wasn't ready to move up yet, I don't think he meant merely that I needed more experience as a general manager. I think he knew that God had brought me to Spartanburg for a reason—and that reason was so I could be introduced to Jesus Christ in Mr. Littlejohn's office on February 22, 1968. I couldn't leave town until I had made Jesus Christ the Lord of my life.

As the 1968 season began to unfold, people still asked the same question: "When is Pat moving up?"

But I noticed that Mr. Littlejohn had begun to give a different answer to that question: "He's ready now."

Mister R. E. never did explain to me why he thought I was ready to move up by the start of the '68 season, but my guess is that he knew I finally had the spiritual stability and purified motives to go with the experience I had gained. And above all, I had Christ. I was ready to move up. I was ready to go wherever God would lead me.

I had a sense that my future was going to work out a whole lot better in God's hands—and I was right. In July 1968, just five months after turning my life over to Christ, I received a phone message to call Jack Ramsay in California. Well, I knew of a Jack Ramsay from Philadelphia. He had coached college basketball at Saint Joseph's, one of the Big Five schools in Philly. I was a huge basketball fan when I was growing up in nearby Wilmington, and I had watched Jack Ramsay coach many an exciting game. He had since become general manager of the NBA's Philadelphia 76ers. But, I thought, this couldn't be *that* Jack Ramsay—he didn't even know me.

When I returned the call, however, I was astonished to learn that it *was* that Jack Ramsay. He was in Los Angeles to work out a deal to trade Wilt Chamberlain to the Lakers—and he was asking *me* to come up to Philly and run the 76ers' front office!

Well, that came as something of a shock. I enjoyed basketball, true enough, but I had spent my life dreaming of a career in *baseball*. Running a basketball operation had never even occurred to me. I thought it over, prayed about it, and talked it through with Mister R. E.—then took the job. That decision turned out to be the biggest decision of my professional career. My life was forever altered by that one phone call from Jack Ramsay. I have been in pro basketball ever since—and I have never regretted taking that fork in the road.

Before I became a Christian, I had always been reluctant to give God control of my life for fear that he would say, "Put on a pith helmet, Pat. I'm sending you as a missionary to Timbuktu." After my conversion, as God opened doors of opportunity for me, I realized that he had been preparing me all along so he could use me right where I was, in the world of professional sports. He didn't want me to abandon my profession. He wanted me to have a ministry that *coincided* with my profession. All the time he had led me into positions involving sales and speaking and radio appearances, he had been preparing me to tell people about Christ in front of churches and civic clubs. I continue to speak for him to this day.

One Christian ministry that became an immediate part of my life was the Fellowship of Christian Athletes. I had been nominated by Rev. Walker to spearhead the formation of an FCA chapter in Spartanburg a few months before my conversion. So I actually was involved in Christian ministry *before* I became a Christian. At first, I was a reluctant draftee. But after my spiritual transformation, I pursued my work for the FCA with enthusiasm and exhilaration—and soon we had scores of athletes meeting together for Bible studies, praying for each other, and supporting each other on teams and campuses around the region.

FCA became my passion for years to come. When Jack Ramsay hired me to work with the 76ers, one of the first things I did was help start an FCA chapter in Philadelphia. I was only in Philly a year before I was traded to the Chicago Bulls. I'm not kidding—the 76ers were trying to trade Chet Walker for Bulls forward Jimmy Washington, and the Bulls, who needed a new general manager, talked Ramsay into throwing me in on the deal. So I went to Chicago and helped start a Fellowship of Christian Athletes chapter there (others who played key roles in launching FCA in Chicago included Ron Morris, who moved from Kansas City to set up an FCA desk in our Bulls office, and major contributors George Halas, owner of the Bears, and W. Clement Stone, insurance magnate and motivational author, whom I met while soliciting their help).

After a couple of years in Chicago, I moved to Atlanta, serving for a year as general manager of the Hawks. Once again, I knew that my mission was to help start an FCA chapter there. I was beginning to feel like a kind of Johnny Appleseed for FCA, as if the Lord was moving me around from city to city so that I could plant a chapter everywhere I went.

After Atlanta, I moved back to Philadelphia for a second and much longer stint with the 76ers (including an NBA championship season in 1982-83). I found the FCA chapter was up and running, and hundreds of athletes were involved, from the high school and college levels all the way up to the pros. The Lord didn't need me to play Johnny Appleseed for FCA anymore. He had something new planned for me.

A Burden for Souls

In 1978, I got a call from the office of Chuck Colson, former White House counsel and Watergate figure. Colson had emerged from one of the century's biggest scandals a changed man—a dedicated Christian evangelist and prison reformer. A major motion picture had been based on the book he had written about his Christian transformation, *Born Again*. The film starred Dean Jones as Colson, with supporting performances by Anne Francis, George Brent, and Dana Andrews. Colson wanted me to chair the committee that would host the premiere in Philadelphia. I was honored—and in the process I got to know Chuck Colson, one of the finest men I've ever met.

It was an exciting venture, and because of the kind of story it was, audiences not only found the movie entertaining but life-changing. Thousands of people committed their lives to Christ as a result of seeing that film. Planning the film's debut was a heady, exciting experience—but on the day after the premiere I was feeling sort of let down. Not that the premiere was disappointing—it was an incredible experience. No, I think the letdown was the result of living on a spiritual high for weeks on end. Once the big event was done, the adrenaline rush was over, and everything was settling down, I was thinking, *Now what?*

I didn't have long to ponder. My phone rang the next day. Dr. C. Everett Koop, the renowned Philadelphia surgeon who later would be named surgeon general by President Ronald Reagan, said, "Pat, Dr. Francis Schaeffer and I have authored a book and a companion film series called *Whatever Happened to the Human Race?* The world debut of both the film and the book will be held at the Academy of Music here in Philadelphia, and Dr. Schaeffer and I would like you to head up the premiere committee. Would you consider it?"

Wow—would I! As a result, these two great men, two of the most brilliant Christian minds of our time, became part of my life. I vividly recall the night before the debut, when I drove to the airport to pick up Schaeffer and his wife, Edith, who had just flown in from their home at L'Abri in Switzerland. As Schaeffer stepped down the boarding ramp, I instantly recognized him, with his trademark beard, flowing hair, and Swiss knickers. Here was one of the greatest theologians of the twentieth century, a mentor to hundreds of young people, and the author of such important works as *Escape from Reason* and *The God Who Is There*—and I eagerly stepped forward to introduce myself and shake his hand.

We gathered up the luggage, got into the car, and headed for the hotel. As we drove along the expressway, with the brilliant lights of the skyline illuminating the night, I glanced over at Schaeffer's profile as he sat next to me in the front seat. His keen eyes scanned the city, and he seemed to be thinking about all the eternal souls huddled together in the City of Brotherly Love. "I'd like to pray over this city," he said.

"I'll pray along with you," I replied.

He shut his eyes and began talking aloud to his heavenly Father—not in lofty theological terms, but in simple conversational terms, as a child talks to an earthly father. Driving along that expressway, listening to that prayer, I felt a sensation deep within me—a tug of the heart, a sense of burden for the souls in Philadelphia, and I silently agreed with every word Schaeffer spoke. It was a moment I'll never forget.

Another unforgettable experience occurred when author Tim LaHaye called and asked me to spearhead one of his Family Life seminars at the Philadelphia Convention Center. More than three thousand people attended the one-day session, and many families were influenced by Tim's teaching.

Another door that opened for me during that period was the sports chapel movement, which was just beginning to take off. During my second stint with the Philadelphia 76ers—from 1974 to 1986—I was the chapel coordinator for the Philadelphia Phillies baseball club. I worked closely with sportswriter Watson Spoelstra, a true spiritual giant and the driving force behind the baseball chapel movement. Waddy remained a close friend until his death in 1999. Every week for thirty years he sent me a handwritten note of encouragement with a verse written out from *The Living Bible*. His last note, penned just before he died, read, "Each day I ask the Lord to elevate my joy meter, and he does. Our Lord is so faithful." Waddy concluded with these simple words from his favorite Psalm: "Smile more."

At that time I would set up the Phillies' chapel services and coordinate Bible studies. Some of the biggest names in baseball were involved—Mike Schmidt, Bob Boone, Garry Maddox, and many others. I also helped set up some of the Sunday services for the Philadelphia Eagles football team and their opponents and spoke at some of them.

One of my greatest thrills was speaking for coach Tom Landry and the Dallas Cowboys, and coach Joe Gibbs and the Washington Redskins. In 1978 we started a chapel service with the 76ers that spread across the NBA. These chapel services were the inspiration behind the God, Family, and Country rallies we staged twice a year after 76ers' home games at the Spectrum. The ball players would share their faith, and top singers like Sandi Patty and Twila Paris would sing.

From 1969 until 1987 I spent two weeks every summer helping run basketball clinics in the Adirondack Mountains of New York. I worked with Norm Sonju, former Dallas Mavericks president, at Camp of the Woods and a legendary evangelist, Jack Wyrtzen, at Word of Life. Those summer experiences shaped my understanding of spiritual truth and allowed me to share those lessons with others.

I had the privilege of speaking before two Billy Graham crusades, one in Chicago and one in Syracuse. What an awesome feeling it is to share a podium with people like Dr. Graham, Cliff Barrows, Ethel Waters, and George Beverly Shea, and tell forty thousand people how the love of Christ transformed my life.

Another amazing experience was meeting a man named Arthur DeMoss in 1974. At the time of his death in 1979, DeMoss was president of National Liberty Insurance Company near Philadelphia. He also endowed the Arthur S. DeMoss foundation, which promotes pro-life awareness and distributes the free evangelistic book *Power for Living* (you've no doubt seen the commercials featuring Reggie White or former Miss America Heather Whitestone McCallum). DeMoss started in business as a bookie in his early twenties, becoming very wealthy by running a couple of horse rooms in Albany, New York. At age twenty-five, he gave his life to Jesus Christ in a tent revival meeting and completely turned his life around.

When I met Art DeMoss, he struck me as a modern apostle Paul— a man whose radical conversion had given him an absolute passion for people's souls. His number one aim in life was to lead people to Christ. Art and his wife, Nancy, would hold huge outreach dinners in their home, inviting some of the most influential people in the nation, and he would share the gospel with them over dinner. There would often be as many as two hundred people at these dinners (which tells you something about the size of their home). Art would have guest speakers—sometimes Gary Player, or Roy Rogers and Dale Evans, or Chuck Colson—and then he would get up to conclude the dinner by offering an invitation to pray and receive Christ.

Now, Art was anything but a polished speaker. There was nothing smooth or slick about him—but he was a doer and a go-getter, and he had an incredible love for people. When he spoke, people responded.

After his death on a tennis court at age fifty-three, I went to see the family. I asked one of his daughters how she was doing. "We're pretty rejoicing," she said with a sad smile. That just about says it all. It's hard to rejoice when a loved one dies, but when you know without a doubt that you'll see him again in eternity, you can be "pretty rejoicing" nonetheless. Bill Bright of Campus Crusade officiated at the memorial service, which was a celebration of a victoriously completed life. Bill asked the congregation, "How many of you came to know the Lord through the influence of Art DeMoss?" There was a lump in my throat as I saw hundreds of hands go up. What a life!

In 1982, I went with a group of Christian NBA players (including Julius Erving) to mainland China—one of the first American groups to visit Red China after the thaw in U.S. relations with China. There, we linked up with missionary executive John Bechtel, who hosted our tour. He told us that as a result of intense government persecution of the Christian church in China, a Christian underground was growing dramatically. New believers were being added all the time, and believers were meeting in house churches rather than church buildings.

"John," I said, "what can we do to help these Christians in China? What is the biggest need they have, and how can we help meet it?"

"That's easy," he said. "The biggest need is for bicycles. There aren't enough pastors to go around, so the pastors have to travel from house church to house church—and they need bikes to get around."

I brought a burden home from China. Everywhere I spoke in the States, I mentioned the need for money to buy bikes for Chinese pastors. We raised thousands of dollars and sent it to John, and I'll never forget what he wrote back: "Pat, we will never know until we get to heaven how many Chinese Christians there are today because of those bicycles."

In 1982, the Lord gave me a new burning issue: international adoption. That remains my hot button to this day. As noted earlier, I am father to nineteen children—four by birth, one by remarriage, and fourteen by adoption from such farflung places as Brazil, Romania, South Korea, and the Philippines. When we reached a point where our family could simply not absorb any more children, my oldest son, Jimmy, said, "You know, Dad, you can't adopt them all. Shouldn't you let some other families help?"

Jimmy was right. So that is my passion now—to spread the word to everyone I meet that there are kids all around the world who need loving parents and a family. Harry Holt, pioneer of international adoption, once wrote, "Every child on earth deserves a home of his own." My message is, "Open your heart, open your front door, and bring these homeless kids home." (For more information about international adoptions, contact Holt International Children's Services, P.O. Box 2880, Eugene, Oregon 97402, telephone 541-687-2202; http://www.holtintl.org/.)

Salt and Light

I look at myself as being in the home stretch of my life, and in this time the Lord has chosen to put yet another passion in my heart—a passion to write. I've been writing books for nearly a quarter of a century, but in recent years God has set this as a priority before me. This is book number eighteen, and I have ideas for some thirty more books I still hope to write. If I publish a book a year, that means I'll be ninety when I get the last book finished—so if I keep getting new ideas for books, I'm going to have to take really good care of myself.

As this book was nearing completion, I was revving up to work on a book about my longtime friend and mentor, sports entrepreneur Bill Veeck. While researching Veeck's life, I tracked down some of the people who knew him. My friend Ernie Accorsi, general manager of the NFL's New York Giants, pointed me to a man who knew Veeck for many years: sportswriter Sam Lacy of the *Baltimore Afro-American*.

I had heard of Lacy for many years but had never spoken with him. I called him, and he was very friendly and generous with his time. He reminisced about Veeck and about baseball in general, and he could even recite to me the roster of the 1924 Washington Senators, the team he admired as a boy. He told me he had seen some great pitchers over the years, including Walter Johnson and the legendary Satchel Paige in his prime. I thought, *Wow! To have seen those guys play, Sam Lacy must have been around a lot of years.* So I said, "Excuse me, Sam, but just how old are you? Ninety-one? Ninety-two?"

He replied, "What are you trying to do? Cheat me? I'll be ninety-six in October, and I'm still writing my weekly sports column."

I thought, *That's awesome. A man approaching a hundred and living his life to the fullest.* It reminded me of that great line actor Mel Gibson used in the movie *Braveheart,* "All men die, but not all men really live."

The Christian life is an adventure—the most exciting kind of life there is. Charles Swindoll put it this way in his book *Moses: A Man of Selfless Dedication*: "If you really want to break the boredom syndrome, commit yourself to Jesus Christ. Life will start comin' at you! You will become effective, empowered from Heaven, and the battle will rage. You never find people on the front lines going to sleep. They're in the fray. The war's exploding. It's terribly eventful when your life counts for Christ. . . . I can promise you one thing: If your walk with Christ is consistent, all hell will break loose, but all Heaven will come to your rescue! You'll be right in the middle of cosmic, high-stakes warfare."

It's absolutely true—the Christian life is warfare—and a grand adventure in a great cause. Two millennia ago, Jesus called Christians salt and light. His words are as true and relevant today as when he first spoke them: "You are the salt of the earth. But if the salt loses its saltiness, how can it be made salty again? It is no longer good for anything, except to be thrown out and trampled by men. You are the light of the world. A city on a hill cannot be hidden. Neither do people light a lamp and put it under a bowl. Instead they put it on its stand, and it gives light to everyone in the house. In the same way, let your light shine before men, that they may see your good deeds and praise your Father in heaven" (Matt. 5:13–17).

The people of Jesus' day knew exactly what he was talking about when he called them salt and light. Salt is a preservative; light gives illumination. Christians are the salt of the world, sprinkled out of God's shaker to prevent cultural decay. Christians are the light of the world, beaming God's truth and love into a dark and sightless existence. God wants us to become involved in the struggles and warfare of this world, calling people out of hopelessness and into a transforming relationship with Jesus Christ. He wants us to share with everyone the story of salvation by grace through faith that is found in his Word.

> Yet to all who received him, to those who believed in his name, he gave the right to become children of God. . . . For God so loved the world that he gave his one and only Son, that whoever believes in him shall not perish but have eternal life.
>
> John 1:12, 3:16

> For all have sinned and fall short of the glory of God. . . . For the wages of sin is death, but the gift of God is eternal life in Christ Jesus our Lord.
>
> Romans 3:23, 6:23

> For it is by grace you have been saved, through faith—and this not from yourselves, it is the gift of God—not by works, so that no one can boast.
>
> Ephesians 2:8–9

> For Christ died for sins once for all, the righteous for the unrighteous, to bring you to God. He was put to death in the body but made alive by the Spirit.
>
> 1 Peter 3:18

This is the message of salvation through faith in Jesus Christ. If you have never received this transforming message into your own life, I urge you to do so right now. And if you already know him as your Lord and Savior, this is the message he urges you to take to your friends and neighbors, to all the people around you. This is the adventure he calls you to. God doesn't want any of us to spend our lives sitting on the bench. So what are you waiting for? Get in the game!

True Success

Throughout this book, I've been talking about success—and Mr. Littlejohn's sixteen rules for success. You might be thinking, "What does faith in God have to do with success?" The Christian faith has everything in the world to do with success. All the earthly accomplishments, all the financial gain, all the power and prestige and reputation in the world would be meaningless if it cost you your eternal soul. Jesus put it this way: "For what is a man profited, if he shall gain the whole world, and lose his own soul?" (Matt. 16:26 KJV).

There is nothing wrong with profit. There is nothing wrong with material gain. But if your concept of success begins and ends with material wealth, then you are destined ultimately to fail. There is a saying that "he who dies with the most toys, wins." Fact is, he who dies with the most toys is just as dead as the one with few or no toys. I've never seen a hearse pulling a U-Haul. In the final analysis, everyone goes into the presence of God empty-handed.

On October 25, 1999, golfing great Payne Stewart and three associates left Orlando on a lear jet. Twenty minutes later the cabin lost pressure, and apparently the four men and the two pilots died instantly. The plane, flying on automatic pilot, finally ran out of fuel over a South Dakota farm.

All six lived in the Orlando area, and their deaths left this community mourning. Stewart had everything—fame, success, wealth, family, friends. But a year before the crash, Payne found out that even with all this, his soul was in jeopardy. He accepted Christ and started the adventurous lifestyle Christianity offers. It changed his life and ensured him a glorious, eternal life with his newfound Savior. And he began contributing to his fellow man, giving away hundreds of thousands of dollars to Christian causes and investing his time in the lives of family and fellow golfers.

I believe in the truth of the couplet that says, "Only one life, 'twill soon be past / Only what's done for Christ will last." The good news is that everything we do in life can be done in service to God. I believe you can run a sports team for the glory of God. My friend from my Philadelphia days, Reggie White, "the Minister of Defense," often said that, as a defensive lineman for the Philadelphia Eagles and later the Green Bay Packers, he "hit hard for the glory of God." I believe you can write books, sing songs, run a corporation, teach school, drive a bus, wait tables, and flip burgers for the glory of God. The Bible says, "And whatever you do, whether in word or deed, do it all in the name of the Lord Jesus, giving thanks to God the Father through him" (Col. 3:17), and "Whatever you do, work at it with all your heart, as working for the Lord, not for men" (Col. 3:23).

Some people say that Christianity and material success are incompatible. But I am convinced that God wants us to be successful. That is why we read in his Word, "Commit to the LORD whatever you do, and your plans will succeed" (Prov. 16:3), and "As long as he sought the LORD, God gave him success" (2 Chron. 26:5).

Being successful doesn't necessarily mean being wealthy. Some of the most successful people in this world have had no material possessions. Certainly, Saint Francis of Assisi was successful, though he turned his back on a sizable inheritance to follow God. So was Mother Teresa, who also chose a lifestyle of poverty. Jesus, though he owned nothing, was the most successful man who ever lived. So it all depends on how you define success.

But there is nothing wrong with making a profit or experiencing material success. When a company that is operated on godly principles makes a profit, good things happen: (1) the company produces goods or services that benefit human society; (2) it provides honorable employment at a just wage; (3) it treats its employees with dignity and a true sense of their worth as eternal human souls; (4) it pays its bills, which in turn allows other companies to make a profit and provide jobs; (5) it is a good corporate citizen, making charitable donations and other enhancements to the surrounding society. A company can only carry out these functions as long as it makes a profit. Failure benefits nobody; success benefits everybody.

Those who say the profit motive is an evil thing are fortunate that they don't have to live in a world without it. A world in which no one could make a profit, in which no one is allowed to excel or succeed, would be a world of misery and poverty, without food, medicine, entertainment, transportation, goods and services, technology, science, education, or any of the other wonderful things that result from people who want to succeed, make a profit, and earn a good living.

God has created us as both material and spiritual beings. We have material and spiritual needs. If, in our search for success, we focus only on our material well-being and forget the spiritual, we will be left unsatisfied. That is the message of Ecclesiastes 5:10: "Whoever loves money never has money enough." It is the message of 1 Timothy 6:10: "For the love of money is a root of all kinds of evil. Some people, eager for money, have wandered from the faith and pierced themselves with many griefs." And it is the message of Pat Williams, who, as a young man, thought he had it all—success, acclaim, material goods, and an inside track to even greater successes ahead. But I'm here to tell you that Pat Williams never knew peace, never knew satisfaction, never knew true fulfillment until he found a personal relationship with Jesus Christ.

I believe I am successful—not because of anything I've achieved in the sports world or as an author or as a speaker, but because I'm doing the work God created me to do, and I'm living the life he created me to live. And Mr. R. E. Littlejohn was successful—not because of his wealth or all the companies he operated or the various church and university committees he served on, but because he lived the life God intended for him. As Pastor Walker wrote, "Mr. Littlejohn was not a great theologian or Bible scholar. Instead, he quietly and consistently lived the Christian life, and that's why he was so admired by Christians and non-Christians alike."

D. L. Moody once said, "All Bibles should be bound in shoe-leather." And in Ephesians 2:10, the apostle Paul says, "For we are God's workmanship, created in Christ Jesus to do good works, which God prepared in advance for us to do." If we are living out God's purpose for us, how can we be anything but successful? Once we have a clear sense of what true success is, according to God's standards, everything comes into focus.

Perhaps, when you started reading this chapter, you thought rule 16, "Have Faith in God," wasn't really a rule for success. But now, I trust you realize that rule 16 is really the capstone of them all. Without a relationship with God through Jesus Christ, the other fifteen rules have no lasting meaning. Only within a context of a relationship with God can we ever be truly and eternally successful. Only as we commit everything we do to the Lord can our plans genuinely succeed.

Here, then, is Mr. Littlejohn's amazing legacy of success, which I've entrusted to you—in shining golden nuggets of wisdom to take with you on your journey toward lasting success and true fulfillment.

1. Sell yourself.
2. Work hard.
3. Keep the communication lines open.
4. Seek out wisdom and advice from others.
5. Be aware of your influence on others.
6. Seek agreement but respect disagreement.
7. Control what you can control—and let go of what you can't.
8. Avoid snap decisions—be patient.
9. Keep it simple.
10. Manage your personal life well.
11. Care about the people you work with.
12. Don't run from problems.
13. Surround yourself with greatness.
14. Be a good listener.
15. Pay your dues.
16. Have faith in God.

So enjoy the road ahead, my friend. I wish you every success along your journey. And who knows? Maybe we'll meet someday—if not in this life, then in the life to come.

I hope so. In fact, I'm looking forward to it!

Mr. and Mrs. Littlejohn with daughters Carolyn (right) and Dixie (left)

Epilogue

Mister R. E. died on February 7, 1987, at age seventy-three. Mrs. Littlejohn died on September 26, 1996, at age eighty-one. Their two daughters, Carolyn and Dixie, still live in Spartanburg, South Carolina. Mister R. E. and Sam would now have five grandchildren and ten great-grandchildren.

Mr. Littlejohn sold his personal companies in 1979. Associated Petroleum Carriers bought back his stock upon his death.

APC still operates today, carrying petroleum products throughout the southeast. In fact, whenever I pass one of their trucks on the highway, I salute in honor of Mister R. E. After reading this book, maybe you'll want to do the same thing.

Notes

1. Tony Mooney, "Ethnic Work Ethic," *Independent,* 28 November 1996, E6.

2. Claudia Wallis et al., "How to Make a Better Student: Their Eight Secrets of Success," *Time,* 19 October 1998, 80ff.

3. David DuPree, "Megastar Still Having a Ball . . . ," *USA Today,* 10 April 1997, 3C.

4. Cited by Deborah Tannen, "The Power of Talk: Who Gets Heard and Why," *Harvard Business Review,* 1 September 1995, 138ff.; electronically retrieved from http://www.elibrary.com.

5. Ibid.

6. Faye Rice and Rahul Jacob, "Managing: Champions of Communication," *Fortune,* 3 June 1991, 111.

7. Cheryl Dahle, "Women's Ways of Mentoring," *Fast Company,* 1 September 1998, 186; electronically retrieved from http://www.elibrary.com.

8. Kim Alexis, *A Model for a Better Future* (Nashville: Thomas Nelson, 1998), 143–44.

9. Ron Willingham, *Integrity Selling* (Garden City, N.Y.: Doubleday, 1987), 87.

10. Sergius C. Lorit, *The Last Days of Maximilian Kolbe* (New York: New City Press, 1968), 27.

11. Quoted by Connie Lauerman in "Don't Freak, but Viorst Has Taken Control," *Dallas Morning News,* 4 February 1998, 3C.

12. Quoted by Michael Warshaw, "Keep It Simple," *Fast Company,* 1 June 1998, 154; available online at http://www.fastcompany.com/online/15/keepitsimple.html.

13. Quoted by Tom Timmermann, "Timeouts Are Coaches' Time In with Players," *St. Louis Post-Dispatch,* 22 March 1998, F3.

14. Ibid.

15. Quoted by Paul Attner, "Older but Wiser: Baltimore Ravens Defensive Back Rod Woodson," *Sporting News,* vol. 222 (28 September 1998), 30.

16. Dale Dauten, "Uncomplicating Simplicity Sometimes Fairly Simple," *Minneapolis Star Tribune,* 22 October 1997, 2D.

17. David Anderson, chairman of Famous Dave's, interview with Ann Sundius, MSNBC Business, 10 September 1997.

18. Julie Ralston, "Papa John's Pizza Maker Follows Recipe for Success," Gannett News Service, 16 July 1996.

19. Quoted by Colleen O'Connor, "Simplicity Pattern," *Dallas Morning News,* 13 August 1998, 1C.

20. Ibid.

21. Steve Berg, "Just Saying Yes to Simplicity," *Minneapolis Star Tribune,* 21 December 1997, 01A.

22. Jim Jones, "Simplicity Trend Gains Momentum," *Minneapolis Star Tribune,* 12 November 1997, 9E.

23. Quoted by Michael Warshaw, "Keep It Simple," *Fast Company*, 1 June 1998, 154; available online at http://www.fastcompany.com/online/15/keepitsimple.html.

24. Ibid.

25. I tell the complete story of my marriage and divorce in my autobiography, *Ahead of the Game: The Pat Williams Story* (Grand Rapids: Revell, 1999).

26. A. C. Green, *Victory: The Principles of Championship Living* (Orlando, Fla.: Creation House, 1994), 155.

27. Ian Thomsen, "Playoff Previews: Show Time! Is Kobe Bryant the Second Coming of Magic or Michael?" *Sports Illustrated*, 27 April 1998, 40ff.;, electronically retrieved from http://www.elibrary.com.

28. Thomas Teal, "The Human Side of Management," *Harvard Business Review*, 1 November 1996, 35ff.

29. Victor M. Parachin, "Seven Secrets for Self-Motivation," *The American Salesman* 43 (1 December 1998) 6.

30. Greg Brenneman, "Right Away and All at Once: How We Saved Continental Airlines," *Harvard Business Review*, 1 September 1998, 162ff.

31. Tom Verducci, "Larger Than Life," *Sports Illustrated*, 7 October 1998, 24ff.

32. Claudia Puig, "Bullock Floats between Hollywood's Reality and Her Own," *USA Today*, 29 May 1998, 12E.

33. Scott S. Smith, "Grounds for Success," *Entrepreneur Magazine*, 1 May 1998, 120.

34. Sharon Phillips, "MDC Communications President and CEO—Interview," *Wall Street Corporate Reporter*, 28 September 1998.

35. *Cavuto Business Report*, Fox News Network, 2 April 1999.

36. Bill Koenig, "Happy Together," *Baseball Weekly*, 11 February 1998, 8.

37. Kwame JC McDonald, "Jackie Joyner-Kersee Awarded Melpomene Outstanding Achievement Award," *Contemporary Women's Issues Database*, 1 March 1998, 4–6.

38. George Will, "The First Michael Jordan," *Newsweek*, 22 March 1999, electronically retrieved from http://newsweekinteractive.org/nw-srv/issue/12_99a/printed/us/so/so0212_2.htm.

39. Keith Miller, *Sin: Overcoming the Ultimate Deadly Addiction* (San Francisco: Harper and Row, 1987), 150.

40. Kevin Allen, "Sabres Coach Nolan Proud of Ancestry and Achievements," *USA Today*, 5 October 1995, electronically retrieved from http://www.elibrary.com.

41. Rick Pitino, "You Must Deserve to Win—Persistence Keeps Us Great," *USA Weekend*, 9 March 1997, 4.

42. Dave McKenna, "Digging Up Bones with Randy Travis," *Washington Post*, 25 June 1999, N13.

43. Laura Ziv, "Life Isn't Going Exactly as Planned? Get Over It!" *Cosmopolitan*, 1 March 1998, 228.

Pat Williams can be contacted directly at (407) 916-2404 or at the following address:

RDV Sports
8701 Maitland Summit Boulevard
Orlando, FL 32810

If you would like to contact Pat Williams regarding speaking engagements, please contact his assistant, Melinda Ethington. She may be reached at the above address or on her direct number at (407) 916-2454. Requests also can be faxed to (407) 916-2807 or E-mailed to methington@rdvsports.com.